# BALLAD HUNTING
## WITH MAX HUNTER

# MUSIC IN AMERICAN LIFE

*A list of books in the series appears at the end of this book.*

# BALLAD HUNTING
## WITH MAX HUNTER

*Stories of an Ozark
Folksong Collector*

SARAH JANE NELSON

FOREWORD BY **ROBERT COCHRAN**

**UNIVERSITY OF
ILLINOIS PRESS**
Urbana, Chicago, and Springfield

Supplemental material can be found on the University of Illinois Press
website and accessed through the webpage for the book.

Publication of this book was supported by a grant from the
L. J. and Mary C. Skaggs Folklore Fund.

Library of Congress Cataloging-in-Publication Data
Names: Nelson, Sarah Jane, 1959- author. | Cochran, Robert,
    1943– writer of foreword.
Title: Ballad hunting with Max Hunter : stories of an Ozark
    folksong collector / Sarah Jane Nelson ; foreword by Robert
    Cochran.
Description: Urbana : University of Illinois Press, 2022. | Series:
    Music in American life | Includes bibliographical references
    and index.
Identifiers: LCCN 2022026744 (print) | LCCN 2022026745
    (ebook) | ISBN 9780252044892 (cloth) | ISBN 9780252086991
    (paperback) | ISBN 9780252054044 (ebook)
Subjects: LCSH: Hunter, Max. | Folklorists—Ozark
    Mountains—20th century—Biography. | Ballads, English—
    Ozark Mountains—History and criticism. | Folk songs,
    English—Ozark Mountains—History and criticism. |
    Ethnomusicology—Ozark Mountains. | Ozark Mountains—
    Social life and customs—20th century.
Classification: LCC ML423.H93 N45 2022 (print) | LCC ML423.H93
    (ebook) | DDC 781.62/13073 [B]—dc23/eng/20220608
LC record available at https://lccn.loc.gov/2022026744
LC ebook record available at https://lccn.loc.gov/2022026745

*To my singing partner Martha Moseley Grace:*
*If not for our childhood predilection for song walks,*
*I might never have stumbled upon Max Hunter's story.*

# CONTENTS

Foreword: The Singer in Me    *Robert Cochran*    ix

Preface    xvii

Acknowledgments    xxi

Introduction: Max Hunter and the Ballad Field    1

1   Singing on the Way to Church    19

2   A Traveling Salesman in Eureka    29

3   Rules of Collecting and How Hunter Got His Songs    42

4   The Child Ballads and Other Bounty    54

5   Singing Grandmas and the Musical Tribes of Stone County    89

6   Circle of Friends    105

7   The Importance of Columbia    120

8   More Than a Hobby    126

9   Max Hunter's Map of the Ozarks    139

10   Max Hunter and the Festival Circuit    145

11   One Eye on the Past and One on the Future    161

Notes    175

Selected Bibliography    217

Index    225

Song Index    233

# THE SINGER IN ME

ROBERT COCHRAN

*Ballad Hunting with Max Hunter* originates in a strikingly oblique encounter. Surfing the internet from her New England home in 2014, Sarah Jane Nelson is mesmerized by a song performance by a young woman Hunter had recorded in his hometown of Springfield, Missouri, in 1975. Hunter has been dead for more than a decade, and Nelson's initial interest centers not on the collector but on the "emotional urgency" of the song's vocal and its "metrically *crooked*" instrumental accompaniment. The single song, however, quickly leads to others no less compelling, and soon enough the sheer size and (even more importantly) the "depth" of Hunter's collection claims Nelson's searching and enduring attention. The volume resulting as the ultimate product of this attention eventually, after persistent trials, not only meets the scholarly standards of a distinguished university press but also satisfies Nelson's own drive to present the labors of a song collector with whom she felt "an immediate familiarity and kinship . . . in much the same way as he would speak about the lives of his singers."

Several important keys to Nelson's study emerge from these originating conditions. It was, after all, "the singer in me" who was first captured by another singer's performance, and Nelson again and again brings a musical performer's perspective to her presentation. She notes Benson and Fleecy Fox of Leslie, Arkansas, as "unique in their habit, not only of singing together but in the fact they did so an octave apart." Listening to a 1958 tape of Hunter singing "Down in the Valley" with his brother Harold, she praises their "perfect blending of voices." Another hint to the singular riches of *Ballad Hunting with Max Hunter* is first suggested in the subtitle of the book, with its top-shelf mention of "stories" given added emphasis by Nelson's reference to the way "he would speak about the lives of his singers."

Here, at the outset, is a hint to the sense of Nelson's reference to the "depth" of Hunter's collection. If she started with and sustained throughout a musician's appreciation for the songs at its center, she ended up writing her book determined above all to communicate her admiration for the collector's astonishingly sustained personal encounters with the singers. Three years into her work, she tells us, Nelson stumbled upon what she calls the *Visits With* portions of Hunter's archive, "a gold mine of untranscribed information that spanned two decades and was buried deep in the larger ballad collection." In this trove she understood instantly what Hunter himself realized gradually and at times grudgingly: that "this may be the most important part of my collecting in the Ozarks." Perhaps the most valuable of this volume's several highlights is Nelson's detailed chronicling of Hunter's wide-ranging interactions with singers, ranging from fugitive encounters with inebriated barflies and an unnamed "escaped convict" who "asked me if he could borrow my car," to repeated visits with seasoned performers like Ollie Gilbert and Fred High.

Academic researchers have routinely chided "collectors" for their failure to record sufficient contextual data, but even a cursory look quickly reveals scholarly interest in singers as characteristically limited in Hunter's day to a handful of questions still centered, in a holdover from the days of historic-geographic focus on origins and transmission pathways, on the songs. Where, when, and from whom was a given song learned? These were the then-standard queries, and beyond them scholarly inquiry only occasionally ventured. Star informants might be taken in hand by collectors or scholars as formal or informal managers—a Leadbelly (Huddie Ledbetter) or a Jilson Setters (James William Day) exhibited in New York or London by the Lomaxes or Jean Thomas. But these are outlier instances, and their handler-produced biographical sketches were highly fictionalized marketing ploys.[1] There were happy exceptions—Edward Ives's and Henry Glassie's pioneering studies with Larry Gorman and Joe Scott (Ives) and Ola Belle Reed (Glassie), Roger Abrahams's work with Almeda Riddle—but Hunter's practice, as revealed in Nelson's scrupulously detailed accounts, went far beyond the day's norm in its exploration of the role of songs in the lives of the singers.[2]

It's also worth noting that Hunter, more than many others, consciously collected repertoires as assiduously as he collected songs (in itself a step toward taking singers seriously as active agents as opposed to biped pack animal "tradition bearers"). As W. K. McNeil points out in his introduction to the 1980 reissue of Vance Randolph's *Ozark Folksongs* (still after forty years easily the most comprehensive survey of traditional music collecting in the Ozarks), Hunter apparently wished at some point that he had done this more systematically, but Nelson's account makes clear that collecting entire repertoires was often his deliberate intention.[3] Hunter also made full use of the advantages of extended and repeated visits to recreate in his recording sessions something of the "intimate performance contexts" characteristic of Ozark traditional singing.

His marathon encounter with Marshall, Arkansas, farmer Odis Bird offers a striking example. As carefully assembled by Nelson from several first-person recollections, it opens with Hunter assigned to driving a truck with no seat cushions, missing gears, "something wrong with the steering," and "the speed of a turtle." Hunter is seated on a board placed directly over the springs, "and boy, if that board had of moved at least six inches I'd have been ruined for life one way or the other." The full day of haying ends "about 6:00 p.m." with the board apparently in place, and Bird rewards a still-intact Hunter by accompanying him to his motel for a recording session: "He sang for me, sang some real good songs. . . . The only thing wrong with that guy was that when it come about midnight I was ready to quit and come back and see him another time, and he felt like he was just getting started."

There's more. A second account of the same day focuses on an interval between the haying and the singing as Hunter waited on the front porch in the company of Bird's father while the son cleaned up for the trip to town. Togged out only in his underwear on account of the heat, and with "a hanky tied around his neck and around his forehead to catch the perspiration," the elder Bird first identified himself as a preacher and then entertained his visitor with a sample of his "way with words." "He said something like this," Hunter recalled: "'I told Brother Jones that if he didn't get right with the Lord he was going to Hell. The old son of a bitch died unsaved and he's burning just as sure as shit.'"

This scene is by no means atypical—Nelson's study features a dozen no less vivid accounts, including one (again collated from multiple sources) describing Hunter assisting Fred High in removing wasps' nests from his well house. The folksong collector emerges from incidents like these as impressively resourceful, almost recklessly fearless, inured to discomfort, imperturbably patient, sharply observant, unfailingly obliging, and (not least) possessed of a "way with words" of his own. I know the reference is graphic, but I'd shy from even beginning to unpack "ruined for life one way or the other." On another occasion, holding forth on the sweeping constraints upon social behavior characteristic of Ozark church congregations, Hunter first listed dancing, card playing, and fiddle music as examples before concluding that "about the only thing left was whittling and then you had better be careful where you got the wood." Holding forth on how the introduction of air conditioning to Ozark homes hampered the transmission of traditional culture by reducing neighborly visits, he produced this gem as capturing current practice: "Your neighbor can die and you don't know it until you read it in the paper, where they buried him yesterday."

On top of the scores of such extended anecdotes revealing Hunter's spectacularly varied relationships with singers, Nelson's work also provides a vivid portrait of the densely reticulated network of singers, collectors, scholars, festival organizers, and audiences who made up the Ozarks traditional music scene in the last half of the twentieth century. They're all here: Vance Randolph and Mary Parler in Arkansas, who inspired and encouraged Hunter's initial collecting efforts; Dolf and Becky Schroeder in Missouri, who assured him decades later of that work's significance; Kansas teacher, collector, and singer Joan O'Bryant, whose death in a car accident in 1964 deprived Hunter of a cherished performing partner; and fellow Springfield businessman/music enthusiast Gordon McCann, who assisted him in his ill-fated adventures at old-time fiddling contests. A huge supporting cast surrounded these headliners—Cathy Barton, Pearl Brewer, Loman Cansler, Lula and Mary Jo Davis, Reba Dearmore, Jimmy Driftwood, Ollie Gilbert, Joe Hickerson, Fred High, Alan Jabbour, May Kennedy McCord, Allie Long Parker, Almeda Riddle, and John Quincy Wolf would make up a small sample, easily doubled or tripled.

The point here is that Nelson's study provides a richly multifaceted portrait of the informally constituted cohort involved in the preservation and celebration of the region's traditional music. Both academic and avocational collectors had published accounts of their interactions with singers ever since John Lomax's *Adventures of a Ballad Hunter* in 1947,[4] but even now only a handful of studies come to mind as matching Nelson's detailed chronicle of a local or regional milieu. Three approximate parallels might be the 2015 portrait of the folk music scene in New York City by Stephen Petrus and Ronald D. Cohen, *Folk City: New York and the American Folk Music Revival*; Adam Machado's text for the awkwardly titled but wonderfully detailed and richly illustrated (and accompanied by four audio CDs) *Hear Me Howling! Blues, Ballads & Beyond, As Recorded by the San Francisco Bay by Chris Strachwitz in the 1960s*; and James P. Leary's monumental *Folksongs of Another America: Field Recordings from the Upper Midwest, 1937–1946*, presenting on five CDs and one DVD nearly two hundred songs in two dozen languages selected from pioneering collections by Sidney Robertson, Alan Lomax, and Helene Stratman-Thomas.[5]

Nelson's approach, to Hunter himself and to the vibrant scene he joined as a young man and enlivened for the rest of his life, never wavers from a baseline sympathy, but she did not arrive at her task blinded by rose-tinted glasses. Hunter's promotion from novice collector, inspired by Randolph's prior example and encouraged by Parler's direct assistance, to at least local recognition as an authority on Ozark traditional life did not fail to enlarge his hat size. Handed a mic and a podium, he over time grew comfortable with imperative expression and ex cathedra pronouncement. At his most self-important, Hunter could come across as an irascible fud. By 1976, when he was at once "master of ceremonies" for the Ozark Folk Festival (with which he'd been involved since the 1950s) and a paid "technical consultant" in charge of music programming at Silver Dollar City theme park, Hunter was issuing orders on everything. He started by patrolling the songs themselves and their presentation, forbidding any instrumentation requiring an electrical outlet and posting lists of songs outlawed for being of too-recent (post-1900) composition. From this he moved on to dress codes for performers—no "watches, make-up, jewelry, open-toed shoes," or "painted nails."

All of this went over poorly with performers and producers alike—"being young, we rolled our eyes a lot," said one of the former. "Unsurprisingly," Nelson notes, "Hunter's contract with Silver Dollar City was not renewed." It's easy, standing back, to sympathize with the temptation here. Blinded by unprecedented applause (and extra checks), the celebrator of tradition fails to recognize the fundamental incongruity of his position. A man who "ran with the purists and resisted commercialization every step of the way" was bound to be a short-term employee at Silver Dollar City. Charged with translating the intimate milieu of traditional song performance to the wider world of professional musicianship, Hunter quickly found that public stages and front porches are strikingly unlike places. Strangers selling tickets to other strangers spending money bring powerful disruptive forces in their wake, and Hunter was neither the first nor the last to founder in the inevitable crosscurrents.

Nelson provides a briefer look at the analogous troubles Jimmy Driftwood experienced as a short-lived program director at the "ideologically troubled" Ozark Folk Center, and, further afield, the whole enterprise of music collecting once featured researchers who shut off their tape recorders when singers struck up songs deemed unacceptable according to varying criteria. Hunter himself occasionally destroyed tapes for bizarre reasons; see Nelson's account of the erasure of Almeda Riddle's "magnificent" performance of "The Maid of Dundee" due to worries over its uncertain or mixed provenance. Feelings at times ran high; witness the brouhaha surrounding future Nobelist Bob Dylan's 1965 Newport Folk Festival appearance with an electric band (apocryphal tales of Pete Seeger taking an ax to power cables). As recently as the late 1990s, a popular and favorably reviewed survey of country music discussed at considerable length and with a straight face the notion of "authenticity" in country music. Garth Brooks took it on the chin as insufficiently rustic in comparison to the hardscrabble roots of Ira Louvin and Merle Haggard.[6]

One prominent bee in Hunter's bonnet when he got going in this vein was an idiosyncratic though vigorously propounded distinction between the use of "Ozarker" and "Ozarkian" as identity markers. The former, he explained to a festival audience in 1977, citing himself as type specimen for the whole taxon, was the genuine article: "'I am an Ozarker' he said, 'because I was born in the Ozarks. I've lived in the Ozarks all my life, my great-great-grandparents came to the Ozarks in eighteen and forty, they lived and they died in the Ozarks on both sides of my family.'" The Ozarkian, on the other hand, foil to this sturdy almost-Osage native, is a latecomer who "moves into the Ozarks, likes it . . . and then in a couple of, maybe, three years, writes back home wherever they came from and says 'I'm a Hillbilly.'"

This distinction falls apart even on first thought of application. Where to draw the line? Might a generous arbiter move the newcomer up to Ozarker status if she or he waited four or five years before writing back to an embarkation point no longer regarded as "home" (nice move, Max), or could a sterner magistrate remand to Ozarkian wannabe rank an applicant whose Ozark ties went back only to his grandfather?

But reading Nelson's account rang a memory bell going back to the late 1970s or early 1980s, when just this topic filled the four or five minutes of my single personal encounter with Hunter. He talked, I listened, and in short order I wrote him off as a sclerotic gasbag. There's no excuse for such boorishness, but I have one. At the time, I was newly arrived from Indiana (not yet even an Ozarkian), hard at work researching a biography of Vance Randolph, and busily crisscrossing the state, bringing Almeda Riddle and Jimmy Driftwood as guests to my folklore classes in Fayetteville. I soon realized that the whole crew of codgers and grannies, for all the "Howdy, neighbors" bonhomie of their public presentations, were privately every bit as jealous of prerogative and intensely competitive with one another as any pampered rock band. The Ozarks are low-altitude peaks (an eroded plateau, actually), but Himalayan struggles occurred for spots at their modest summits.

Entering Mountain View for a first meeting with folklorist W. K. McNeil, I noted a large billboard featuring the Rackensack Folklore Society, only to notice as I drew closer that it had been defaced. I was astonished. Who works up vandalism-level animosities over dueling folklore societies? The standard charge, freely traded in every direction, was of "inauthenticity," a term almost by definition introduced by outsiders but quickly picked up by savvy locals. A 1950 interview with banjo player Booth Campbell offers an early instance. Campbell was a favorite of Parler's, a regular on the regional festival circuit, and one of five stars in the nationally broadcast 1954 CBS television special *The Search*. He often appeared costumed in what was described as a Confederate Army uniform and was known for his belligerent version of "I'm a Good Old Rebel." Already a veteran interviewee, Campbell is quick to volunteer his credentials. Vance Randolph has recorded thirty of his songs for the Library of Congress, "for historical purposes," he reports. Campbell's elder brother Frank, also present, intervenes at one point to remind him the interviewer is interested in "authentic folklore of the Ozarks."[7]

Festivals and talk of festivals in the Ozarks had been around for fifteen years or so by 1950—plenty of time for writers like Randolph, promoters like Otto Rayburn, and performers like Campbell and Jimmy Driftwood to figure out what was currently playing well on the folklore stage. Authenticity was almost too good to be true—impossible to define with anything close to precision but easily presented in sharply binary terms: I and we are authentic embodiments, true Ozarkers; you and they are commercialized hucksters, ersatz Ozarkians. Given this appeal, it's no surprise that the whole issue has enjoyed a very long shelf life. Randolph and Parler, as knowing as anyone on the scene, were perfectly capable of penning certifications of legitimate folkiness as liner notes for friends (Joan O'Bryant and Hunter himself) when they headed into the studios as performers. Even McNeil, who had little use for Driftwood (his passing mention in the *Ozark Folksongs* intro gives his name as "Jimmie," a spelling Driftwood hated), gives Campbell a pass. Factor in differences in time (Driftwood was thirty-five years Campbell's junior) and the younger man's remunerative songwriting success, and drawing an authenticity line between the two requires a pen of extra-fine nib. Both were gifted showmen eager for the limelight who boasted Ozarker pedigrees worthy of comparison with Hunter's.

Such scuffles also figured prominently in the "Ozarks expert" arena. Interviewing friends and associates of Randolph for my biography, I was informed—directly by two and obliquely by four others, both male and female—that my research could more profitably be directed toward themselves. The hills were alive, I concluded, with cantankerous oldsters; every hollow harbored a diva Queen of the Hillbillies, no crossroads lacked its cracker-barrel sage, bitter feuds were everywhere. This got old very fast, even as I fell hard for Randolph's unique combination of unceasing labor and send-up schtick. (He did his work diligently but dedicated *From an Ozark Holler*, a short-story collection, to "Agnes, Mabel, and Becky," a then well-known brand of condom, and published *The Truth about Frankie and Johnny, and Other Legendary Lovers Who Stalked across the American Scene* as the work of "Belden Kittredge.") These same tensions surface in Nelson's study; in addition to the extended treatment of Hunter's struggles with festival promoters and the briefer references to Driftwood's troubles at the Ozark Center, she reports Hunter's description of Springfield's own "Queen of the Hillbillies," May Kennedy McCord, as "a little bit hard to handle" and herself suspects Kansas City singer and high school guidance counselor Loman Cansler of "deliberate subterfuge" in "not sharing authentic songs" with Hunter. But—and this is the point here—her remarkably full account differs from my own short-shrift dismissal most obviously in its remarkable generosity to all parties.

Reading Nelson now, forty-plus years after my encounters with her subjects, has thus been both a revelation and a bit of a rebuke. After all, the man I dismissed as a rancorous crank was remembered by his youngest daughter as distinctive most of all for a gentle, encompassing empathy. Her father was, she recalled, "a people person . . . very mild mannered." Then even this formulation struck her as too bland. "His kindness," she added, "was a bit overwhelming." Any parent worth the name could settle comfortably into a casket with such an epitaph, and I'll not soon forget the image of Hunter stopping by cemeteries to add his condolences at the funerals of strangers. "If it looked like there was a small crowd," the same daughter recalled, "he'd join them, just to help send this person on."

This seems like a good spot for ending: Hunter with his head bowed in an Ozark cemetery. If I in my youth was at least in some sense an appropriate biographer for "rascal" Vance Randolph (Roger Abrahams's label), this engaging, thoroughly researched, and deeply sympathetic study makes it abundantly clear that Sarah Jane Nelson's instinctive sense of "immediate familiarity and kinship" with Hunter has been right on the money.[8] Max Hunter was a remarkably gifted collector, happily at home in the world where he worked so diligently and successfully, and Nelson's *Ballad Hunting with Max Hunter* brings both the man and his mountain world to vivid new life.

# PREFACE

One evening back in August 2014, I was combing the internet for new traditional song material when I stumbled upon the Max Hunter Folk Song Collection. The very first song I listened to is now a standard among folk and blues artists; it was a 1975 recording of Krisanne Parker of Springfield, Missouri, singing "Careless Love." But this was no ordinary rendition. There was an emotional urgency in the singer's voice that—combined with the seamless but metrically *crooked* guitar accompaniment—reached out over four decades of time and grabbed me by the throat.

I probably listened to that recording about a dozen times that night and stayed up well past midnight, listening to other singers and songs in the collection. From the outset, the depth and breadth of Hunter's material was so astonishing that I immediately endeavored to find out as much as possible about both the collector and those individuals who shared both their stories and songs. I did most of my research from my home base in New England, knowing that this would be a long journey, both geographically and logistically, but I would soon be heartened to learn that I was just one more New Englander who had fallen in love with Ozark balladry. One might ask why I chose to write about a man whom I had never met and who lived in an area that was unfamiliar to me. But, as has been said before, biographers do not choose their subjects; the subjects choose them. From the moment I discovered Max Hunter and his work, I felt what can only be described as an immediate familiarity and kinship and an urgency to tell his story in much the same way as he would speak about the lives of his singers.

While to some extent I could turn to collected materials in Hunter's hometown of Springfield, Missouri, and to the State Historical Society of Missouri in Columbia to ferret out details on his life and work, getting biographical information on the lives of Hunter's ballad bearers—most of whom are long gone—proved more challenging. I cast the widest net possible, and each day was a new adventure, reminding me that the nature of this research is serendipitous to the extreme. Krisanne Parker, who grew up during the peak of the folk festival frenzy in the 1970s, would prove one of the most elusive of Hunter's singers. It took me two years to track her down, and when I finally did, she surfaced just long enough to share her valuable memories and reflections with me before receding into the diaspora of time and geography. This, and similar experiences along the way, made my race against time all the more compelling.

Historical forgetfulness has inevitably accompanied alterations in the landscapes of the Ozarks. Indeed, several organizations that sit at the helm of folk music in the Ozarks—including the Ozark Folk Festival at Eureka Springs, Arkansas, and Silver Dollar City in Branson, Missouri—seem to have lost track of Hunter and his most critical contacts. During the two decades that have passed since his death, photographs, correspondence, and other memorabilia pertaining to his collection have become few and far between, scattered from Washington, D.C., and Fayetteville, Arkansas, to Framingham, Massachusetts, and both Springfield and Columbia, Missouri, among other places. In reconstructing the life of Max Hunter and his singers, I have been constantly reminded of the fragility of collective memory.

It took a trip to the Springfield–Greene County Library to discover that a professor within an hour's drive back in Boston had over one hundred hours of Ollie Gilbert songs on tape. And it was three more years before I stumbled upon Hunter's *Visits from the Ozarks* (or *Visits With*, as he often referred to them) audiotapes—a gold mine of untranscribed information that spanned two decades and was buried deep in the larger ballad collection.

I can hardly recall the details of the twisty trail that brought me into conversation with a bass-playing professor at Wichita State University who provided me with valuable leads and materials on Joan O'Bryant, Hunter's singing partner. And more recently, the creative endeavors of Ozark community builder Joshua Heston led me to his *State of the Ozarks* online newsletter, which provided an interesting anecdote on David Prickett, who sang but one glorious song for Hunter.[1]

Whenever I lost heart or lost my way, all I had to do was return to Hunter's recordings, which never failed to reenergize me. Listening to the warm voices of Fleecy and Benson Fox singing their uniquely gentle version of "Blackest Crow" or stumbling upon a primitive and hypnotic version of "Rosemary and Thyme" was enough to remind the singer in me why it was so important to share the story of Hunter and his extended musical family.

Then there were the unpredictable rewards of the research itself: having long and inspiring conversations about Hunter and the Child ballads with Folk-Legacy Records' Caroline Paton;[2] being the first person to ever perform a Crankie story scroll (about Hunter's life) at the Berklee College of Music;[3] and going on to do the same for families at the New England Folk Festival. And then there was the night my daughter and I participated in Joshua Heston's collaborative arts night in Hollister, Missouri. The opening of the digitized Ozark Folksong Collection at the University of Arkansas in 2015 provided essential fodder where Hunter fell short. But like Parker herself, the lives behind some of the most captivating voices in the Hunter Collection remain shrouded in mystery.

This journey of discovery has continued throughout the writing of Hunter's story, and I only regret that I cannot give equal attention to every singer and every song in the collection. Each time I fell under the spell of one ballad or ballad singer, I found myself stumbling upon yet another old gem. I heartily encourage readers to enjoy their own exploration of the Max Hunter Folk Song Collection while keeping in mind that the ballads I chose to write about reflect my own musical tastes and literary biases. Spending time with the Hunter Collection also added dimensions to my life as a performer. I began to understand that singing isn't merely a form of entertainment; for so many, like "Aunt" Ollie Gilbert, Raymond Sanders, and Almeda Riddle, it was both a way of seeing the world and a matter of emotional and (often) spiritual survival. I'd like to think that this form of storytelling still keeps humanity afloat.

# ACKNOWLEDGMENTS

So many people led to my success with this project, but the person who first comes to mind is my forever friend and singing partner Martha Moseley Grace. Martha and I grew up in Princeton Township, and when we weren't mucking horse stalls, we spent a lot of indolent New Jersey days singing the good old stuff as we wandered through the woods and fields, most of which are miraculously still there. Martha is the individual who first brought the Max Hunter Folk Song Collection to my attention, thus propelling me into my most ambitious writing project to date.

I got to know editor and Hunter enthusiast Becky Schroeder just in time, and she served as my guiding light throughout the initial writing of this book. In her first email reply to me, she wrote, "Max deserves a biography," and coming from her, these simple words carried enormous weight. I'm sad that she won't be around to read the final product, but without her insight into Hunter's life, the stories she shared, and the materials she and her husband made available to persons like me, it would never have been written. Conversations and correspondence with Hunter's eldest daughter, Linda Bangs, were essential to my understanding of Hunter as a family man as well as a song collector. I cannot thank her enough for both her generosity and her steadfast support throughout this project.

Throughout the writing of this book I have often returned to Adam Davis, the indefatigable director of the Missouri Folklore Society, for both contacts and information. Such was also the case with performing artist Cathy Barton (before her death in 2019), who devoted much of her graduate work to documenting Max Hunter's journey as a ballad collector. Barton's husband

and musical partner for life, Dave Para, also took time out of the couple's busy performance schedule to respond to my inquiries. Other Missouri Folklore Society editors who came to my aid include Jim Vandergriff and Lyn Wolz. Dr. Alexandra Gregory's early attention to the Child ballads in the Hunter Collection also enriched this biography.

I am grateful for the community grant from the Country Dance and Song Society, which made it that much more feasible for my daughter Emma and me to go on a second research trip—this time to Springfield, Missouri. It is there that we met Michael Price—librarian extraordinaire—who helped guide us through the labyrinth of Hunter materials and has been an invaluable contact throughout my ongoing research. So many skilled librarians came to my rescue, chief among them Heather Richmond (early on in Columbia), Aryn Denette at the University of Central Arkansas, and Judith Gray at the American Folklife Center, among others.

Mark Bilyeu, a talented musician who has helped keep the Hunter Collection alive, has been one of my greatest cheerleaders. Speaking of the younger generation of Ozark ballad singers, I am thankful for the beautiful vocals of both "Julies," Julie Henigan and Julia O'Reilly, who shared stories of their festival years with Hunter. I completely understand that looking back on these times was both a joyous and melancholy experience for them both. Henigan's scholarship also gave me a much-needed critical perspective on Hunter's ballads. The inspiration Judy Domeny Bowen found in Hunter's collection and the beautiful recordings she has made also fueled my writing.

My project also benefited from the incomparable record keeping of musician and fiddle tune collector Gordon McCann, who held on to years of news clippings on his friend Max Hunter. Marie Demeroukas, of the Shiloh Museum of Ozark History, went above and beyond in helping me to locate photo materials.

Thanks go to Mark Foley, the bass-playing professor at Wichita State University who enthusiastically offered to locate essential materials on Joan O'Bryant, and to Ozarks scholar Brooks Blevins, who sent an early note of encouragement and guidance, and whose own writings have informed and inspired me throughout this process. Speaking of Arkansas, I am particularly grateful to Susan Gilbert Kemp (whose husband had just become the Chief Justice) for putting her family matters temporarily on hold in order to send me essential materials on her grandmother.

Back home in New England, I am thankful for the variety of support I received from my music friend Bob Phillipps, whose beautiful guitar accompaniment and (yes, Bob) warm vocals graced our CD *On the Trail of*

*Max Hunter: To the Ozarks and Back Again* (Nelson CD, LPL072821, 2017) as well as fiddler and gig partner Cathy Mason, who immediately got on board with my Max Hunter obsession. A huge note of appreciation goes to Anita Danker, who served me tea, lent me the illuminating tapes of Ollie Gilbert as well as other important materials, and spoke of her husband's passion for Ozarks music.

I wish I could name all of my friends in the folk music and education community, and those whom I've not yet met, who contributed to my Go-FundMe campaign. They know who they are, and without them (some of whom made multiple donations) my work would be incomplete.

Thanks, too, to contra dance evenings at the Concord Scout House, which brought me into contact with two men who might think of themselves as somehow tangential: Harvard anthropologist and author Steven LeBlanc, who gave me authorly wisdom that I didn't want to hear, and my husband, Andre White, whose motivational pep talks and assistance with certain technical aspects of the manuscript allowed me the time and focus for the storytelling itself.

Late in the research game, I owe an enormous thanks to all of the incredibly responsive staff in room 306 of the Meyer Library at Missouri State University. Shannon Mawhiney, in particular, unearthed some incredibly helpful resources that were buried deep in the McCann Collection.

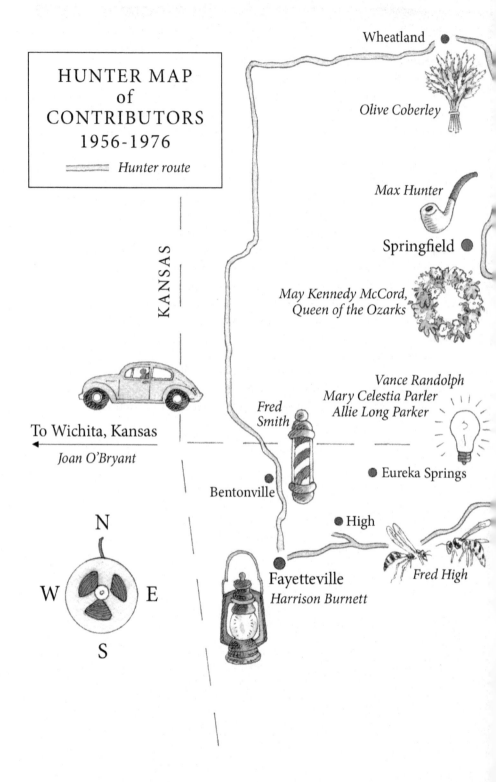

HUNTER MAP
of
CONTRIBUTORS
1956-1976

Hunter route

Wheatland

Olive Coberley

Max Hunter

Springfield

May Kennedy McCord,
Queen of the Ozarks

KANSAS

Vance Randolph
Mary Celestia Parler
Allie Long Parker

Fred
Smith

To Wichita, Kansas

Joan O'Bryant

Bentonville

Eureka Springs

High

N

Fayetteville

Harrison Burnett

Fred High

W    E

S

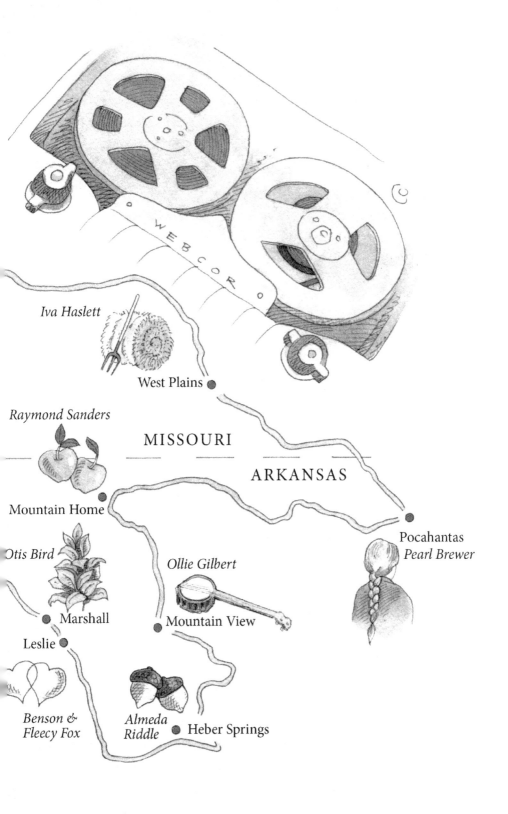

Iva Haslett

West Plains

Raymond Sanders

MISSOURI

ARKANSAS

Mountain Home

Otis Bird

Ollie Gilbert

Pocahantas
Pearl Brewer

Marshall

Mountain View

Leslie

Benson &
Fleecy Fox

Almeda
Riddle

Heber Springs

# BALLAD HUNTING
## WITH MAX HUNTER

# MAX HUNTER
# AND THE BALLAD FIELD

From 1956 through 1976, Max Hunter, a traveling salesman with little formal education, sought ballads throughout the Ozark region, recording nearly sixteen hundred traditional songs from more than two hundred singers. His remarkable song catching and ballad hunting drew upon, intersected with, and influenced cultural currents within and beyond the span of his life and the territory in which he lived, worked, and traveled. The urban son of country parents, Hunter grew up in a house filled with old songs, but beyond this domestic setting, he'd given little thought to the fragility of his musical inheritance, and he had no idea of the preservation work that had already taken place on Ozark soil and well beyond. With regard to background, geography, and time, Hunter was a world away from nineteenth-century Harvard University, where most early ballad studies began. But his transformation from a guitar-strumming businessman to a song preservationist happened almost in an instant, although the depth of conviction that followed would develop more slowly.

## Harvard's Early Influence

No individual contributions to culture take place in isolation, even when we are initially unaware of those who have laid the groundwork before us, and such was certainly the case with Hunter's own ballad work. A full century before the Missouri collector entered the field, Francis James Child,[1] Harvard's first English professor (and indeed America's), was hard at work on creating a systematic approach to gathering, identifying, and cataloging song materials.[2] Child's ballad preservation efforts were at their height from the mid-nineteenth century until his death in 1896 and were just one manifestation of an anti-modern, romantic movement driven by the realization that unstoppable social, political, economic, and industrial forces were altering the world at an accelerating pace. Published incrementally between 1882 and 1898, his groundbreaking volumes of *English and Scottish Popular Ballads* contain variants of no less than 305 ballads.[3] Anthologized from a variety of preexisting sources, such as popular broadsides,[4] manuscripts, and correspondence with English and Scottish scholars, many Child ballads can be traced back to the fourteenth century.[5] For Child and his contemporaries, the narrative folksongs contained therein were cherished fragments of lost worlds. Historically looked upon as the crown jewels of any Anglo-American collection, the presence of such materials in Hunter's collection gave it all the more ballast.

After Child's death in 1896, ballad studies gained an even firmer footing at Harvard under the direction of Child's successor, George Lyman Kittredge. Among Kittredge's early accomplishments was the editing and posthumous publication of Child's fifth and final volume and the seminal words he used to introduce these materials. "A ballad is a song that tells a story, or—to take the other point of view—a story told in song" would be echoed and distilled by folklorists for decades to come,[6] most notably expanded upon by Gordon H. Gerould in 1932: "A ballad is a folksong that tells a story with stress on the crucial situation, tells it by letting the action unfold itself in event and speech, and tells it objectively with little comment or intrusion of personal bias."[7] These features stood in contrast to many eighteenth- and nineteenth-century ballads (sometimes attributed to known authors), which often relied on first-person narration, not only to "tell" the story but also to *react* to its contents, often in an unrestrained maudlin or moralizing manner.[8]

Given the broad variety of ethnic communities that comprise the United States, it's worth keeping in mind that when these folklorists spoke of ballads, they spoke primarily of Anglo-American songs that had been passed down in English as opposed to materials in other tongues and traditions.[9] Following the work of Child, the methodology for future collectors was developed further by Cecil Sharp,[10] a turn-of-the-century British folksong collector who in 1916 teamed up with his assistant Maud Karpeles to cull the southern Appalachian Mountains for English ballads. They succeeded in their quest, thus permanently expanding the conversation between British and American song chasers on both sides of "the pond." All of this early twentieth-century activity would impact the ways early song collectors and folklorists nation-wide went about their work.

Adolf Schroeder, a patron of Missouri folk music and a professor of Germanic studies at University of Missouri–Columbia,[11] saw great irony in the fact that each folklorist, from Child forward, seems to have been driven by the finality of their mission. Shining a light on the arbitrary nature of dates repeatedly drawn in the sand, Schroeder commented, "Cecil Sharp believed that the 'last generation of folk singers must have been born not later than . . . say 1840.'"[12] As Schroeder went on to say, with characteristic humor, "Why the chain of tradition snapped at that particular point he [Sharp] could not determine."[13] This sense of urgency, in combination with the intriguing travelogue of Sharp's and Karpeles's treks over the rough Appalachian terrain, created an aura of romanticism around song collecting. And although perceptions of a disappearing song field may have been premature, there is no question that these concerns generated productivity well before the last Ozarks sweep.

## A New Englander in Missouri

When Hunter first started recording ballads, he would not have been familiar with the names Child, Kittredge, or Sharp. Nor was he aware that his song-chasing activities in Missouri stood (in part) on the shoulders of Connecticut native Henry Marvin Belden,[14] or, more accurately, on those of Belden's students who had done the actual fieldwork some thirty years before Hunter became active. But these earlier influences were in the song-collecting soil all around him, and a generation of ballad bearers had already been touched by them.

In 1903 Belden established the University of Missouri's first English Club, which was comprised of students, many of whom happened to enjoy the singing of old songs.[15] When a student (likely Maude Williams[16]) got up and sang an ancient ballad during an early club meeting, this event triggered a "lightbulb moment" for Belden, who was thrilled to defy the naysayers. The importance of this moment was highlighted in a history of the Missouri Folklore Society: "Child's belief that traditional balladry and song had not survived into the late 19th century was shared by many of his contemporaries and adopted by many of the scholars who followed him. Belden recognized the significance of his discovery that 'many such songs were known and sung by the country folk in Missouri,' and his students soon became aware of the importance of their mission."[17]

The year 1903 was also the first time that Belden sent his students into the field, and while the bulk of their collecting would be finished by 1917, it would be twenty-three more years before his life's work, *Ballads and Songs Collected by the Missouri Folk-Lore Society*,[18] would see the light of publication.[19] Needless to say, this collection was a landmark event in the world of Missouri folklore. Luckily for Belden, he received considerable financial and academic support from Mary Alicia Owen, a writer and fellow folklorist who devoted her life to collecting the folklore of Native Americans and African Americans in Missouri and to whom he would dedicate his collection.[20]

The scholarship coming out of Harvard during the early twentieth century, particularly during Kittredge's long tenure there, catalyzed conversations between folklorists all across the country, and Belden was no exception. From 1916 to 1917 he would take a leave of absence from his post at Columbia to study with Kittredge. Kittredge, in turn, would have a major impact on how Belden went about his work and was an essential link in the cultural exchange between New Englanders and Midwestern folklorists. Missouri scholars Susan Pentlin and Rebecca Schroeder made special mention of "Belden in Missouri" and "Louise Pound in Nebraska,"[21] among other notable folklorists who "led the way in promoting the collection of both traditional British ballads and native American songs in their areas." It was no exaggeration to say that "a virtual fever of collecting to preserve the American heritage of song swept the country, reaching its peak in the 1920s and 1930s."[22] All of this was going on before Hunter's time.

Due to the time and place in which he did his work—a predominantly white, Protestant state in a time of prolonged segregation—most of Belden's singers were the descendants of Anglo-European settlers, a limitation of which he was aware, suggested editor Rebecca Schroeder, who contributed Belden's biographical sketch to the *Dictionary of Missouri Biography*.[23] The following statement from Belden also suggests a moderately inclusive mindset: "It does not appear that ballads in Missouri belong to any particular age, sex, or class of society," the Missouri collector once observed.[24] As the founder of the Missouri Folklore Society, Belden tried to address this lack of diversity by encouraging the collection of materials from a broader segment of Missouri society, a task largely delegated to Owen.

Unlike collectors who had preceded him, Belden did not put the Child ballads on a pedestal.[25] Because of his abiding interest in homegrown songs of American origin, he succeeded in gathering, what was for his place and time, a remarkably broad mix of song materials;[26] personal "ballet" books of lyrics occasionally provided by his contacts included an eclectic array of songs that appealed to the unschooled singer, who was generally unconcerned with balladic origins.[27] As described by folklore librarian and editor Lyn Wolz, "Stall ballads (i.e., sheet music sold at fairs or sometimes copied from newspapers), sentimental ditties, the works of local minstrels, and what Child called 'popular ballads' existed side by side in the repertory of Missouri folk singers," and Belden's collection was richer because of this.[28]

Of all the collecting activities that took place between the early years of Belden's efforts and the publication of his work in 1940, none are more important and directly applicable to Hunter's own collecting work than those of Arkansas transplant Vance Randolph,[29] who was writing down, meticulously annotating, and publishing ballad texts from both Arkansas and Missouri well before 1940.[30] By the late 1920s, Randolph found himself in the intellectual spheres of both Louise Pound, who encouraged his dialect studies,[31] and Belden, who championed his ballad work.[32] Randolph, a prolific author, had already starting amassing songs for what would become his greatest opus of all, his four-volume *Ozark Folksongs*,[33] which would be published incrementally from 1946 to 1950 on the heels of Belden's collection.

But Randolph and Belden were hardly the only collectors in the region. A paper coauthored by Randolph and his longtime friend Ruth Ann Musick (a scholar in her own right) provides an engaging overview of song gathering in Missouri.[34] Infused with their collective wit, it illuminated some common themes in ballad collecting during the first half of the twentieth century.[35] Not surprisingly, Randolph and Musick made ample mention of Belden's students, who mostly followed in the footsteps of Child and Kittredge: "These collectors brought in text only, and made no attempt to record tunes."[36] (A star among them was Goldy Hamilton, who collected thirty-eight songs.) Outside of academia, attention was also given to Ozarks enthusiast Otto Ernest Rayburn,[37] who created his own ballad section for Randolph in his monthly *Ozark Life* magazine in 1929 and sporadically printed lyrics in others of his regional publications, such as *Arcadian Magazine* and *Arcadian Life*.[38]

During the 1930s, Hunter's hometown of Springfield featured prominently in song-harvesting activities among Missouri columnists (in particular), although the majority of these individuals were non-academics who simply used partial lyrics to spice up their stories. Balladeer journalist May Kennedy McCord often included local ballads in her "Hillbilly Heartbeats" column,[39] as did Lucile Morris Upton for the Springfield *Leader-News* (in later years Upton would interview Hunter about his own fieldwork).[40] In a different vein, Emma Galbraith (also of Springfield) purportedly collected as many as 208 songs (and their tunes) in Greene County while assisting Federal Writers Project director Geraldine Parker of St. Louis, but Galbraith's promised manuscript never surfaced.[41]

During this same time period, other Springfielders also offered up song collections that never came to fruition—among them, singing grocer Ben Rice and his son David, both of whom were recorded for the Library of Congress. Randolph and Musick also included this tantalizing tidbit: "Paul Holland, head of a printing company in Springfield, knew many old songs, some of which he consistently refused to have recorded by folksong hunters. In carefully chosen company, back in 1934, Mr. Holland sang a highly prized 'family ballad' (Child 250) which he called 'Andrew Bardeen' and believed to be virtually unknown outside the Holland clan."[42] Written in 1951 on the cusp of the growing folk revival, the paper presented Randolph and Musick's contention that the reason behind so many incomplete song projects was the disapproval of local society toward this material, which many preferred to keep buried:

> A few years ago many progressive Missourians, particularly in the southern part of the state, seemed rather ashamed of the old songs. Some of these citizens thought that ballad-hunters and other folklorists were "glorifying the backwoods" in such a manner as to minimize the advantages of modern industry and agriculture. . . . But recently there seems to be a more enlightened public opinion. Books on folklore are reviewed without heat in Missouri newspapers, and the conservative State Historical Society now looks with favor upon folksong collectors.[43]

Beyond Springfield, Randolph and Musick made special mention of prolific newspaperman C. V. Wheat, out of Aurora, who published "Songs and Ballads of Yester-Years" in the Aurora *Weekly Advertiser* from 1934 to 1942.[44] Historian and author Charles Van Ravenswaay, who would go on to direct the Missouri Historical Society for over a decade, collected up to two hundred folksongs in 1935, many of them from Black singers.[45]

But in the end, all of these efforts paled in comparison to the achievements of both Belden and Randolph, the latter of whom would dedicate his *Ozark Folksongs* to the Missouri professor. In addition, Belden would serve as an invaluable resource not only to Randolph but also to nationwide collectors such as John and Alan Lomax, both of whom intermittently corresponded with him on behalf of the Library of Congress. Indeed, Belden's sparse but insightful annotations enhance our own understanding of the Ozark songs, and there is a profound satisfaction in discovering the long timeline of ballads that have survived so many centuries on Ozark soil. And although Hunter was never interested in publishing per se, Randolph's collecting methods and level of achievement would blaze a trail for the younger song chaser. Taking the accomplishments of both Belden and Randolph into account, it is hardly an overstatement for folk music scholar Norm Cohen to conclude, "Between the two of them they inaugurated and closed out the first four decades of Ozark folksong scholarship."[46]

## Looking to the Ozarks

When Max Hunter came onto the scene in the 1950s, many key events had already taken place on the national timeline of ballad collecting. By 1922 Louise Pound had published *American Ballads and Songs*,[47] which was groundbreaking in terms of both its level of scholarship and its broad geographic sweep, and by 1928 poet and song chaser Carl Sandburg had published his one-of-a-kind book *The American Songbag*, which would inspire artists and writers for generations to come. This is also the same year when Robert Winslow Gordon convinced Library of Congress administrator Carl Engel to establish the Archive of American Folk Song, a branch of the library that would eventually become part of the American Folklife Center.[48] And by the end of 1936, John Lomax had recorded 116 ballads from Emma Dusenbury, a blind ballad bearer from Mena, Arkansas, who had since passed away and whose story would come to embody the allure of the ballad chase. Folklorist Sidney Robertson Cowell had already teamed up with the Lomaxes and Charles Seeger to record a wide swath of folksongs from Appalachia to the Ozarks.[49] Also during the mid-1930s, hundreds of individuals had been propelled into fieldwork through jobs created by the Works Progress Administration (WPA) under Franklin D. Roosevelt's New Deal policies.[50]

Despite all of these activities, there was still a deep and invisible vein of Ozark balladry that had not yet been touched, let alone recorded. In 1931 Randolph observed, "The last sixty years have brought some changes to the Ozarks, of course, but it is astonishing how insignificant these changes are, as compared with those which have occurred in more enlightened parts of the country."[51] Randolph's use of the word "enlightened" reflects the complicated relationship he had with this region, at once suggesting that Ozark inhabitants were benighted in comparison to those from other parts of the country, while at the same time expressing deep affection for the culture in which he chose to immerse himself.

Eighty years on, Arkansas scholar and writer Brooks Blevins would make similar observations, noting that cultural and economic shifts have taken place "at a pace that lagged a generation behind other American places,"[52] a time lag, he argues, that has been greatly amplified by almost a century's worth of folklorists and writers, many of whom he believes were temperamentally resistant to change: "The Ozarkers of the foothills, creek bottoms, and mountain hollows had never been as isolated and as unconsciously immune or consciously resistant to modernizing influences and brushes with the outside world as folklorists and travel writers had suggested."[53]

Blevins, a historian by training, has a sweeping disciplinary grievance against folklorists—those in the Ozarks region in particular: "Folklorists, professional and amateur—Vance Randolph chief among them—impacted the public's perception of the Ozarks as they did few other regions."[54] Regardless of the merits or weaknesses of Blevins's complaint, there is no doubt that swimming against the current of the Ozarks as an *idea* rather than a place on the map has been no easy task. The moment that Harold Bell Wright came out with his book *Shepherd of the Hills* in 1907,[55] the romanticization of the region stuck like glue to the American imagination. Who could possibly resist the melancholy and mysterious Daniel Howitt ("The Stranger"), let alone John Wayne, who would portray him in the film version, which came out in 1941. The book, filled with moonlight, "forest-clad hills,"[56] pipe smoke, tragic young lovers, and old men in tattered hats, became a teacher's pet of the tourism industry. In their book on regional tourism, Lynn Morrow and Linda Myers-Phinney put it this way: "Wright's book served as the first national promotion of the Ozarks, and boosters used it to institutionalize scenery and landmarks."[57]

But while the Ozarks have historically received less attention than other places, Blevins has rightly suggested that this region's late-blooming balladry was well worth waiting for: "By the post–World War II era . . . the rural Ozarks was, along with parts of rural Appalachia, the most fertile field for collecting remnants of Anglo-American folkways and music."[58] Blevins, who has spent much of his academic career looking at the Ozarks and *perceptions* of the Ozarks from all angles, also had this to say during the 2015 opening of the Ozark Folksong Collection at the University of Arkansas:[59] "The Ozarks certainly possessed the requisites for the incubation of anachronism. The region, or at least vast, rural stretches of it, was and is poorer and more isolated than most other places in the United States. And poverty and isolation are two of the characteristics most associated with the survival of traditional folkways,"[60] particularly those, like ballads, that relied on oral transmission.

Raised amid the burgeoning postwar sprawl of Springfield, there is no question that Hunter, a man of a down-to-earth temperament and sharp observational skills, nonetheless harbored some idealistic notions about the Ozarkers who lived beyond the city limits. Having once declared that "the Ozarker is the finest," he simultaneously voiced his disapproval of the social strictures he saw around him and expressed skepticism toward long-held regional beliefs and practices, despite his lifelong fascination with them. He was temperamentally predisposed toward trying to get things right, a trait that those around him would either admire or find tiresome. Hardly a grammarian, words nonetheless mattered deeply to Hunter, and he had no patience for euphemism. Speaking on the topic of death, he once observed of his fellow Ozarkers, "They usually refer that they 'have passed on,' 'have gone to heaven,' 'have left this world,' or something like that. For some reason, they seem hesitant to use the words 'died' or 'dead.'"[61]

If anyone had asked Hunter point-blank whether the Ozarks and its people were exceptional in comparison to other parts of the country, he would surely have answered yes, but he was far less likely to romanticize the region, certainly not to the degree of his older friend Randolph, who (a full quarter of a century after Wright) would paint this alluring picture:

One has only to leave the broad auto roads and go back a few miles into the hills to find himself in a different environment, among people who have until very recently been curiously isolated from the outside world, and whose way of living has changed very little since their sturdy forbears wandered west from the southern Appalachians more than a century ago. There are men in the Ozarks today who sleep in cord beds and hunt with muzzle-loading rifles; there are women who still use spinning-wheels and weave cloth on homemade looms; there are minstrels who sing old English ballads brought over by the seventeenth-century colonists.[62]

During an interview in 2005, Springfielder Gordon McCann—whose voluminous and meticulously documented collection of Ozark fiddle tunes is housed at Missouri State University and who would work alongside Hunter during local music events—weighed in on the cultural advantages of this region's comparative isolation: "Everywhere else folk music had been 'mainstreamed,' but we still had it here" (meaning region-specific fiddling styles and repertoire). At the same time, McCann acknowledged that "all this is very fragile,"[63] a sentiment that proved to be the driving force behind both his and Hunter's impulse to collect.

## Two Springfielders

Hunter and McCann, two pragmatically minded businessmen, were undeniably drawn not only to the music of their contributors but also to the anachronistic lives their musical acquaintances appeared to lead. Although they would sometimes be at odds with each other, McCann picked up some collecting tips from observing his older acquaintance's successes and mistakes. McCann first got the collecting bug after attending a Saturday night jam at Emanuel Wood's Ozark Opry just south of Springfield: "It was about as much atmosphere as you'll ever find. Every Saturday night there was a mixture of people, almost from another century."[64]

For his part, Hunter was constantly on the lookout for that direct window through which only *he* could see; this happened when he recorded the ninety-one-year-old Olive Coberley while perched on the edge of her bed, and when he finally located the forlorn and inebriated Herbert Philbrick in a local tavern. It happened repeatedly throughout his twenty years on the road. But regardless of his preservationist impulses, he worked diligently at bringing cultural artifacts, unembellished and unaltered, into the future.

Early on in their collecting days, both Hunter and McCann had to learn to navigate around occasionally reluctant sources. When McCann first started collecting fiddle tunes, he observed that "people were suspicious of that tape recorder." He related how hoedown champion Lonnie Robertson later confided to him, "First, when you come over, I purposely made mistakes in the tune."[65] But McCann's acquired skill as a guitar accompanist would go a long way toward helping him forge strong and natural connections with the local musical community. In the case of Hunter, whose oftentimes stubborn provincialism might have proved a hindrance to success, his status as a businessman native to the area greatly enhanced his ability to tap into song sources. Though he traveled in wider circles than McCann, Hunter was rarely viewed as an "outsider," and this enabled him to collect far more than the music itself.

There is little doubt that despite Hunter's distance from cultural hotbeds such as New York City's Greenwich Village, Boston, San Francisco, or Chicago, the revival of interest in folk music during the decades of the 1950s and 1960s influenced the energy with which he went about his ballad-collecting work. In his exploration of the folk revival, author Robert Cantwell reminds us "that the 'folk' are rarely such to themselves."[66] W. K. McNeil has also given some thought to the term we use so loosely: "The only criterion that modern-day folklorists assign to the folk is that . . . he or she must be involved in folklore. This can lead to a circular definition," or to no meaningful definition at all, he concludes.[67] As for Hunter, having been reared in a conservative, blue-collar milieu, he would not have identified with such "folk" as the culturally sophisticated, well-educated, often left-leaning urban and suburban youth who became so intent upon preserving and celebrating regional music.[68]

Hunter's definition of "folk" would have applied to the material he sought rather than to himself.[69] Nor was he positioned to be a national influencer in the folk revival, although he would eventually forge working relationships with those, like Alan Lomax, who were. Add to this his reluctance to engage in the political activism or social debates that often went hand in hand with folk events—in fact, he actively disliked songs with a "message" or political lyrics. Nor did he spend much time on college campuses, where, as cultural scholar Ronald Cohen expressed it, "folk activities mushroomed" during the second half of the twentieth century.[70] Living on the southern edge of the Midwest, Hunter was far from the Northern institutions that set their sights on preserving and understanding the comparatively "exotic" Southern folk culture.[71]

If, as Cohen characterized it, "the folk revival proceeded on two parallel, slightly divided tracks," one of which was concerned with authenticity and the other focused on folk music as a commodity, Hunter ran with the purists and resisted commercialization every step of the way.[72] Indeed, the neatly packaged performance was of least concern to him.[73] Focused as he was on local culture, the revival might have entirely passed Hunter by had he not been drawn to the possibilities of the festival scene. His concern for collecting ballads in their natural state, regardless of their aesthetic appeal, would bring him into conversation with both academic and non-academic folklorists who shared his values.

## Hunter's Start

By the mid-1950s, when Hunter first began to collect, he would capture the next generation of Missourians singing many of the same ballads as those that first appeared in the Belden collection. Although Hunter made every effort to limit his collecting activity to pre–World War II songs sung in southern Missouri, northern Arkansas, and (occasionally) Kansas, the collection encompasses a wide range of materials from nineteenth-century Anglo-American broadside ballads (aka "stall ballads") composed in response to specific events, to approximately two hundred variants on Child ballads,[74] as well as "native" American ballads (meaning songs that originated in the United States).[75] Geographically speaking, Hunter's collection would ultimately be wider in scope than that of Randolph or Belden.[76]

A few of the names of those Hunter recorded may be familiar to contemporary readers, due in part to the efforts of collector John Quincy Wolf Jr., an English professor at Southwestern at Memphis,[77] who collected mostly from the Arkansas side of the Ozark range and devoted much of his life to discovering and cataloging important singers.[78] Hunter collected songs from Stone County, Arkansas, residents "Aunt" Ollie Gilbert as well as her close friend and neighbor Jimmy Driftwood.[79] He also collected several songs from Almeda Riddle, whose songs were previously recorded by Alan Lomax and included in *American Folk Songs for Children* as part of Lomax's Southern Folk Heritage Series,[80] and whose life was well documented in her autobiography, written in collaboration with Roger Abrahams.[81] Close to home, Hunter recorded Johnny Mullins, the "singing janitor" of Springfield, who would become famous for the songs he penned for Loretta Lynn and other Nashville folk.

Alan Lomax, who made sweeps through Stone County, Arkansas, in both 1959 and 1967,[82] occasionally seemed to be collecting in parallel with Hunter, and although they would eventually correspond, there is no record of the two men ever having met. On the spectrum of "armchair" folklorists versus those who ventured into the field,[83] Hunter's approach to song gathering can best be compared to that of North Carolina's Bascom Lamar Lunsford, who also started life as a salesman and (in the opening words of his biographer) "would cross hell on a rotten rail to get a folk song."[84] They had other elements in common as well; while Lunsford's musical performance skills were more advanced than Hunter's, it is interesting to note that both men got into the recording habit simply for the pleasure of expanding their personal repertoires.

## Songs and Stories

The songs Hunter would go on to capture covered the full emotional range of human existence. It is both startling and discomfiting to hear some of the darkest murder ballads sung in the high, sweet soprano voice of Fran Majors of Fayetteville, Arkansas, or to hear the voice of ten-year-old Betty Lou Copeland unflinchingly making its way through the brutal story of "Notchville Girl." Sometimes it is the very absence of emotion in a singer's voice that speaks volumes about the times they lived in or through.

Most of Hunter's contributors sang without accompaniment. Those who played guitar did so with a minimum of adornment and only with a few major chords.[85] He observed, "Aunt Ollie Gilbert . . . could play the banjo, but she did so rarely. . . . It was just something she would do to take a little break, to give her voice a rest or something like that. . . . And I can think of one or two that did use a musical instrument that would have been better off if they didn't."[86] This lack of instrumentation immediately laid bare not only the skills of the singer but perhaps more importantly the qualities of the lyrics themselves.

What song scholars Fiona Ritchie and Doug Orr had to say about Appalachian balladry could just as easily be applied to its successor, Ozark balladry: a cappella singing "underscored the communally held philosophy that traditional singing was not about the singer and the performance. The old ballad stories were owned by no one and yet by everyone: generations of singing families and communities. The singer's job was to give the song a voice."[87]

In addition to the stories that folksongs and ballads naturally contained, singing was a form of entertainment, especially among young people. During a 1958 recording session, Lucy Quigley, who lived just south of Eureka Springs, spoke fondly of singing parties and song competitions that moved from house to house during her youth. In addition to her comments about the rarity of instrumental accompaniment, her narrative implies differentiation on the part of the community between "approved" songs (such as those from hymnals) and more traditional material:

> All those good Christian people would say, "Now get the songbook." Whenever we'd get done, they'd make us sing out of the songbooks then. We'd have the best time, and then we'd go [to] some of the rest of the houses next time. Whoever sang a new song got the prize—a new handkerchief or something . . . just to have fun—or pins or something. There would be twenty-five or thirty of them. We'd just sing—oh, sometimes a man, Jerry Evans, would come with his fiddle and he'd play for us. Never had no other instruments. Oh, the boys had French harps [harmonicas] and things, but they never could play them.[88]

But gaining insight into the lives of those who sang for Hunter has necessitated going well beyond the materials he left behind, for interviews (at least early on) with sources were the exception rather than the rule. In this respect Hunter was typical of non-academic folklorists, but in other ways— such as his consistent documentation of the time and place in which ballads were recorded—he exceeded them. In his chapter on "Ballad Collectors in the Ozarks,"[89] writer Norm Cohen addressed this issue head on: "While the nonacademics often preserved important materials that can reveal much regional lore, their materials are unfortunately of distinctly less use for later scholarly analysis because they generally lack any information about the informants, where and when the songs were collected, and where or when they were learned."[90] Hunter consistently supplied us with the "where" and the "when," even when other information was missing, and one can certainly argue that the time Hunter might have devoted to note taking was instead allotted to being particularly "present."[91]

As to his sources, some of Hunter's contributors were highly skilled and self-aware in their artistry, such as young college students like Wise Jones or Krisanne Parker, or torchbearers like Almeda Riddle, but the majority of his ballad bearers had no pretentions about being true "performers." As Hunter observed, "They do not think of themselves as singers. Most of them claim their voices are not good."[92] Such was certainly the case with a Mrs. Lee (Floy) Huskey of Blue Eye, Missouri. Even though Mrs. Huskey protested, "I don't think I can sing good enough for your tape,"[93] she nonetheless bestowed upon him a handful of songs in a tuneful soprano voice. But since Hunter was consistently focused on the authenticity of the ballads that he recorded rather than musical aesthetics, quality of voice was the least of his concerns. He was far more apt to be moved by the Ozark singer's ability to inhabit the lyric stories and to impart a deeper meaning, "even the songs that the singers sang that they outwardly didn't seem to understand, yet their inner selves seemed to know what the song was about."[94] Hunter understood that the Ozark ballads constituted a musical DNA of sorts.

### From All Walks of Life

Hunter, whose recording activities picked up just as other Ozark collectors were winding down, always insisted that his ballad collecting was an *avocation* rather than a vocation, that it was mostly about the experience itself:

> Some of the places I have been to collect were almost at the end of the proverbial "no-where." Down in hollows that were two miles down hill, over glorified wagon trails, country roadside tavern[s], on top of small mountains that overlooked large rive[r]s and wide valleys, into homes where the very barest of necessities were visible, into the finest homes in the community, into farm homes where the independence of country living was everywhere, into service stations, hotel lobbies, jewelry stores, into sheriff[']s office[s], into county operated homes for the poor, into city and county schools, anywhere I could find someone with a song.[95]

The above passage reflects a distinctly American brand of romanticism as might be found in the work of Woody Guthrie or Carl Sandburg, because it shows Hunter's awareness of the importance of collecting in a wide variety of settings and from people in all walks of life. That said, like Belden and Randolph before him, Hunter was a product of his ancestry and the time and place in which he lived and worked, and he did not seek out racially diverse sources. In his own hometown, with its history of racial violence and segregation,[96] there was a parallel current of Black music coming out of the all-Black Lincoln schools and houses of worship,[97] but if this cultural phenomenon interested Hunter, he never made mention of it. Occasionally he included annotations that hinted at the African American origins of some of his materials, like that of "The Tiehackers Song" as sung by T. M. Davis: "Mr. Davis said he used to hear the negroe workers sing this song while driving spikes on the rail ties," he wrote. Indeed, Hunter's largest source of gospel songs came from Ollie Gilbert, a white grandmother from Arkansas. Overwhelmingly, Hunter and those who came before him were focused on Anglo-American balladry sung by white singers of European ancestry.[98]

While approximately 150 years of song scholarship have given us a greater appreciation for our vast musical inheritance, some scholarly treatises on Anglo-American balladry have done us a disservice by creating artificial divides within repertoires. Only a handful of Hunter's contributors concerned themselves with the types of songs they were singing; in fact, they were more likely to categorize songs by subject.[99] Belden, who himself eventually came up with more than a dozen song classifications, acknowledged the divide between the academic world and that of its human sources: "For to the student of folk-song it soon becomes apparent that the distinction attempted by Child and more definitely by Gummere between 'genuine' and 'vulgar' balladry does not hold for the singers of 'song ballets' nowadays."[100]

In other words, the development and accumulation of a region's repertoire was deeply democratic and unsystematic. The night that Hunter visited with Joe Walker at a beer tavern in Eureka Springs, the inebriated Walker commingled songs about whoring and copulation right alongside ancient Child ballads.[101] In February 1968, when Hunter taped Boyce Davis, a musically inclined lawyer and newspaperman from Lincoln, Arkansas, Davis supplied the collector with a potpourri of personally composed ditties and popular songs, in addition to two Child ballads. Overall, Hunter's songsters were far quicker to identify from whom they had learned their material and to recall songs by subject rather than by title. As observed by Belden, "Ballad titles are of course quite unreliable as a means of identification."[102]

The people Hunter spent time with over a twenty-year period rarely thought of themselves as singers, tradition bearers, entertainers, or even storytellers, although they were all of the above. They simply thought of themselves in the context of family, church, and community, all of which were tightly interwoven. Song scholar and performer Julie Henigan,[103] a native of Springfield, has written at length and with great clarity about the interrelatedness of story and song: "The performance of narrative songs (called 'ballads' by folk song scholars) constitutes a form of storytelling with a long history in the Ozarks. . . . This practice was at once contiguous and continuous with the folktale tradition, occurring, as it did, primarily in intimate performance contexts, and sometimes employing the same narrative in either form: ballads often appear as spoken stories and singers were not infrequently also storytellers."[104] In short, songs or stories were of the same fabric.

Such was the case with raconteur William Eden of Monte Ne, Arkansas. Eden had a particularly rich repertoire of American ballads (or what Alan Lomax categorized as White Desperado songs) with which he felt a personal connection. Almost every song that Parler and Hunter recorded had a "backstory" from Eden, and the tales he had learned along with the songs were of equal importance to the singer. Such is certainly the case with "California Joe," which Eden claimed to have learned from a Missouri schoolmate by the name of Tildy Phillips. As though he himself had been at the scene, Eden frequently interrupted his singing to describe Joe's reunion with a girl named Mag in cinematic detail. The song begins with Joe's rescue of the girl, presumably from marauding Indians, and continues forward to Joe and Mag's reunion and likely marriage; but due to the immediacy of Eden's narration, it is often unclear as to where the commentary begins and the verses end.[105] This was also the case with Arkansas balladeer Ollie Gilbert, who regularly propped her songs in between anecdotal "bookends." In short, the boundaries between modes of expression were entirely fluid.

Such recitations on the part of contributors showed how strongly they related to the characters about whom they sang. During the 1958 recording of W. H. Shelly of Cabool, Missouri, the elderly singer repeatedly broke out in sobs as he made his way through "Little Darling" and "Little Colleen." Although Hunter's annotations on this session were characteristically sparse, he noted that the eighty-year-old Shelly had suffered a stroke eighteen months before and that "he had tears in his eyes and his voice broke very badly, from memories of days gone by." Such moments emphasized the emotional bonds between the singers and their songs and left a deep impression on the young song collector.[106]

The manner in which Hunter's sources carried their songs and the often private and domestic settings in which they chose to share them stand in contrast to many of today's practices. In this perfectionist age of YouTube, high-tech recording studios and music conservatories now offer an abundance of traditional music courses,[107] and singers can now spar for the most aesthetically pleasing performance, thus losing sight of songs as conduits of culture and continuity. Regionalism in traditional repertoire, while studied, is fast disappearing, and there are strong currents of both competition and collaboration within the folk music community. Artists are constantly reminded to take an old song—or a new song written by someone else—and "make it their own." But overall it is difficult to imagine how the songs we now choose to sing will leave a navigable trail back to who we were when we sang them or what was, in the broadest sense, the landscape of our lives.

Max Hunter's contributors didn't have to worry about any of this. For the most part, songs were handed down through a long and seamless line of oral transmission, and these materials resided deep in a collective memory that went back for generations. Nor would these songsters have categorized their repertoire as "folk" songs, as expressed by Jimmy Driftwood (one of Hunter's most famous and knowledgeable balladeers):

> When I was a boy growing up in the Ozarks, we never heard the term "folk music," but we sure played a lot of it. My dad taught me my first tunes on the guitar, sitting out on the porch those long summer evenings. . . . We played a guitar my grandpa made from a fence rail and an old ox yoke. Wintertimes we would often huddle around the fireplace till bedtime, singin' and pickin'. Saturday nights several families often got together to sing songs like "Barbara Allen," "Old Joe Clark," or "Knoxville Girl"—ballads as old as the hills.[108]

Unlike some of the academic collectors who preceded him, Hunter had no folkloric disciples to send out into the field and was very much a one-man operation. That said, it would be a mistake to conclude that the line between folklorists who conducted their own fieldwork and those who did not falls neatly along academic versus non-academic lines. A number of folklorists, many of whom were professors, did do their own collecting at one time or another: Harvard graduate Robert Winslow Gordon would fall in love with fieldwork in Darien, Georgia (often to the detriment of family life and his relationship with the Library of Congress); novelist and folklorist Dorothy Scarborough (who championed Randolph's work in the Ozarks) taught at Columbia University and spent much of her life in the field collecting songs from African Americans and Appalachian sources;[109] and Herbert Halpert (a visiting professor at the University of Arkansas in 1960 and a close friend of Randolph) spent geographically diverse time in the field collecting ballads both for the WPA and for his own research purposes.[110]

In the case of Hunter, his status as an academic outsider initially insulated him from the century-long chorus of folklorists, starting with Francis James Child, who repeatedly claimed that their own contributions to the field of balladry were but swan songs. And while Hunter inarguably arrived late on the ballad-chasing timeline, the course of his life is a reminder that we often embark upon our greatest adventures in a state of relative unawareness.[111]

# 1

# SINGING ON THE
# WAY TO CHURCH

Max Franklin Hunter was born on July 2, 1921, to Ethyl Rose and Roy Hunter in Springfield, Missouri, just a few miles north of Ozark, where his older siblings had already come into the world. Hunter could reach at least as far back as his great-great-grandparents when tracing his family roots, and all of his ancestors came to the Ozarks region from such Appalachian states as North Carolina, Georgia, and Tennessee.[1] As one journalist expressed it, it was "a migration from one set of mountains to another that carried the culture of eastern Tennessee, eastern Kentucky, and western North Carolina into an entirely new region."[2] This migratory path west was common to a majority of early Ozarks settlers, most of whom came from the Appalachian region, and census data, as described by author Norm Cohen, bears this out: "In 1860, for example, only half of all Missourians had been born in that state, while a quarter came from Kentucky, Tennessee, Virginia, Ohio and North Carolina (in order of decreasing importance)." In addition, at least half of Arkansas's population consisted of Tennessee transplants.[3] Not surprisingly, many of the ballads Hunter and others collected would have traveled this very same route.

As for Hunter's own family history, Hunter's paternal great-great-grandfather, Isaac Redfearn, came from North Carolina and was a veteran of the War of 1812. After the war, Redfearn was rewarded with land grants that amounted to eight hundred acres around Bois D'Arc, where he and his wife, Penelope, began to settle around 1843.[4] The land was eventually divided up among the Redfearn children: two hundred acres to the sons and one hundred acres to the daughters when they married. Hunter's ancestors on both sides were mostly farmers.

Hunter's maternal great-grandparents, Malinda (Byrd) Gideon (1828–1907) and William Carroll Gideon (1824–1863), both came from Tennessee. Hunter loved to regale audiences with a Civil War story that made it down through generations of his family, describing how Grandmother Gideon supposedly "made biscuits and bacon sandwiches and would stand along the road handing out these sandwiches in hopes of keeping the men [Union soldiers] away from their home." He went on to say, "It didn't work all the time, but they apparently fared better than some of their neighbors."[5] As for his great-grandfather, Hunter recalled that William C. Gideon was "reared among the pioneers of the Ozarks" and that he married Malinda Byrd in 1845 at the age of twenty-one. A Greene County historical paper states that William Gideon had 480 acres of land in Christian County before the Civil War and attained much more afterward. We also know that he was a Methodist who started life as a War Democrat and ended life as a Republican and that, in the words of a Greene County historian, he "was a man of quiet and peaceful disposition."[6] Gideon, who became a recruiting officer during the Civil War, was a victim of a vigilante slaying and died in December 1863. He was thirty-nine years of age.

Hunter's maternal grandparents were Emma Jane (Gideon) Rose (1870–1950) and Edwin ("Bud") Rose (1866–1929), who scraped up a living by running a boardinghouse near Ozark, Missouri, where Hunter's grandfather doubled as postmaster for many years. Ethyl Rose (1890–1965), Hunter's mother, was the oldest of several daughters and had two prominent uncles: Thomas J. Gideon, who narrowly escaped death from a musket ball during a Civil War battle, and James J. Gideon, who earned the nickname "Sleepy Jim" both because of his tendency to ponder things deeply and because he apparently "had a knack for sleeping in the saddle," as described in a local history of Greene County.[7] Both Gideon brothers rose to prominence in Springfield due to their lawyerly skills. As Hunter once remarked, "The Gideons down in Christian County and King County were well known. They were doctors, lawyers, sheriffs, some how they were in politics in one way or the other."[8] But none of these prominent professions appear to have continued into the next generation.

Hunter's paternal grandparents were Isaac Hunter (ca. 1837–1915) and Hiley (Foster) Hunter (1850–1910), both of whom suffered a grueling journey westward from Tennessee, having, according to Hunter's eldest daughter, "buried two sons and a daughter along the roadside on the way."[9] Once they settled down in Ozark, they had four more children, all of them sons: William, Roy (Hunter's father), Charles, and John. Grandfather Isaac was one of the few Hunter ancestors who did not make a living off of the land, and it seems likely that he and Hunter shared the "salesman" gene. As described by his grandson, "He [Isaac] was a little of everything, *except* a farmer. He was a trader; he'd trade anything for anything . . . whether it was your pocket knife or your buggy. He'd trade. He didn't get rich, but he never did get threw out of anywhere. Some people can do that and some can't; he just could."[10] Hunter's grandparents would remain in Ozark, Missouri, for the remainder of their lives.

Hunter's father, Roy, was born in 1887 in Ozark and passed on some vivid recollections of a strict childhood in his mother Hiley's house. It is likely that the tone of the household was set by the hardscrabble lives that Hunter's paternal grandparents had thus far endured. In retelling his father's narrative, Hunter combines elements that are characteristically both grim and humorous:

> [Grandmother Hiley] was an invalid for about thirty some years, and I think for fifteen of those years she was in a wheelchair. . . . She took care of her family. . . . If one of them [boys] needed a whipping by Dad or one of his brothers, she'd tell 'em to go out and cut a limb off the tree and bring it to her. They'd go out and cut the limb off and bring it to her and she'd give them a switching right there in the wheelchair.[11]

The city Hunter was born into was about one hundred years old at the time of his birth. Part of southwestern Missouri, Springfield grew up quickly on the edge of the agriculturally rich Kickapoo Prairie and was soon to become the terminus of railroads that traveled both north/south and east/west.[12] Hunter's father worked in the Eisenmayer flour mill—the largest mill on the northern outskirts of town—for thirty-two years, twenty-seven of which he served as its superintendent.[13] According to Hunter, his parents kept "the biggest garden in the neighborhood," and he recalled how much he hated weeding as a child because his mother insisted that he do it by hand. And then there was the stacking of wood. During public presentations in his later years, Hunter was fond of claiming that he was from "a poor family, probably a little below middle class."[14]

But while an early photograph (taken before he was born) shows Hunter's parents in a cramped and sweltering kitchen in Ozark, Missouri—Ethyl in a sleeveless and unkempt house dress and Roy in a crumpled shirt open to his narrow chest—this picture would later be replaced by portraits of a well-groomed couple. The newer photos would show Roy in stylish ties with a pen in the engineer's pocket of his dress shirt, well-polished shoes, and a hand on his hip, and Ethyl smiling at the camera from the passenger seat of the latest family Ford (likely a convertible). By the time Hunter was a teenager, his family had a house with two front porches, and to all appearances they had worked their way solidly into the realm of the comfortable middle class. Curiously absent from Hunter's recollections are any mention of the Great Depression, likely because his position as the second-to-youngest child insulated him from some of the family's economic struggles.

Hunter's childhood home stood on West Division Street (at the time unpaved), so named because it set the boundary between North Springfield (established in 1870 when the St. Louis–San Francisco Railway, better known as the Frisco Line, came through) and Springfield. Hunter described it as "a dirt road and you went a little farther out and you went to the stockyards, which was outside the city at that time."[15] Regardless of the degree of their economic struggles, Hunter spoke proudly of his parents: "I don't think there were any more honest people in the country than they were."[16] Music, folk beliefs, and religiosity commingled in the daily lives of the Hunter children, and singing came naturally to most of them. As Hunter summarized, "So I just grew up with music; it wasn't anything that I acquired or learned later."[17]

Indeed, Hunter had the good fortune to be born and raised in a city that enjoyed a rich musical life of its own, including everything from early jazz

The house where Hunter was born on West Division Street. (Courtesy of the Hunter family)

and parlor music to fiddle tunes and folksongs. Springfield particularly fell under the twenty-year influence of *Hillbilly Heartbeats* radio show host May Kennedy McCord. To quote fiddle tune collector Gordon McCann (born a decade after Hunter), "Growing up here, you didn't have much choice really of what you were listening to, but you were pretty well raised on KWTO [radio] and country music. . . . By osmosis, you were gonna know what it was whether you liked it or not."[18] (Although it took place before Hunter's time, Springfield was active enough in homegrown music that as early as 1934 the city was chosen for the All-Ozarks Festival.[19])

In the early years, Hunter's immediate family attended a variety of Christian services, including Baptist, Presbyterian, and Methodist houses of worship, and local society columns indicate that the Hunters were actively involved with the religious life of the community. In 1926 the local paper made mention of Roy Hunter—then president of the Christian Endeavors chapter—in

Max's parents, Ethyl and Roy Hunter. (Courtesy of the Hunter family)

connection with an effort to establish the Broadway Presbyterian Church, which held meetings no less than every night of the week. Later that year, in December, Max's older brother Harold had taken over his father's role with the Christian Endeavors chapter and was leading the singing portion of church services at the aforementioned church. Ethyl Hunter's name appeared in a 1927 news column when she "entertained" a gleaning class from the Broadway Presbyterian Church.[20]

But of all the services the young Hunter attended in his childhood, the one he found most memorable was at a Baptist church: "There are a lot of songs that start, even during the preaching. . . . Somebody'd get up and start a song like that and the whole congregation—even the preacher—get in and sing. After they went up and down the family [starting songs], and a few of the neighbors, then they'd quit and he'd go to preaching again."[21] While such experiences fed the young Hunter's interest in music, and singers in particular, his attitude toward religion would remain ambivalent throughout his life.

In addition to the church, his mother, Ethyl, was a primary musical influence in his life. In Hunter's words, "She played piano and sang a large number of songs [as did his sisters], ranging from ballads like 'Barbara Allen' and 'The Drunken Fool' . . . to more recent Victorian parlor pieces such as 'The Blind Child' and 'The Little Rosewood Casket.'"[22]

Hunter had two older brothers, Harold (the firstborn), followed by Charles Eugene, and a sister on either side—Pauline being five years senior to Max, and Doris (Dottie) being the youngest. Gifted with a deeply resonant voice that no doubt served him well in his adult life as a Methodist minister, Harold's musicality rubbed off on young Max, who recalled, "The very first thing I learned to play was my brother's French harp, and we lived in a two-story house and my brother wouldn't let me play it when he was there, but when he was gone to work . . . I'd sneak upstairs . . . and start blowing on it and learned to play that first, even played it so much it made my mouth sore. The guitar came much later."[23] With regard to his familial acquisition of music, Hunter never did learn to read musical notation.[24]

Born over a span of sixteen years, the Hunters were a slim, attractive bunch with high foreheads and straight, earnest brows. Max, slight in stature and wiry in build, had a clear gaze that gave the impression of an alert, quietly ambitious individual; a high school photo of him displays a freckled, self-confident youth with an engaging smile. Compassionate by nature, he would grow into a good-humored man who moved at his own measured pace while observing the world around him.

Max Hunter in his junior year at Central High. (Courtesy of the Hunter family)

## Homemade Remedies and Beliefs

In addition to the practice of Christianity, Hunter's early life was steeped in Ozarks folk culture, although he wouldn't have perceived it as such at the time. By the mid-1970s, his talks for universities, libraries, and other civic groups would be infused with memories of Ozark family traditions and ideas while at the same time poking fun at them:

> I have seen my Grandmother Rose place a cobweb on a bleeding cut.[25] Some stop bleeding quickly and others took a little longer. Who knows? Maybe they were ready to stop anyway. . . . It seems the worse the medicine smelled and tasted, the better it was for you. (If the first remedy didn't work, then another was tried. If none of them worked, you were too far gone, and might as well get ready to pass on.)[26]

Hunter's recollections of the homemade remedies he had witnessed and experienced in his youth most certainly fell under the spell of Vance Randolph, who, along with a proliferation of titles, authored a book on "mountain medicine" and Ozark beliefs as far back as the 1940s. Randolph wrote, "The hillfolk, however, seem to feel that the efficacy of a treatment varies directly with its unpleasantness—bitter tea is always best, and the more a poultice hurts the better they like it."[27]

In the spirit of Randolph, Hunter documented family cure-alls with un-flinching enthusiasm: "When my father or his brothers would have an ear ache, my Grandmother Hunter would have them urinate in a cup and would very slowly pour this in their ear. My dad said it worked." Roy Hunter also claimed that stump water ("rain water found in a hollow stump") was a palliative for rheumatism. As recollected by her son, Hunter's mother was particularly fond of making an anti-itch salve from lard and sulfur. "It took quite a stay in the washtub to get the salve off. It had got rather brittle and we didn't have any inside plumbing in our house," he later recalled.[28] Hunter said that his mother rarely bought medicine, preferring to concoct her own,[29] but as she was the parent of five children, it seems most likely that she did so out of economic necessity.

Woven into the fabric of his childhood were memories of the Everly family, whose musical matriarch, Gladys Everly, was frequently visited by visions, premonitions, and significant dreams. Once described by Hunter as "closer than kin," Elmer and Gladys Everly (referred to as Uncle Elmer and Aunt Gladys by the Hunter children) came to Springfield in the early 1920s by way of Kirksville, Missouri. Possibly because he was significantly younger than his brothers, Hunter had a particular attachment to the Everly family, who likely first met Roy and Ethyl Hunter at the local Methodist church. Hunter had fond memories of falling asleep on the rug while the two couples played

Brother Harold with Aunt Faye in 1979. Faye supplied stories about the Rose and Gideon ancestors. (Courtesy of the Hunter family)

cards together late into the evening, and the Everlys' eldest daughter, Bertha (Lamar), used to babysit Max in his early years.

Born in Kirksville, Missouri (near the Iowa border), in 1891, Gladys Everly had what might be construed as an active imagination, and her belief in her own psychic powers and in paranormal phenomena played a prominent role in the Everly household. In the words of Bertha, "She was very superstitious and she had an enormous wealth of old wives tales she depended on a lot. . . . There were a lot of things you just didn't do . . . because something would happen to you if you did."[30] Lamar said that her mother once claimed to have seen smoke coming out of the floor "and going right back into the ground"—a sure sign of death—near her sister-in-law Martha, who died soon after.[31] And although Aunt Gladys was a flatlander, her view of the world was certainly similar to that in Randolph's description of Ozarkers: "Many trivial happenings are regarded as presages of an approaching death. A bird flying into the house, or a ringing in the ears. . . . The falling of a window-sash at night,"[32] and the list goes on. In fact, Everly's view was so riddled with "signs" that her daughter once remarked that her mother was always on the verge of dying.[33]

Hunter recalled how an evening croquet game between both families was brought to a screeching halt when Aunt Gladys claimed to see a "spook" of some sort on the Hunters' upstairs porch. Lamar's father, an itinerant Methodist preacher who worked for the Frisco Line between strikes, expended a good deal of time and energy on allaying his wife's endless fears, and both Roy Hunter and Elmer Everly once attended a spiritualist meeting in order to, according to Hunter, "prove that this was a bunch of hooey."[34] This and other heroic measures on the part of Uncle Elmer, such as staging a false séance (complete with hand knocking) and then revealing himself from beneath the dinner table, never did succeed in changing Aunt Gladys's mind. Late in life she had so many near-death-and-back-again experiences that her surgeons affectionately dubbed her "Lady Resurrection."

Folkways and eccentricities aside, both families shared a love of music, and some of Hunter's earliest memories were of Aunt Gladys singing the songs she had learned in her childhood in Kirksville[35]—songs like "After the Ball" and "The Old Hickory Cane" as well as Child ballads such as "Nightingale" and "Lady Margaret"—selections he would later record. Aunt Gladys was also an indefatigable pianist who occasionally sat at the piano well into the night while joined by her musical sons at country gatherings down in Barry County near the southwest junction of Oklahoma and Arkansas. A few years before her death in 1972, Gladys Everly addressed one of her journal passages to Hunter. In it she detailed her early musical life, including long lists of the songs her parents had typically sung. Everly recalled how in her early years

Hunter's sister Doris ("Dottie") in 1956. (Courtesy of the Hunter family)

her "parents spent the evenings singing without the benefit of any musical instrument." She wrote, "It was the custom to sing ballads as well as sacred songs." As in the Ozarks, sacred hymns, parlor songs, and traditional ballads were of equal importance to singers.

Both the Everly and Hunter children shared memories of singing at home and on the way to church. Hunter particularly recalled outings in his father's Model T Ford: "It wouldn't climb the hill and we all had to get out and walk. And Dad had to turn the car around and back the car *up* the hill. I always wondered why we did that. Come to find out it didn't have a fuel pump on it. The gas runs by gravity."[36] Hunter, who would later discourage young festival performers from using vocal arrangements in their ballad singing, greatly enjoyed harmonizing with his siblings during long car rides.[37] Like the Sunday church bells chiming as a backdrop to his mother's "Orphan Girl" or the cooing of his youngest daughter behind "Darling Little Joe," singing was an entirely domestic affair. One need only observe the number of songs Ethyl Hunter enthusiastically contributed to her son's collection or hear the perfect blending of voices in the 1958 recording of Harold and Max singing "Down in the Valley" to understand the importance of music making in the Hunter family.

# 2

# A TRAVELING SALESMAN
# IN EUREKA

The harmonies that pervaded Hunter's childhood extended themselves into his years as a young adult. He married his high school sweetheart, Virginia Mercer, on Christmas Day 1939. Looking back decades later, the Hunters (with voices gently overlapping) told tales of their wedding day:

> MAX: And she had pneumonia the day before . . .
> Virginia: The week before.
> M: And I knew that all it would take to get her well—that I had that hidden power. Some people have it and some don't!
> V: And when you . . . came out with that minister, they had a rose. Only it wasn't a bud, it was a long-stemmed rose, and you had pinned it on, the whole thing.[1]

Soon after he and Virginia were married, Hunter apprenticed to her father, Myrl, who ran the Mercer Refrigeration Company in Springfield. There was no thought of further schooling. Years later Hunter explained, "Oh, I graduated from high school and I took a few engineering courses at Drury College. . . . It was related to the work I was doing. I had no desire to go on to college, never even when I was a kid."[2] During their married years, the Hunters and Mercers attended the Campbell Street Methodist Church in Springfield and often shared meals together. While the Mercer family was seemingly less musical than Hunter's birth family, Virginia's aunts were known to have sung songs into the neighborhood's communal phone line upon request, and she had a lifelong appreciation for her husband's work.[3] Hunter would stay with the Mercer company for thirteen years, after which he moved on to the John

Max and Virginia's wedding day, December 25, 1939, at the Campbell Avenue Methodist Church. (Courtesy of the Hunter family)

Rhodes Refrigeration Supply Company in 1952.[4] It was during his employment with the Rhodes company that he began his song-collecting activities. By this time, Max and Virginia had three daughters and one son.

Back in the 1950s, when Hunter started recording folksongs during his sales trips through the Ozarks, he was not thinking about the illustrious line of song catchers who had gone before him, and he could not have foreseen that copies of his tapes would end up at the Library of Congress—or that his field recordings would one day become universally accessible to anyone connected to the internet. Nor was he thinking about how prominent folk musicians in the decades ahead would delight in performing his material. He was thinking only about his job selling refrigeration and industrial control parts, bringing home money for his family of six—the youngest born in 1957—and taking up a musical pastime that would keep him entertained and less than lonely while he was on the road: "Why I started collecting old songs, as a hobby, I don't rightly know and I don't think I am too interested in trying to find out. I just did."[5]

At the time that Hunter received his first wire recorder (circa 1955), he was completely unaware of where his musical pastime would lead. He received the recorder from Virginia's father, and although it is unclear precisely which model Hunter used, most wire recorders of the time evolved from an earlier Danish invention called the Telegraphone.[6] This machine, which would have had a lot of novelty appeal for gadget enthusiasts like Hunter's father-in-law, was likely a welcome step forward, given that it recorded more cleanly than the hiss and scratch of the earlier phonographs.[7] Wire recorders were primarily used by journalists with the Armed Forces Rapid Service during World War II. As vividly described by one audio historian, "In a testimonial to its portability, one reporter strapped a wire recorder onto his chest and jumped out of an airplane, describing the descent by parachute for later broadcast."[8] As Hunter described it, this early recorder had a wire that ran from one spool to the other: "The only thing you did on that wire recorder—if you wanted to erase anything all you had to do is run it between your fingers and it just wiped everything off."[9]

At about the same time that Hunter acquired the audio recorder, he also purchased a ten-dollar guitar from a secondhand store, and although he often referred to this instrument as a musical "crutch,"[10] his guitar served as a loyal traveling companion during his twenty years on the road. He made a habit of recording songs during his sales rounds, but early on they weren't from live performers; they were from the radio or a jukebox. When he got to his motel room at night, he'd learn the songs and tape himself singing the

Hunter's father-in-law, Myrl Mercer, seated in the red 1956 Chevy that Hunter used for collecting trips. (Courtesy of the Hunter family)

lyrics. He had a warm and straightforward baritone voice, but he sang and played at the same loping tempo throughout his life, never taking himself too seriously as a performer. Hunter once quipped, "Gee whiz, I couldn't understand why I wasn't in the movies and everything else!"[11] While he got in the habit of recording songs purely for his own pleasure, he soon became intensely interested in the singers themselves. His daughter Linda Bangs said, "His first trips into the hills were defining moments for him."[12] Soon he would leave solitary singing and the low-capacity recorder behind. Hunter later reminisced:

> But the first trip I ever made I borrowed that wire recorder and then it wasn't very long after that that I got a great big old monster of a thing, tape recorder, it took two men and a go-cart to carry it in and out. And I wore that thing out and got a Webcore [sic], and then eventually had to buy the third Webcore. Probably the reason I bought the third one was that I had to have the heads replaced on the first Webcore and then it got to bothering me that maybe the thing was gonna slow down. . . . I've still got both of the last two and then the one that has [been] repaired five or six times.[13]

Although Hunter's life as a salesman enhanced and indeed enabled his work as a collector, it is less clear as to how this growing "hobby" was viewed

Hunter in his twenties. (Courtesy of the Hunter family)

**Max Hunter**

1240 WEST WESTVIEW
SPRINGFIELD, MISSOURI 65807
417-882-7763

COMMERCIAL ICE SYSTEMS

Hunter's business card.

by his employers. While a 1962 news story stated that Hunter, owner of Thermal Supply, an industrial supplies and air-conditioning company, "does his ballad collecting on holidays and weekends,"[14] this company, along with the others he worked for, has long since changed hands and kept scant records (if any) on employees, so this statement remains unsubstantiated.

Regardless of the individual companies he worked for, Hunter seems to have developed a regular sales route that covered mostly southern Missouri and northwest Arkansas. He typically traveled south from Springfield into Arkansas border towns like Bentonville, Fayetteville, Eureka Springs, and Mountain Home; then northwest toward Marionville and Joplin, Missouri; sometimes as far west as Wichita, Kansas; and then north toward Webb City and Lamar, Missouri, before returning home. Journalist Ted Anthony, whose investigations into the history of "The Rising Sun" ballad led him to the Hunter Collection, found a musicality in the very names of the places Hunter touched upon: "His stops included places like Hog's Scald Holler, Hemmed-in Holler, Skunk Holler, Lost Valley, and Eureka Springs."[15]

## The Eureka Moment

Eureka Springs, a dot on the Ozarks map that would have the most impact on Hunter's life as a collector, was a pivotal point in the evolution of national folk festivals. The town was home to a onetime Ozark Folk Festival, which took place in March 1934. The festival was one of several talent-scouting events designed to spark interest in the upcoming National Folk Festival, to be held in St. Louis in April of the same year. Spearheaded by three folk luminaries—Ozarks ballad singer and soon-to-be radio personality May Kennedy McCord, Arkansas-based writer and folklorist Vance Randolph, and festival originator and promoter Sarah Gertrude Knott—this event was unlike previous festivals in that it actively welcomed participation on the part of musicians and audience members from a variety of ethnic backgrounds and regions. This development occurred largely as a result of Knott's comparatively forward-thinking and inclusive mind-set.[16] Knott's vision stood in contrast to the character of Virginia's White Top Festival (begun in 1931), which was bedeviled from the start, not only by a dysfunctional cohort of organizers but also by its direct appeal to white, middle-class male performers and locals who could actually afford to pay the entry fee.[17] Aside from its location and a partial overlap in the cast of characters, Knott's first Ozark Folk Festival was, by all accounts, well attended and a great success,[18] but it bore no direct relationship to the event Hunter later attended in the mid-1950s.

Although it is likely that he first attended the Ozark Folk Festival in Eureka Springs in a previous year, it was October 1957 when, traveling on his habitual 150-mile sales circuit, Hunter stopped here once again. The way he tells it, he got up and sang of his own volition: "Well, I was smart enough to know if you were going to a folk festival, you should have a folk song."[19] But since Hunter's name doesn't appear on the festival flyer until 1959, it is far more likely that he maneuvered his way onto the performers' list, possibly with the help of his hometown musical acquaintance May Kennedy McCord, a mover and shaker at the festival who was a headliner on the program each night. One of the songs Hunter chose to sing was the humorous betrayal song alternately known as "Our Goodman," "Three Nights Drunk," and other titles as well. The lyrics will no doubt be familiar to many readers: "Well, I came home the other night / Just drunk as I could be / Found a hat on my hat rack / Where my hat ought to be." Commented Hunter, "When I first heard that song I thought it was just . . . kind of a country song that maybe somebody'd made popular on the radio. It isn't. It's an old English ballad" (Child 274 to be exact).[20]

The decade-old festival Hunter attended that weekend reeked of commercialism; from the start it was an event tailored to bring in tourists who were hungry for a glimpse of hillbilly culture.[21] The "Original" (or "Annual") Ozark Folk Festival (as it's now laboriously referred to) was first held in October 1948, almost a decade before Hunter's arrival on the scene, and was the direct outcome of a cry for cultural preservation on the part of author and publisher Otto Ernest Rayburn, a newcomer to Eureka Springs, who produced and directed the festival from 1952 to 1959.[22] But Rayburn was also a proponent of tourism, and, according to Brooks Blevins, the authenticity of the festival had long ago been built on a false foundation: "The vacationers who had been promised electric lights and hot showers in their mountain bungalows

May Kennedy McCord, October 1958. (Photograph by Hunter, courtesy of the Springfield–Greene County Library)

had also been promised real hillbillies by the travel writers and incidentally by the folk tales and songs in Rayburn's *Ozark Guide*. They received only the former."[23] Blevins went on to aptly describe the cultural paradox behind the entire event: "In 1948 Eureka Springs revived its Ozark Folk Festival to re-capture the hillbilly spirit that the town had never possessed. But the staged musicals and dances and the Indian relics and factory-made corncob pipes were less than authentic."[24]

Hunter's frustration with the festival's lack of authenticity planted a seed: "What I heard that night was a country-western and [just about] anything else, but I stuck to my guns and got up and sang."[25] His remark about "any-thing else" music was entirely accurate. Given the milieu, it is hardly surpris-ing that Hunter's traditional streak caught the attention of Ozark folklorists Vance Randolph and Mary Celestia Parler, who just happened to be sitting in the audience. The way Hunter tells it, Parler came backstage at the start of intermission and gave him Randolph's address, urging him to meet with the folklorist the very next morning.[26] In later years, Hunter would fondly recall the moment when he was, in essence, both discovered and sent on a cultural mission. At an after-festival party at festival emcee Bob Duncan's house in Eureka Springs,[27] Hunter got to speak a little more with Randolph and Parler: "Vance told me . . . he was getting ready to leave because he hadn't heard any folk music." The way Hunter remembers it, he sang three or four folksongs, whose authenticity immediately caught the elder folklorist's attention. Never above hyperbole, Hunter quoted Randolph as saying something to the effect of "He must be out of his mind. Because that's the only folk that we had heard on the whole program."[28]

The next twenty-four hours would be a whirlwind of activity that would propel Hunter into a lifelong project. Sunday morning, in addition to other post-festival gatherings, he visited Randolph at his home in Eureka Springs: "The second visit was rather serious, there wasn't very much fun in that one because he [Randolph] had made up his mind what he wanted to tell me." Hunter was told not to leave town before talking with Parler at the university: "I contacted her on this same trip and she give me the same speech."[29] Vance and Mary "kinda twisted my arm . . . but one of the things they both told me [was] . . . we can't tell you *how*, we just tell you *what* to do . . . and they are right. I don't think anybody can tell anybody else *how* to collect in the field."[30] Any advice the sixty-five-year-old Randolph had for Hunter was already written down in the senior collector's early titles, such as that found in *The Ozarks: An American Survival of Primitive Society*: "The collecting of this material is a delicate and difficult matter at best, and the man who simply rides up to a mountain cabin and asks somebody to sing old songs will never hear any songs worth recording."[31] Back in 1931, Randolph the "furriner" claims to have resorted to singing an ancient ballad *wrong* in order to get his source to sing it *right*,[32] a measure Hunter never needed to take. Randolph justified this practice by saying, "The successful collector must either be introduced and vouched for by someone whom the natives know and trust, or he must cultivate the hillman for himself, and lead up to the subject of balladry by slow and easy stages,"[33] an approach that suited Hunter the salesman to a T.

Randolph and Parler—not yet married—recognized that Hunter was in a unique position to collect songs, and as they detailed in the liner notes to his Folk-Legacy recording, before Eureka Springs Hunter had a very different pastime: "He began collecting folksongs after he paid a handsome price for a set of 'matched .41s' and suddenly realized that his pistol collection was becoming too expensive a hobby for him to continue. He sold his pistols, bought a tape recorder, and turned his immense energies to the collecting of songs, instead."[34] While the anecdote regarding pistols may be just that, that weekend in October 1957 was decidedly a turning point for Hunter.

As Hunter himself once put it, "Where another person would have maybe one or two chances to collect from a person, I am back in the territory four weeks later and do not have to push for the material. . . . Collecting a little each time over the period of a year adds up to much more than the other way. Not only that, but I have been able to become better acquainted with the person, see as much as I hear."[35] Being observant of an individual's circumstances and personality came naturally to Hunter the salesman and helped him build relationships with his sources.

## Early Encounters with Other Collectors

When Hunter first began his quest for traditional songs and their singers, he did so with a minimum of training. In 1958 he sometimes traveled down to the University of Arkansas at Fayetteville to attend Parler's ballad-collecting classes, and as evidenced in the Ozark Folksong Collection, he taped several of her own collecting sessions—likely under her guidance—both on campus and in the field. But most of the time, when he wasn't getting advice from Parler or Randolph, Hunter worked off of sheer gut instinct. This instinct was the result of both temperament and ancestry, and there is no doubt that having family roots planted deep in Ozark soil helped him connect with persons who might otherwise have shut him out.

It was during this same visit to the Ozark Folk Festival in 1957 that Hunter also made the acquaintance of another guitar-strumming ballad collector from Missouri—Loman Cansler, an individual who, in contrast to Hunter, was generally more comfortable on stage than collecting in the field. Cansler was on the festival program that year and ended up at the same after-festival singing party as Hunter. They also met in Hunter's hotel room (likely the following morning), where Cansler sang Hunter ballads that the greenhorn collector enthusiastically documented as "songs from my grandfather." Years later, Cansler's depiction of this session was ambiguous: "Well, unfortunately, he saved the tape of me singing 'Poor Boy'. . . . I hope I told him it wasn't a family song," but this was less than clear in the retelling. The song was, in fact, from a popular songbook titled *Frontier Ballads*.[36]

Years after Hunter's first conscious foray into recording, Cansler added this caveat to what was likely a deliberate subterfuge on his part: "In the '50s I was a little reluctant to share my songs because they might fall into the wrong hands. And in the '50s you may recall that there was quite a bit of commercialism of folk music." He then went on to reveal another motivation in not sharing authentic songs with Hunter that day: "I wanted to give my own interpretation of the songs. So that would be another reason why I probably sang Max Hunter['s] 'Poor Boy' instead of one from my family or one I had collected."[37] Regardless of whether Cansler purposely concealed material from Hunter that day, his guardedness was a direct reflection of how his identity as a performer often took precedence over his work as a cultural preservationist. Having spent most of his career as a school guidance counselor in the Kansas City area, he was a seasoned musical performer who recorded traditional songs from well beyond the Ozarks region.

Although both men had grown up with ballads in their ears, it wasn't until he was a student at University of Missouri–Columbia that Cansler got a notion to collect ballads: "One day I was back in the stacks at the library and I came across books by Henry Belden and Carl Sandburg. I glanced through them hurriedly and I realized, 'my goodness, they're talking about stuff I grew up with.'"[38] In short, from the start Cansler's impulse to collect was more intellectual than social. He had a particular interest in the psychological meanings embedded in the old songs. This was the opposite mind-set of Hunter, who once had this to say about the survival of Child ballads in the Ozarks: "I have heard two explanations of why they knew and could sing the old songs." One argument was that the well-to-do had more time on their hands to learn these songs, and the opposite argument was that singing "of lords and ladies" had particular appeal for poor singers. But, concluded Hunter, "To me, it's not important why. I'm glad they did for whatever reason."[39] While Cansler's analytical interest in balladry led him to contribute journal articles to places like the *Southern Folklore Quarterly* and the *Kentucky Folklore Record*, it appears likely that his scholarly bent sometimes got in the way of his fieldwork. Cansler was the first to admit that he often had a challenging time locating singers:

> I might talk a little about the difficult aspect of collecting that I found, especially in an area where you did not know anyone [and] they didn't know you. . . . This has been the hardest thing for me to do is to get across to people who aren't educated in folksongs. . . . Usually I would just say old songs rather than folksongs—old songs that people grew up with and sang. Usually they would refer me to an ex–music teacher or to the local history buff or the newspaper editor of the town. Everyone but the right people.[40]

One of Cansler's greatest difficulties in locating singers was his reluctance to "go into bars and places that I didn't feel quite as comfortable . . . [due] to my upbringing," he once admitted while comparing his field methods to those of Hunter.[41]

And even though the folk revival was at its height, Cansler was aware that many cultural factors could get in the way of singers wanting to share their material. He once surmised, "I think what was happening here back in the '50s and '60s—there was a stigma attached to people who knew superstitions, maybe they were superstitious themselves, or knew folklore (and I'm talking about the whole genre now). If they knew the ghost stories and the tales and the songs, they must be ignorant or low-class people."[42] While both men made deliberate efforts not to stereotype their contributors, Hunter in particular displayed a knack for keeping the proverbial door open—an ability that Randolph and Parler recognized from the outset.

The 1957 Ozark Folk Festival was significant in that in addition to meeting Parler, Randolph, and Cansler, Hunter was introduced to a new singing partner, Joan O'Bryant, a charismatic and accomplished folklorist from Wichita State University who regularly performed traditional songs on television as well as on the live stage. Because Hunter met O'Bryant at the same time and place that he met Parler and Randolph, the four of them became close friends. Hunter says, "She [O'Bryant] got in a lot of collecting in Kansas, and then when she came over to see Vance he got into a lot of father/daughter talk with Joanie. And I think from that time on she changed her method of collecting, and I think Mary helped her do a lot of cataloguing by the University."[43]

From the Ozark Folk Festival on forward, Randolph and Parler took Hunter and O'Bryant under their collective wing. But, while they didn't tell Hunter exactly how to go about collecting, they did tell him what *not* to do; first off, they told him to "stop erasing" simply in order to make room on the low-capacity wire recorder,[44] and to get better equipment so that he could record more than one ballad at a time. Looking back, Hunter had this to say about his early efforts:

> The end results of my first collecting was one of the finest and most completely fouled up collections of good, bad, and otherwise songs that was ever collected. . . . Then, I met a man and woman that changed the picture. . . . From that time on, the songs that I collected were sang to me by people that had learned their songs, not from a record, not from a book, not from the television or radio, but from some other person. There [might] be a few that used their "hand written ballet book" that helped them remember the words, but even this would be a very small number.[45]

Through conversations with Randolph and Parler, Hunter was coming up with a definition of authenticity that he would stick by for the remainder of

his life as a collector. One year after meeting his new friends, he wrote a letter to Cansler reflecting on this process: "My ideas and interest has changed
considerably, this past year. I now keep all the tapes I collect and try to sing
the song exactly as it was sung for me. As you know this can be quite a chore.
This past year I have collected about 225 songs. To date 24 Child Ballads." And
his relationship with Parler was now more that of collaborator rather than
student: "All the songs I collect I let Mary Parler dub off for the University
of Arkansas."[46]

If Hunter was overdramatic in describing this change of approach, given
that he had only started "dabbling" with ballad collecting shortly before he
met Randolph and Parler, his new mission was coming into sharper focus:
"It didn't take very long after I started when I began to know it was important. This was a way of life that people were losing, and it was never coming
back."[47] And although Hunter began to visit his new friends on a regular basis,
and to draw inspiration from the lives they had thus far led, it is important
to keep in mind that the young salesman and the Ozark folklorist were at

Vance Randolph, Joan O'Bryant, and Max Hunter in Fayetteville. (Photograph by Mary Celestia Parler, courtesy
of Special Collections, University of Arkansas Libraries,
Fayetteville)

very different stages in their lives when they met. As observed by Donald Lance, a University of Missouri linguistics professor who helped document Hunter's work, "Hunter did not meet Randolph until the latter was over 60 years of age, was no longer active in collecting, and had turned over most of his papers to several university libraries and the Library of Congress."[48] And for Randolph, who had already completed his four-volume opus, *Ozark Folksongs*, stumbling upon Hunter must have given him new hope for the preservation of traditional balladry.[49]

In turn, conversations with his Arkansas friends energized and motivated the youthful Hunter, who was twenty-eight years younger than Randolph. Randolph and Parler realized that Hunter wouldn't have to make elaborate plans to cram all of his recording into rushed, one-shot visits when seeking out their songs; he would have repeated opportunities to collect from the same individuals. As Hunter said, "I had a job that allowed me to do this and if I couldn't get all of it this trip then leave the door open, I'll be back within a month, and take up where we left off.[50] Hunter often described his song-collecting work as play: "It was something I enjoyed; checking in at night at the motel and getting your tape recorder and going out and visiting somebody you didn't know and never saw before and wasn't sure where they lived; knocking on a total stranger's door and spending the evening with them."[51]

# 3

# RULES OF COLLECTING AND HOW HUNTER GOT HIS SONGS

## Taking His Time

As previously alluded to, Hunter's success as a collector can be attributed to several factors, not the least of which was his good fortune in being taken under the collective wing of Randolph and Parler. Both folklorists could provide a disciplined and experienced perspective that Hunter might otherwise never have been privy to. And without prescribing specific field methods, they enabled Hunter to arrive at strategies that would bring both his vocation and newly discovered avocation into a workable alignment.

At least early on, recording folksongs was just a sideline and Hunter took neither his hobby nor himself too seriously. His approach to potential contributors was one of humility: "Just remember, when you go to visit—you're not doin' them a favor, they're doin' you the favor. Just be yourself. If you're not the right kind of person, they'll run you off anyway."[1] Hunter knew that if he carried any sense of superiority, he would lose his foot in the all-essential door.

But the door remained remarkably open. As one year extended itself into twenty, it would be hard to overstate the strategic importance of Hunter's repeat visits. Among those he recorded most often were balladeers Ollie Gilbert of Mountain View, Arkansas; Allie Long Parker of Pleasant Valley Community, Arkansas; Harrison Burnett of Fayetteville, Arkansas; Fred High of High, Arkansas;[2] and Olive Coberley of Wheatland, Missouri. Visits with these singers proved especially rewarding not only in the friendships that developed but also in that these individuals were often the purveyors of the highly sought-after Child ballads. Oftentimes a repeat visit to a musical contact simply meant getting a more complete version of a song, as in the case of Allie Long Parker's "Battle of Pea Ridge." When Hunter met with Parker in January 1958, she had just one summary verse of the Civil War battle song, but when he saw her again three months later, she gave him four.

In addition to his frequent drop-ins, Hunter's other rule was never to be in a hurry: "If you're gonna go somewhere and expect to . . . collect within 30 to 45 minutes or an hour, forget it. *Take plenty of tape* and go out there and plan on staying anywhere from half to three-quarters of a day. . . . You may get invited to dinner. They may want to show you out in the field, out in the barn, in the house, all kinds of things. *But just don't go pushy.*"[3] This unhurried approach was all the more reason for Hunter to do the majority of his fieldwork solo, since having anyone else along would have interfered with this pace. According to his elder daughter, Linda Bangs, her father would occasionally hunker down for the night after a song session: "On one or more occasions he would sleep in a barn loft or on someone's floor. One morning he woke up surrounded by four big, stinky hound dogs. He said that was the last time he was going to carry candy bars in his pockets."[4]

Every now and again Hunter's wife, Virginia, would accompany him on collecting trips, and her husband's slow winning over of songsters likely proved maddening. Bangs remembers her mother's description of a visit to the homestead of Odis Bird, one of Hunter's most enthusiastic sources:

> She went with him one time . . . into Northern Arkansas, and she sat in this old rickety truck with an old bottle—I think the water was in an old milk jug . . . and he was helping some guy load some hay. It was evening and by the time they got through it was night and here she'd been sitting in this old truck with this jug of water. And I guess by the time they got back to the motel she was on the irate side. . . . And they got back to the motel, and he took out this old crumbly piece of paper and spread it out on the table, got his guitar and started singing it. Then he said, "See, while you were sittin' in there with that old jug of water, this is what I was getting." Once she heard the song he had gotten . . . all was forgiven. He didn't take her all the time but every once in a while. . . . It seems like every time he would take her down to that area she gets stuck sittin' somewhere.[5]

Occasionally, when they were at home together on the weekend with no plan to travel, Hunter would hear from somebody somewhere singing a song

```
1. To try and make my collection one of the finest
2. To collect only within the Ozarks area.
3. To try and keep the song exactly as I found it.
4. To try and keep out feedbacks of commercial recordings.
5. That I will not knowingly give any song to any singer
   if I believe they may change it in any manner.
6. To make my collecting fun and enjoyable.

With these few rules, I continue to hunt for old songs.
```

Max F, Hunter

Hunter's "Rules of Collecting" as found in his bound volumes. (Courtesy of the Springfield–Greene County Library)

he needed, at which point he and Virginia "would argue back and forth for a while, but nine times out of ten, off they'd go . . . to Timbuktu—half the time some place she'd never heard of."[6] Living with a man who was so driven and, at times, single-minded was undoubtedly a challenge. But despite the moments when Virginia Hunter no doubt felt marginalized, according to her daughter, Virginia became her husband's strongest ally: "Once Mother realized what was going on and she could see what he was doing and how passionate he was about it, she was open to all aspects of it."[7]

Early on, Hunter went on collecting trips, not with his wife but with Mary Celestia Parler and other folklorist friends, and much of what we know about his sources can be attributed to Parler's diligence in interviewing the individuals they recorded. Such was certainly the case with their visit to ninety-six-year-old William Eden of Monte Ne, Arkansas, one of the first people Hunter taped. In between ballads, Eden, born in 1863, shared some memories of his youth, much of which was spent in Oklahoma:

And my father, he bossed me. I belonged to him till I was twenty-one. . . . And I never went to but one dance. I went a-huntin' one night— what I mean, possums and coons, things like that. . . . And I had went and helped clear [furniture] for some neighbor, and they give a dance. And I asked Father if I might go by and see em dancin'. And he said I could go by and watch em dance one change, and for me to go on then a-huntin'. And that's the only time till after I was twenty-one that I ever went to anything like that.[8]

Indeed, dancing was often frowned upon.[9]

Parler's interview with Eden indicates that he had vivid recollections of when, where, and from whom he'd acquired certain of his ballads, a characteristic he shared with many of Hunter's other raconteurs. When Parler asked him about the first song he ever learned, Eden quickly replied that he was about ten years old when he heard an uncle sing "A Pretty Fair Maid in Yonders Garden": "He tuck me to church with him one night, and as we come back, he sung that—we was a-horseback—I rode Paw's horse and he rode his'n. . . . Then the next day, I believe he sung it again, and I learnt it." And once he heard a song he liked, he'd sing it to himself—a musical habit that surely caught his neighbors' attention: "All along the road people knew where and when I'd . . . go to town and [come] back, you know. They'd hear me singing along the road."[10]

These are the sorts of recollections that would fall into Hunter's lap when he put aside his sales work for the day. He soon fell into a nocturnal rhythm, which served him well: "After supper is the best time to collect songs—when they have sat down [and] are relaxed, the chores are over and no one is sleepy yet."[11] One evening in May 1958 remained particularly vivid in Hunter's memory, both for its pleasantness and because it provided an outsider's perspective on the work he was doing:

> I was going out to see Ed Stilley [raised by Fannie Prickett] who lived out by Allie Long Parker.[12] I invited Bob [a salesman friend] to go with me . . . below Eureka, down in Hogscald Holler. . . . This was a warm summer night, beautiful night, the moon was shining as big as a horse tub. Got out, and we went in and visited with Aunt Fannie and Ed and they sang for me, and Bob, like a gentleman, sat on a little stool in the corner, and was one of the best listeners that you could ever want. On the way back to town, there wasn't much said, but the most important thing that Bob asked me was, what'n the hell I wanted with those songs. They were songs that Bob had never heard. However, he admitted that he had a good time. He enjoyed it. . . .
>
> There was a stream running right in front of Aunt Fannie and Ed's home, and we had to walk from where the porch was to where the car was and we had to cross this little stream on a foot bridge, and on the way out we heard this frog croakin', but it sounded like it was in a barrel. . . . We asked Ed what that noise was, and Ed said "sounds like a snake is swallowing a frog and the frog is croakin' down in the snake. He's not got it all swallowed yet." And he went back and got a little flashlight . . . "let's

see if we can find it." . . . Finally Ed hollered, "well, here it is." And here was this snake that had this frog down in its mouth, and you could see the frog legs, still stickin' out. It didn't bother us, we didn't bother it.[13]

Spending time with song carriers occasionally meant not taping them at all: "Sometimes when I would go see the people that had sang for me, I didn't collect anything, and sometimes the reason was there was some type of a family problem. And I got acquainted well enough that I was a good listener and sometimes I could hear about these family problems which didn't involve me at all."[14]

This experience of having to delay collecting activities is hardly unique to Hunter. Reflecting on her student days in the field, ethnomusicologist Nicole Beaudry wrote the following: "I learned that I could not instruct people to work when and how I thought they should. . . . On both my first and second trips to an Inuit community, I had to wait for two to three weeks before any concrete work could be accomplished." It wasn't until sometime later that this researcher understood the value of slowdowns or interruptions, which often came in the form of spontaneous storytelling: "At the time, I was still unaware of the learning process that was taking place in spite of my apparent unemployment."[15] Beaudry was learning that what happened *before* and *between* the harvesting of sought-after material provided essential context and connection: "Often, when hoping to record songs, I have been surprised (and, I confess, a little annoyed) at the number of stories the Dene always come back to.[16] Had I been reluctant to listen to these, I would really have missed a lot."[17]

Despite Hunter's very different circumstance, both he and Beaudry understood that the heart of fieldwork lay in the relationships forged between researcher and subject, the nuances and definitions of which remain a lively topic of discussion among folklorists.[18] For Hunter, none of the time spent in conversation with his sources ever felt wasted. His younger daughter, Jenny Sweet, referred to her father as a "people person . . . very mild mannered." And she added, "His kindness was a bit overwhelming."[19]

Hunter once mentioned how he stopped at a cemetery close to the Arkansas line to share his condolences with sheer strangers. This happened more than once, according to Sweet: "If it looked like there was a small crowd, he'd join them, just to help to send this person on."[20] But time spent in the company of strangers also meant less time at home, and there are indications that his presence was missed. Six years after her father's death, Sweet commented, "He was gone a lot," and it was a special comfort to have him home, regardless of the fact that he spent a good deal of time in the utility room working on ballad transcriptions. "He was there. That's all that really mattered," she later reflected.[21]

The affability that helped Hunter succeed as a salesman certainly came into play in his song work. He acknowledged, "Now, not everybody can collect. I know some people that's tried to collect and they laugh at the wrong time. You might as well go home. Your visit is over. . . . You laugh *with* the people. Don't laugh *at* the people."[22] Hunter's respect for Ozarkers and their history made itself felt, for unlike most collectors, he was rarely turned away: "I've sent people back where I've been, to the same people, to collect and they didn't get anything. . . . I just feel like that I had just a little better percentage record than most people."[23]

When Hunter wasn't pursuing singers recommended by Parler and Randolph, he relied on one of the most important tools in his toolbox: his innate ability to *read* a house. When asked how to go about collecting, he had this to say: "I don't have the slightest idea. . . . When you drive up in front of a house, if you can't feel it—that you're either going to collect or not—you might as well drive on home."[24] This is where his powers of observation came into play: "I would look where I was going . . . whether the gate was about to fall off the post or whether it was on there tight, whether the chickens were running around in the yard, or whether the cows were up on the porch. I don't know, there was just lots of things that you saw."[25]

Patience and persistence also played a large role: "I went places where . . . when I drove up I took the tape recorder in with me—never saw the people before in my life and got them to sing." Alternatively, he said, "I went a few places where I didn't get anything the first trip; I didn't ask for anything. I felt that I had better just go and make friends and then come back the second time. There's nothing in the [world] that'll tell you this."[26]

Mirroring the attitude of his mentor, Vance Randolph, Hunter claimed to have a particular intolerance for so-called collectors who tried to gain favor with their sources by "blending in":

There was some people [likely college students] came down from Chicago, and they stayed all night at the motel and when they got up the next morning . . . they thought, well, where we're going, we'd better dress up like they do, so they put on overalls and all kinds of straw hats that looked like somebody had stepped on them, and when they got there, the people they met had cleaned up, had put on a little better clothes, they were expecting company and they thought they should take off their clothes they wear out in the field and here the idiots that showed up . . . they put people down.[27]

However apocryphal this anecdote might have been, this was nonetheless Hunter's way of saying that he—who had never set foot in college—would never act *that* foolishly.

## Only the Ozarks

When it came to collecting songs, provenance was of first concern to Hunter, and he remained vigilant regarding songs that tested his geographic boundaries. From day one, he set firm limits. "My collection is strictly for the Ozarks," he once commented while a guest of Dr. Adolf Schroeder at the University of Missouri–Columbia.[28] But beneath this seemingly simple declaration were layers of complexity; the Ozarks, as Hunter perceived them, was less a place of cultural and environmental shift where various populations came and went (as it had been since the coming of the railroads in the late nineteenth century),[29] and more a place where his ancestors, and those of his ballad bearers, had settled long ago. And it was easier for Hunter to declare that he collected songs *in* the Ozarks than to say *of* the Ozarks. If he was concerned about out-of-state influences on the repertoires of Herbert Philbrick (who spent time in both Illinois and Kansas), Raymond Sanders (who had lived in both Kentucky and Washington State), or Glenn Ohrlin (a collector of cowboy songs who came from Minnesota), he did not dwell on it.[30]

In keeping with his conviction to collect only while *in* the Ozarks, Hunter was leery of ballads that were composites of other versions:

> I've had people stop by my house and visit with me and sing songs from Colorado, from Florida, from various places—Chicago. . . . I record all of these people and when they go home the next day or so I rub it all off. . . . I wanted a song called "The Maid of Dundee." I don't have it. But I went one time to visit with a lady that knew the song.[31] Now, when she got through singing, I had the finest "Maid of Dundee" that had ever been collected in the world. . . . It told the whole story—details, just as you don't find in folk songs. . . . When she got through singing, I asked the lady where she got it. She knew part of the song as a child. She had learned it in the Ozarks. Then she had met somebody in California that knew part of the song and some that she didn't know. . . . Now when she gets home she has this beautiful, wonderful "Maid of Dundee" that any collector . . . you'd let 'em cut off your arm for it. When I got back to the

motel, I sat there and I think I cried. I really do. I think the tears come down my cheeks. I rubbed that off that tape. Why? Well, first I've got to live with Max Hunter.[32]

At least a decade after erasing that recording, Hunter (then well established in the ballad-collecting world) had this to say: "If I had kept that complete version and had kept it in my collection, folklorists from all over the country would've jumped up and down on my neck."[33] By then, in addition to his own conscience, he had a reputation to maintain: "If I tell you that I've got a song, you count on it. . . . Robin Hood songs. . . . We just don't get some songs in the Ozarks. Vance Randolph in forty years never collected a Robin Hood song."[34]

Hunter was less consistent in weeding out composed versus traditional material. Although he would later expound on the idea that composed songs were not true "folk ballads" and were therefore of little interest to him, a number of contemporary compositions nonetheless eked their way into his collection. Unattuned as he was to popular song culture, this likely happened by accident, at least early on. Take, for instance, 1959, when he recorded six zesty ballads about life behind bars from Chloe Bain, a news-of-the-town columnist from Hermitage, Missouri. Several of Bain's songs, including "Twenty One Years," were written by Nashville's prolific hall-of-famer Bob Miller. Later on, as he became more discerning, Hunter deliberately omitted songs that were commercial in origin or that came from anthologies.

## Documentation

Finding and recording singers and their ballads was one matter, but documenting the songs for posterity was quite another. Although Hunter certainly had an easier time of traveling to and from his songsters, and although he had technological advantages over earlier adventurers (including Randolph), he still came home to some of the same documentation challenges. When Hunter returned from his many days on the road—typically Monday through Thursday—his family would help him hoist the heavy reel-to-reel Webcor tape recorder into the house. Often it would end up in the laundry room (aka his "office"), where he would hunker down at a desk and table that he'd set up for the purpose and begin the long and arduous process of transcription.

As described by one local journalist, Hunter would "play his recordings over and over until he had all the lyrics copied down in longhand and he had learned the tune exactly."[35] Methodical by nature, Hunter would write down the lyrics in pencil long before he would type them. At the same time that he referred to his collecting activities as fun, he also acknowledged the tedious aspect: "If you work continually with just a little bit of a break for a cigarette or a coffee, I don't think you can do it in eight hours . . . and that's eight hours of listening to a tape."[36]

Early on, Hunter made the decision to transcribe the tapes himself because other people would "anticipate things" and would lose the local flavor of the songs: "For example, they may sing 'earl-eye' for 'early,' . . . or 'quick-lye' for 'quickly.'"[37] Although he arrived at these methods through his own process of trial and error, there was nothing particularly groundbreaking in Hunter's approach; many academic and non-academic folklorists had adopted the same or similar strategies. H. M. Belden, working thirty years earlier and without the benefit of audio equipment, made the same choices. But Belden, being in the academic fold, took special care to add footnotes to questionable words. Hunter wrote down ambiguous wording without hazarding interpretations, and many words are spelled out phonetically, without the modern conventions. He once remarked, "Sometimes I get some new words that way. I don't know what they mean, but they're new words."[38] By 1976 the following upper-cased note, authored by Hunter himself, accompanied his collection:

YOU MAY BY THIS TIME BE CRITICAL OF THE WAY I HAVE PUNCUATED [sic] MY TRANSCRIPTIONS OF THE SONGS. IT IS MY BELIEF, THAT MY JOB IS TO GET THE WORDS OFF OF THE TAPE THE BEST WAY THAT I CAN AND KNOW HOW. IT TAKES ABOUT TEN (10) TO TWELVE (12) HOURS TO TAKE THE WORDS OFF OF THE TAPE AND THIS IS DONE BY THE USE OF A PENCIL SO THAT I CAN ERASE WHEN I HAVE TO. THEN, FROM THIS I TYPE THE TRANSCRIPTION. THIS IS ONE "HELL" OF A JOB. SO, SINCE I AM DOING THE WORK, I'LL PUNCTUATE THE WAY I WANT TO.

Hunter's collection is certainly characterized by the unaltered state of its contents, but his purist approach to transcription is often problematic for those musical performers who choose to honor his original notations. There are innumerable examples of mondegreens among the transcribed lyrics, not the least of which is Reba Dearmore's "The Peacefullo Farm," which was undoubtedly "The Peaceful Old Farm." In addition to the writing down of "garbled or incomplete" phrases,[39] the mishearing of orally transmitted lyrics is a given, and it is up to individual judgment as to whether Hunter was overzealous in his "purist" approach to transcription. Musical performer

Cathy Barton, a longtime Hunter friend and documentarian, reiterated this approach: "[Max was] very truthful and deferential to his sources,"[40] a quality she greatly admired.

Hunter took the songs as they were delivered and diligently documented them as such, even when the stories (let alone the individual words) didn't make much sense: "I will not change a song. And some of the songs . . . have obvious mistakes in them. . . . I'm going to sing it just like the person sang it to me."[41] In the written introduction to his collection, Hunter talked about "the natural hazards" of orally transmitted material, which "change[s] nearly all our songs. . . . This is not the fault of the singer or neither is it wrong. . . . I believe you should never tell a person they are singing a song wrong, unless of course you wrote the song." And then, sounding very much like Randolph, he added, "But any person that changes the song from the way they collected it is a damn fool and don't know what they're talking about, let alone being honest with the person that sang it for them."[42] But just below the surface of Hunter's bluster was his naiveté with regard to the creative life of several of his sources, many of whom admitted to altering lyrics to satisfy their artistic sensibilities.[43]

## The Good, the Bad, and the Ugly

The same conviction that kept Hunter from altering nonsensical words carried through in his refusal to modify gruesome or socially unacceptable lyrics. Once, as a guest of Adolf Schroeder at the Festival of Missouri Folk Music and Dance, Hunter spent considerable time explaining the context for lyrics that the audience would no doubt have found offensive. One of the songs he sang, "A Sailor Cut Down in His Prime," was a variant of "The Streets of Laredo." This particular sailor had syphilis, Hunter told his audience: "It was a known fact that those who had it, and had it bad, their bodies *did* rot and they *did* smell," hence the six fair maidens carrying the six (fragrant) white roses.[44] During this same program he sang "The Jew's Garden," a variant of Child 155 in which the "Jewess" cuts off the head of a child who wandered into her garden. Ollie Gilbert's version does not spare us the details:

VERSE 7
She pinned a napking o'er his face
An' pinned it with gold pin
Then called for a vessel of gold
To catch his heart blood in, in, in
To catch his heart blood in

And similarly in Allie Long Parker's rendition:

VERSE 6
She took him by th lily white hand
An' led him 'cross th hall
An' with a broad sword cut off his head
An' kicked it against th wall, wall, wall
An' kicked it against th wall

Hunter explained, "Many of our old, old folk songs are bloody and I don't find any racial problem with songs."[45] This was a common refrain for the Missouri collector, who, in addition to acknowledging a song as a product of its time, had enough of the contrarian in him to enjoy keeping his educated audience off balance: "I know some people who sing this . . . change a word because they think there's some racial problem with it. I don't. It's a known fact that things like this [murder] did happen, and if you don't think so, look in 'The Prioress's Tale' in Chaucer, and see if you don't read the same story." In the aforementioned ballad, the headless boy continues to sing about Christianity as depicted in the Fran Majors variant:[46]

VERSE 7
Go bury my Bible at my head
My prayer book at my feet
And when my schoolmates calls for me
You tell 'em that I am a sleep, o sleep
You tell 'em that I am sleep

Once, mid-concert, Hunter corrected the youthful singer Judy Domeny Bowen after she sang "The Brown Girl." "He didn't throw the head after he cut it off; he *kicked* it," Hunter made a point of telling both Bowen and the audience.[47] In addition to probable racist messages in "The Brown Girl," a quick keyword search on the Hunter Collection website yields a number of racial slurs that make reference to African Americans.[48] Despite the fact that Hunter was reared in one of the whitest, most Protestant counties in all of Missouri, in a town that had its own racially violent history, he rarely mentioned his feelings on matters of race. During the same concert in 1977, he told the audience, "I don't care if you're white, black, green, blue, whatever. I don't care whether you wear your hair long—I wear mine short because it's my head and I want to. You wear yours long. I don't care what you do with it . . . doesn't have anything to do with what's inside of you, anyway."[49] Hunter often struck this egalitarian note, although it is hard to know how deep it truly went.

Hunter's tirelessly literal approach to song transcription certainly ran contrary to many of the collectors before him who could not resist changing a word or a tune here or there in order to create a more cohesive narrative or to enhance the song's aesthetic appeal.[50] The British expatriate poet Robert Graves—coming from a long line of English songbook makers who were (to varying degrees) more focused on popularization and performance than preserving original texts[51]—was completely transparent (not to mention cynical) about his approach to ballad emendation:

> Most ballad anthologies nowadays are "scholarly" which means that the editors feel obliged to print each ballad exactly as it occurs in one of the many variant versions still surviving. But unless such a version happens to be superior to all others in every stanza, this seems unjust to the reader. . . . Ballads are nobody's property, and if careless singers or illiterate printers have claimed the right to spoil them, who can deny us the right to guess how the originals went?[52]

Looking back on her family's involvement in her father's work, Linda Bangs realizes that Hunter's diligence was met with some derision on the part of his children. "Every once in a while he would ask us to listen to a tape and tell him what we thought a word or phrase might be. All we thought we were hearing were old-sounding people with twangy voices singing funny songs and pronouncing words wrong," recalled Bangs. "Little did we know!"[53] Virginia Hunter recalled many nights when her husband would come home from collecting and go straight up to the bedroom and shut the door: "And then he would transcribe what he had collected."[54] There were times when he couldn't make out certain lyrics: "He'd call the children and I up into the bedroom, and we'd sit there real quiet like, and we'd listen."[55] Then they would debate what the mystery word was and come up with a consensus. This activity was a "labor of love" and Hunter was as enamored of the singers as with the songs themselves.[56] In fact, he once remarked with characteristic irony, "I have a priceless collection that is worthless, at least in a monetary way."[57] Given that Hunter never paid his sources to sing for him, and given that he did not receive any compensation for occasionally performing their songs, the importance of the ballads they chose to share with him lay largely in their acts of generosity.

# 4

## THE CHILD BALLADS AND OTHER BOUNTY

### Early Contributors

The year 1958 was a landmark one for Hunter, who was finding his stride as a collector. This was due to a number of factors, not the least of which was his unofficial apprenticeship to Mary Parler (of the University of Arkansas), for whom he had made several hours' worth of ballad recordings that would populate his collection as well as her own. In addition, he had purchased recording equipment with a larger storage capacity. It also helped that Hunter was in his sixth year with the Rhodes refrigeration company, which meant he had established relationships with customers along his sales route, and if his clients weren't singers, they served as conduits to those who were. The individuals Hunter recorded during that period and the experiences he had in the field would fuel his collecting efforts for years to come.

One of the first people Hunter deliberately collected from was Virgil Lance, whom Parler had first visited back in 1953. Lance was a well-spoken man who worked at a ferry dock on Lake Norfolk and lived a few miles west of Mountain Home, Arkansas.[1] He was important to Hunter and Parler because of a repertoire that stretched back "across the pond." As Lance expressed it, his forebears "come over when my people was run out of England on account of Prince Charlie."[2] Said Hunter, "I called Virgil up one night and found out his wife Virginia was going to some kind of ladies meeting at the church and this would be a good time to come and visit, after she left. She didn't think too much of his singing and anybody that wanted to come out and listen to him she thought was out of their mind."[3] Hunter enjoyed two sessions with Lance, but these visits were more than a decade apart, the first in February

1958 and the second in April 1969. Hunter described his time with Lance as highly rewarding, and the pleasure Lance took in singing is palpable in all ten of the ballads he shared.[4]

Apparently, an unbroken thread of musicality stretched from generation to generation in the Lance family. In addition to the many songs he learned from both his father and grandfather, Virgil had a daughter of whom he was quite proud. A 1954 recording captures Carla Lance's supple fourteen-year-old voice singing her father's own sentimental composition "Where the Ole White River Flows," a song that Hunter would capture Virgil singing eleven years later.[5] Oddly, Hunter makes no mention of this being the original composition of the dockhand; therefore, it is unclear as to whether he assumed that it was traditional. Regardless, Lance apparently took as much pleasure in authoring songs as in singing them; Parler and O'Bryant collected another of his creations, "My Home in the White River Hills," during a recording session in 1958.

In 1969 Hunter would visit Lance again, this time capturing a spirited rendition of "Bill Stafford," a song that Parler had collected from Lance more than a decade earlier under the better-known title "The State of Arkansas."

Virgil Lance, circa 1958. (Photograph by Hunter, courtesy of the Springfield-Greene County Library)

Allie Long Parker in front of her home, July 1958. (Photograph by Hunter, courtesy of the Springfield–Greene County Library)

Replete with inedible meat ("His beef I couldn't chaw") and poor pay ("fifty cents a day"), this first-person narrative is an iconic and cynical "drifter" song. It describes the narrator's dismal experience of being hired to work as a "swamp angel," draining land. Lance claimed to know a good deal about two songs in particular: "Lovely Jane" (earlier recorded as "Sweet Lovely Jane") and "Erin's Green Shores" (earlier recorded as "Rose of Erin"), both of which he believes came over with supporters of Charles II, otherwise known as the Cavaliers. Lance described them as "men who fought for Prince Charlie, who was run out of England when he made a try for the throne. . . . They came to me from my grandfather, who came from the Mountains of Tennessee and Virginia."[6]

Allie Long Parker of the Pleasant Valley Community (near Hogscald Hollow) is another Arkansas source Parler shared with Hunter early on. Parker had a colorful repertoire that included local broadsides, Child ballads, and native Ozark ballads, and she learned the majority of her songs from her father, James Long, whom she called "a terrible hand to sing," an expression that Randolph and Parler defined as "he sang well, loved to sing, and knew many songs."[7] Some of the songs she sang, such as "Sing Low, Laurie O," about the Battle of Santa "Fay," could be traced as far back as her paternal grandmother, who was married to a sea captain. Time spent with Parker helped Hunter develop his sixth sense for ancient balladry.

## Child Ballads and Broadsides

In addition to Hunter's knack for locating useful songsters, he regularly applied this intuitive approach to ballad collecting. When asked by Cathy Barton how he knew a song was "important," Hunter replied:

> I can't tell you that either. . . . It happened on the "Nightman";[8] it happened on several songs. . . . I had a Child's [ballads] collection, but I wasn't too familiar with it when I got "The Jew's Garden." But there was something that told me that that was an old song. Well, with that one I didn't have to look it up, because I went from Pleasant Valley Community [where] Allie Long Parker sang it for me . . . near Eureka Springs and I stopped by to see Vance and while I was there, I decided I'd play my tapes so he could hear it. Vance knew it immediately and plus some of the other songs she sang for me. . . . Of course, I had to make seven or eight trips to collect from Allie Long Parker before she ran out of songs.[9]

We know regrettably little about the life of Allie Long Parker (who carried these old songs), although we can gather—from brief exchanges between herself, Hunter, and Parler—that she was a genteel woman who greatly enjoyed visits from song gatherers.[10] We also know that she kept ballet books of song lyrics on paper tablets and wallpaper.[11] Like many other singers, Parker often did not know the titles of songs, as in the case of "The Mermaid," which Hunter immediately recognized as a fragment of Child 289. She gave Hunter his one and only version of Child 002, "Rosemary and Thyme"—a veritable laundry list of demands between lovers—which she sang in eleven detailed and hypnotic verses. The "Long" in Parker's maiden name was entirely appropriate given the length of many of her ballads. But she was by no means singular in this regard, and many of the songs in the Hunter Collection run even longer. As the Missouri collector himself once remarked, "The traditional singer is hard to start, and hard to stop."[12]

In addition to the frequent presence of kings, queens, princes, and princesses in these songs, the Child ballads certainly have a savagery that would

have alerted Hunter about their authenticity. As time went on and he became more knowledgeable, he gave a great deal of thought to their longev-
ity: "Why should some of the bloodiest songs, you know, a guy taking his
girlfriend by the hair, which is a pretty cruel way of getting rid of anybody,
is dragging them and throwing them in the river. Why should a song like
that hang around for three or four hundred years?"[13] Hunter was hardly the
first person to ponder this question.

In addition to Hunter's vigilance regarding the occurrence of Child ballads
among Ozark singers, his collection includes a large number of Broadside
ballads as well, the most popular of which seemed to be the gruesome story
of the "The Knoxville Girl," sung by as diverse a group of performers as Paralee Weddington, Fred High, Reba Dearmore, and T. R. Hammond, among
others. Although each variant has its virtues, probably the most musically
striking is that provided by David Prickett (with help from his musical sister
Lucy[14]), whose all-absorbing rendition leaves a brief but memorable trail in
the Hunter Collection. It appears likely that we would have heard more from
this skilled singer had Hunter not run out of tape, something that happened
more often in his less experienced days of collecting back in 1958.

Certain of the native American ballads in Hunter's collection were composed by his sources, as in the case of "The Baggage Coach Ahead," a song delivered to Hunter by its seventy-six-year-old author, T. R. Hammond, with an
unusual wealth of biographical detail from the author himself: Even though
it originated outside of the Ozarks, this song and its singer left a deep impression on Hunter, who returned to his motel in North Osceola, Missouri,
that night and recorded some biographical notes about its author. Hammond
said that the song started as a poem that he composed about the loss of his
young wife and his sad return home with their infant son. As told by Hunter,
"After they had been married ten months and three days, Mr. Hammond's
wife died and left him with a child that was twenty-eight days old. Mr. Hammond brought this child back to Oklahoma and her [his wife's] parents for
burial, and the story that is told in the song . . . actually happened."[15]

But something about the song or the author's commentary troubled
Hunter: "Mr. Hammond had no reason to tell this story to me if it wasn't
true, and I checked around Osceola, and his reputation is above reproach.
I wondered at the time Mr. Hammond was telling me this story—I have no
reason to doubt it, but I still wonder." It is likely that Hunter's skepticism came
from this individual's oddly detached narration of a pivotal personal event.
Although Hunter learned that the child went on to become a commander in
the U.S. Navy, the subject of the ballad remained nameless both in the song

and in their conversation. In a rare addendum to the lyrics, Hunter wrote, "This is one of the most unusual contacts I have found."[16]

In April 1958, Hunter collected only one song from Bessie Owens of Batesville, Arkansas; it was the "Johnny Lee Ballad," which was composed by the Reverend John Crafton, who served as the first pastor for Freewill Baptist Church in St. Paul, Arkansas. Written in 1886, it tells the story of two young boys who are sent out into a blizzard by Lee's father:

> You now must go to mill
> Tho the snow hit got so very deep
> He could hardly climb the hill.

On their way to the mill, they stop at "Uncle Sam's," where the older of the two boys, Nathan Bailey (age eighteen), offers to go on without his ten-year-old companion, Johnny Lee. When Nathan returns to his uncle's house:

> The boys then got their supper
> But lay upon the floor
> And there they nearly froze to death
> They slept so near the door.

In the morning, they start on the trek home, but Johnny Lee dies of exposure to the elements. Not surprisingly, given its author, the ballad ends on a note of redemption:

> The neighbors gathered and buried him
> Upon th west hillside
> But on th resurrection morning
> He will not be denied
> But may he ever have a home
> In that happy land of bliss
> Where there'll be no more sorrow
> Or stories told like this.

According to local legend, Lee's negligent father was sent to prison for three years.[17]

In 1958 Hunter collected a number of songs from Springfield resident J. W. Breazeal. Breazeal was unique among Hunter's sources in that he often sang religious songs, some of which were composed hymns or parlor ballads. In formal prose, he once explained his musical tastes: "I have been a great lover of music, and especially of old sacred music. For about fifteen years I went with a group of singers . . . singing out of *The Old Christian Harmony* and *Work and Worship* songbooks. . . . I served from '34 until '45 as the leader of that band; and still, where we sing, I lead. . . . I also have an *Old Four Notebook*—just four notes: so, la, fa, me. And instead of the seven, we just have the four."[18] Breazeal was referring to shape-note hymnals that made social singing more accessible to community members, who could quickly be taught to sight-read through a system of geometrically shaped and easily recognizable notes.[19]

Nineteen fifty-eight was also the year that Hunter first recorded Pearl Brewer from Pocahontas, Arkansas. Listening to Brewer's recordings, it is easy to understand why she was a favorite among several collectors, including Parler, who brought her to Hunter's attention. Parler first collected from her in May of that same year, and Hunter followed up both in November and the following May. His correspondence includes a copy of an impassioned letter that Parler wrote to Brewer two years after she and Hunter had first collected from this singer, and it reflects the high esteem in which Parler held Brewer:

> In the seven years that I have been collecting folksongs, I have collected 41 Child ballads, but never as many as nine from one person—except from Mrs. Brewer!!! . . . [ballad titles listed]. Don't get the idea that the only songs of yours that are valuable are the Child ballads. You sang Joanie and me 49 wonderful songs, and you sang about three others for Max Hunter that you hadn't sung for us. . . . I know you have others that should be preserved here at the University of Arkansas. When you and I are forgotten, the tapes will be in the library, keeping the old songs for another day and other folks who might not know about them if you had not sung them for me in the summer of 1958.[20]

Pearl Brewer's popularity as a ballad bearer was also recognized by those in her community: "A student from the University [of Arkansas] heard some children in Pocahontas, Arkansas, singing 'Hangman, Hangman, Hold Your Hand' (Child 95). The children said they had learned it from their 'Grandma Brewer.'"[21]

The little we know about Brewer comes from a brief portrait written by fledgling folklorist Sue Jackson, who visited her six years after Hunter. It is clear from Jackson's notes that Brewer greatly enjoyed sharing her songs with ballad hunters: "I was not quite sure what to expect, but her eagerness to sing for me made me a little less apprehensive. . . . She was a tiny woman with long black hair which she wore in braids wound on top of her head. Her smile was radiant, and I fell in love with her the minute I saw her. . . . Then she told me that she learned practically all of her songs from her uncle when she was a little girl."[22] According to Randolph and Parler, this was a "blind uncle who lived in her home."[23]

Thanks to that unidentified uncle, Brewer was a repository of several Child ballads, most of which she delivered with drawn-out cadences that were very much her own. Brewer was the source for a musically hypnotic and modal version of "Two Sisters," which she called "The Old Woman Lived on a Sea Shore," a variant of Child 10. In contrast to her winsome personality, Brewer seemed particularly fond of murder ballads; she gave Hunter his only two versions of "Down by the Greenwood Side" (Child 20, also known as "The Cruel Mother"), in which two infants are murdered and come back to haunt the murderer. This is one of several British songs that had not been caught by Henry M. Belden. Randolph and Parler found Brewer's version particularly artful and wrote of "the chilling impact of this beautiful ballad of guilt and supernatural,"[24] speaking specifically of the intensity of the second-to-last stanza:

O Mother, dear Mother, we once were yourn
All alone and lone
You neither gave us coarse nor fine;

Pearl Brewer, November 1958. (Photograph by Hunter, courtesy of the Springfield–Greene County Library)

You killed and buried us under a stone,
And prayed to the Lord it'd never be known,
All down by the greenwood side.

Brewer also sang a fragment of "The Wild Hog" for Hunter—one of only two versions he collected of Child 18—alternately referred to as "Sir Lionel" and "Old Bangum," among other titles.[25] The popularity of this ballad has stretched over centuries, most likely due to the primal depiction of the hunt itself and the presence of a witch figure, suggesting a fight between good (the hunter hero) and evil (the wild boar/witch). She also provided him with one of his six "Brown Girl" (Child 73) variants, which she referred to as "Lord Thomas."

In addition to the Child ballads, Brewer knew several broadside ballads such as "The Taylor Boys" as well as native American ballads. Time spent with this source always proved fruitful, and there is little mystery as to why she was so popular among ballad hunters.

A rarely mentioned rejection came in the form of a Mrs. Shepherd in Osceola, Arkansas, who, according to Hunter, "had a treasure trove of stories and memorabilia about the outlaw Jesse James."[26] Hunter was under the impression that she hoped to make money off of her songs: "She wouldn't sing for me, she wouldn't sing for Vance, she wouldn't sing for anybody. . . . And that's the only person who ever told me 'no.'"[27] In one of many conversations between himself and Dolf and Becky Schroeder, Hunter again indicated that he occasionally came home empty-handed: "Mary Jo Davis probably had as good a voice and could sing her mother's songs as good as anybody. And her sister . . . sang some for me. She had a good voice but she wasn't as good as Mary Jo. Mary Jo got married, and when she did, why I think her husband was opposed to her singing. She just clammed up."[28] Hunter thought this inhibition had much to do with the husband's religiosity, which led Mr. Davis to believe that (in Hunter's words) folksongs "was real bad songs" due to their generally unacceptable content.[29] Hunter did manage to get at least two songs out of Mary Jo Davis and several more from her mother, Lula Davis, who was known to be "a really good singer."[30]

Hunter's comments regarding Davis are important because they point to societal strictures around musical performance, particularly on the part of women, and one is left to wonder how many female voices were silenced by such attitudes. This is a theme that comes up again and again. When contributors were asked to sing, the songs they chose to share were determined by conscious and unconscious factors that ran deep. Depending on the personality of the individual, he or she sometimes reflected on the morality of the song and whether it would be "acceptable." One contact refused to sing a song because it was just plain dangerous. Hunter recalled:

> I will not call names or dates, but recently I had a visit with a man that lives in the Bald Knob country. And as you recall, the Bald Knobbers were quite a notorious band at one time. But I asked this gentleman if he knew the Bald Knobber's song and if he would sing it for me. He said he knew the song but would not sing for me. The reason—that he knew a man very well that got his head blew off for going down the road on horseback singing that song. He knew the man that done the shooting; he knew the man that got killed; he knew the sheriff; he knew the lawyer; he knew the places; and he was pretty close on some of the dates. And the feeling that still exists, even though it is not talked about, the old timers still hesitate to talk to the outsiders too much either for or against that organization.[31]

Much has been written and much has been said about the Bald Knobbers, a vigilante group that sprang up in post–Civil War times, first in Taney County on the Missouri-Arkansas border, and then spread to other counties as well. Hunter's predecessor Randolph, who had a knack for extracting "personal, or secret" material (as noted by W. K. McNeil),[32] collected a version of the song, and his sources credited its origin to Andrew Coggburn, who was in the habit of mocking and speaking out against the Bald Knobbers. Coggburn is likely the man Hunter refers to who "got his head blew off for . . . singing that song," and the man who "done the shooting" was likely a reference to Bald Knobber leader Nathaniel Kinney.[33] Randolph and many writers before and after him have been fascinated by the Bald Knobbers.[34]

Regarding the perceived propriety or impropriety of specific songs, lessons were introduced early in childhood. Speaking of visits to neighbor's houses for spelling "matches" and song sessions, William Eden recalled that "anything that was out of order, they didn't allow it."[35] Others were less concerned about the effect of their selections and simply enjoyed themselves. Frequently, individuals did not know or did not care about the titles of their songs, which varied greatly, but tended to categorize their repertoire by subject matter and by their source.

## Hard Lessons

Lessons well learned are often those that are most painful. One early recording session proved a casualty of the one-wire tape recorder, which had an extremely low storage capacity. Hunter located one of his oldest ballads, "The

Dewey Dens of Yarrow," after chasing down the elusive Herbert Charles Philbrick of Crocker, Missouri, a man who could most often be found in the local
tavern (when, according to Hunter, he could be found at all).[36] The following
anecdote from Hunter, which describes the afternoon that refrigeration cli-
ent Clarence Carroll first introduced him to Philbrick, shows the amount of
corralling it sometimes took to get people to sing for him:

> So, we went into this little tavern . . . and sure enough there was Mr.
> Philbrick settin' up at the counter, up at the bar, on a stool, talkin' to
> some of the fellows there. So he [Carroll] and I went in and we stood
> and talked with Mr. Philbrick a few minutes. . . . I suggested that we
> move into a booth, which we did. . . . Well, after a while I asked Mr.
> Philbrick if I could bring my recorder in and also told him I had my
> guitar with me and he could play it. So he said "All right." I went out
> and got the guitar and tape recorder and brought it back in. And we all
> started singin'. Mr. Philbrick would sing, and I'd sing, and after a while
> everybody in the tavern was standin' around the booth. Crocker, Mis-
> souri is not very far from Fort Leonard Wood. There's a lot of soldier
> boys that are stationed at Fort Leonard Wood but live at Crocker and
> Dixon and various places around. Well, before the evening was over, we
> had a real good crowd. In fact, I doubt if that tavern had done as good a
> business in a long time or I'd doubt if he's done as good a business since.
> But anyway, Mr. Philbrick sang for me "The Dewey Dens of Yarrow."
> . . . In fact, he took my guitar and he *untuned* it, or tuned it the way he
> wanted it and played and sang somethin' about a Mexican gal.[37]

But soon after this recording session, Hunter hurried back to his motel
room, wrote down the words to "The Dewey Dens of Yarrow," and then erased
the recording to make room for something else. He would always look back
at this irreversible error with the deepest regret: "And at that time, on these
songs and interviews, I was just taping the people and the songs and then
destroying the tape, or using it over."[38] This was a turning point for the novice collector: "This is probably the only person that I was unable to go back
and to get to sing for me the songs they had sung for me the first time. And
if ever anything would leave an indignation or memory on your mind, the
importance of getting as much on the tape and keeping the tape as this one
situation did, none other had ever impressed me like this one did."[39]

Hunter went on to say, "I did make several trips after that to find Mr. Philbrick. And on the one or two times that I did find him, Mr. Philbrick was in
no condition to sing. . . . In fact, he didn't know what his [own] name was."[40]

"Setting [*sic*] in the swing at the Sherwood Motel in Eureka Springs, Arkansas," October 1972. (Courtesy of the Springfield–Greene County Library)

A later interview with Hunter shows the single-mindedness with which he pursued this most slippery of songsters. He described the time he visited Crocker immediately following the death of Philbrick's wife: "I drove over to Richland and went to the funeral home and he [Philbrick] had just left there, but they said that when he got there he must have been stopping at every beer tavern on the way. . . . I . . . stayed all night in Waynesville [Missouri] and I got up real early in the morning and drove up to Crocker just about the time he was getting out of bed. I got him before he had a chance to get down to the tavern."[41]

While Hunter failed to recover the coveted Child ballad, his uncharacteristically thorough interview with Philbrick on October 28, 1959, yielded rich fodder about the lifestyle of this seventy-two-year-old who nonetheless gave him a few other songs.[42] Born in Ottawa, Kansas, in 1886,[43] Philbrick spent his earliest days in Lincoln, Illinois. He and his brothers took jobs at the Hardin glass plant in Fort Smith, Arkansas, and at two plants in Kansas. He enjoyed the hot work in the winter but far less so during the summer months. He also made a living as an apple packer. As to how he acquired his songs, Philbrick said, "I always liked music. Why, I'd get around somebody who knows every song. I'd just stick around with him 'til I learnt it."[44] Hunter asked Philbrick if he still played the guitar, to which he responded, "One of my boys got a fiddle and the other one a guitar, and . . . the kids got to rompin' 'round and they busted it." Philbrick then went on to describe the enjoyment he took in playing music for barn dances and frolic dances. When Hunter asked him if he ever got paid, Philbrick gave this anecdotal response:

> Sometimes we'd be pretty lucky to get 50 cents, sometimes a dollar, a dollar and a half. . . . You'd get enough for gas or a little chicken to eat on the next day. That's about all. . . . We mostly went in for amusement. Sometimes we'd get somebody else to play for us and we'd dance a little. We used to play at the Wilson Ranch in Oklahoma. . . . I used to play down there. Them cowboys, they do lots of dancing. . . . Because they don't have no fun, just ride, ride all the time, and then dance in the night. You could sit and play all night . . . and I played up until 9 o'clock the next morning before they quit. Old . . . John McCluskey, he was the foreman there. . . . He'd barbecue a beef. . . . All you'd have to do when you got hungry was go up there and help yourself. . . . And they had a little drink on the side. I never got to where I couldn't play, but I got feelin' pretty good![45]

This interview concluded with Hunter addressing both Philbrick and (in the largest sense) posterity, likely in an unconscious effort to console himself over the loss of the Child ballad: "I did want to . . . let the people know there was a Herbert Philbrick that *did* live in Crocker, Missouri, and that we *did* spend the afternoon together—I think one of the finest afternoons I've spent in a long time. . . . We drank a few beers and sang a few songs." And then Hunter sounded a particularly wistful note: "I wish that the two little songs you did sing for me, about the little Spanish girl and the 'Dewey Dens of Yarrow,' could've come back to your mind, but I still travel this territory."[46] Then a heavy-hearted Hunter, trying to forge a deeper connection with a man who clearly did not remember his interviewer's name, said, "Mr. Philbrick, among other things that has affected your life, about a year ago your wife died, and that kind of changes a man's life too." Philbrick, who had been married for forty-nine years, replied, "I'm just like a stray dog. I just run here and there and go somewhere for company. I just can't stand it to stay here by myself too much."[47] Then, reflecting on the three sentimental songs he sang for Hunter during that final visit,[48] the old man shared his own thoughts with future listeners: "If this can do anybody any good, why I'm proud of it. . . . I know them little old songs . . . they got a lot of good meaning to them. . . . All they can think about today is Honky Tonky."[49] Philbrick died three years later, in 1961.

## From Strangers to Friends

Songs that went unsung were by far the exception. Time spent with musical acquaintances created an emotional bond that seemed to travel in both directions; it also created a trail of memories that amounted to some peak experiences for the collector himself. Take Hunter's account of his visit to the homestead of illicit tobacco grower Leander Witt of Hindsville, Arkansas, in 1958:

> We set out on the porch and chewed and spit [tobacco]. . . . He sang and he was warm and in the background you can hear on this tape this frog is croaking every once in a while. And every time I play that tape, there's something goes up and down my spine, that that few minutes *will never be again*, and Leander Witt is dead, and nobody is ever going to experience what I did with that fine old man. So, this is all built into a collector, I think.[50]

Hunter's ability to collect was enhanced by the ease with which he made friends of strangers. In the words of his daughter Linda, "I think he was the type of person you could talk to five [or] ten minutes and you felt like you had known him forever. He had that way of making you feel comfortable in his presence. . . . By the time he was through [collecting], if somebody in their family passed away, they [his contacts] would notify him . . . and if he was able, he would go to their services."[51]

While at the time of recording Hunter may have found the presence of background noise a nuisance, these ambient sounds provide important clues about the lifestyle of the singer, clues that, by and large, Hunter was not in the habit of documenting through written or recorded field notes.[52] Hunter himself was emotionally stirred by the sound of the frog croaking. It brought him back to a particular moment in his own life, and, aesthetically speaking, these sounds serve to make the setting more palpable and put any listener more "in the moment." One need only listen to the sound of acorns raining down on Almeda Riddle's metal roof as she sings "Lady Margret" to understand.

Hunter had several noises to contend with during visits to Allie Parker in 1958: there was the running of her husband's saw during the taping of

"Johnny German" and the chattering of canaries, which set the cadence for many of her songs during a November session. Regarding the birds, Hunter apologetically asked Parker to relocate them during the session.

Early on, Hunter realized that he'd never be able to get the songs he wanted if he was a stranger to his sources. Sometimes this involved taking some risks. His son David once described his father's openness to people from all walks of life: "He got to meet and talk to some people that we wouldn't even walk up to. He called them 'down-to-earth hillbillies.'"[53] Hunter explained, "The only way to learn is to get involved. Now, I've been involved sometimes in people's lifestyles that maybe I didn't approve of, full well knowing that either my brains or my fists was gonna have to get me out of it."[54] But Hunter, reserved by nature, seems to have consistently chosen the former.

In later years Hunter would enjoy regaling audiences with his many song-chasing adventures, one of which involved helping deliver stump whiskey over state lines. He describes what it was like waiting in the truck while the bootlegger went on his "errands." Hunter was instructed to "'set in the truck, and if you hear anything or see anything you either flash the lights or honk the horn.'" Hunter pointed out that "he was delivering moonshine. . . . He had put the whiskey on a stump and picked up his ten dollars." When they passed a tavern on the way home, Hunter suggested they stop for a beer, but the bootlegger firmly declined because he was concerned that he "might get in trouble," as Hunter remembered it, with more than a touch of irony.[55] Not all of these adventures sat well with Hunter's wife, Virginia. Their daughter Linda recalls, "Dad would take moonshine from Missour[i] down into Arkansas, which was a big no *no*. . . . Mother, . . . at first I think she was absolutely mortified; drink and whiskey was not even allowed in our house. . . . But later she got the humor in it."[56]

Another collecting trip brought him into contact with an escaped convict. As Hunter tells it, "I . . . loaned my car one time to a guy that had escaped out of the penitentiary and had been gone for two weeks, and they was looking for him—I didn't know it though."[57] Here's one iteration of the story as told by Hunter:

A young fellow stopped me on the highway before I got into town. . . . Some of the local citizens didn't care much for him and some may have had their reasons. Well, he asked me if he could borrow my car to go get his girlfriend. . . . He said he would have my car back in one hour. . . . I told him I would put the keys under the floor mat. . . . After the young fellow had been gone only a few minutes, one of the local people told me that the fellow had recently escaped from one of the state prison

Hunter traveled to many folk festivals in this truck. (Courtesy of the Hunter family)

farms and had been hiding out in the area for the last few weeks. . . . I had the feeling that it just might be possible I had lost a car. But I decided to wait and see.[58]

At the appointed time, another person brought Hunter his keys with a "thanks" from the escaped convict: "This young fellow was caught, served his time, came back, got married and is making a good father."[59] Hunter also found himself in the company of outlaws when he occasionally taught refrigeration classes to prisoners from the Springfield State Penitentiary. Although Virginia Hunter was less than thrilled when her husband came home with such stories, she eventually reconciled herself to the inherent hazards of his fieldwork.

Then there was the time he was invited to a shivaree for a newly married couple in Ozark County, Missouri, when the party came to a sudden halt due to a commotion in front of the house. "[The] mother and her daughter was out breaking the windshields out of people's cars," Hunter said.[60] He later found out that the daughter (who was possibly pregnant) had been "jilted" by her boyfriend and this was her and her mother's way of expressing their displeasure. Hunter said the fight came to a natural end, likely because "they run out of rocks. . . . Anyway they went out and talked it over and after quite a bit of cussing they drove off." Hunter, who called this the "dirtyest" fight he ever witnessed, once claimed that he didn't have to look for adventures; he simply needed to "be around at the right time."[61]

## The Singing Postman

Hunter had particularly vivid recollections of his pilgrimage out to fellow song collector Fred High of Carroll County, Arkansas, with whom he visited several times. Decades later, while visiting with the Schroeders, he gave a detailed description of Fred's now legendary one-man village:

> Fred used to have a store and a grocery store and . . . now he was the Postmaster there . . . and he had a little route around. . . . And when Fred was running the mail route, the women [his wife and sister] would run the grocery store and the post office. . . . He had built a church—you go on 'round the curb, and across a little creek and then go on across the other side of this little valley and here was the High Community Church. . . . And the cemetery was right behind this building. There was a sign, when you come either direction, that Fred had put up on just a post, that said Population 3. Well, this was right. It was Fred, his sister Sukey, and his wife Janie. I don't remember which died first, but when one of the women died Fred went and changed the sign to Population 2. When both of 'em had died, he changed it to Population 1.[62]

Hunter once observed, "High lived all his life in a log cabin within 40 feet of where he was born."[63]

Hunter knew that helping with ordinary or even "extraordinary" farm chores would help him gain favor with ballad bearers, and he did so whenever he was able. This took on practically heroic proportions during one summertime visit to High's place circa 1959:

> When I drove up . . . I saw this gentleman standing out on the west side. . . . The only way I knew it was Fred was by his height, and the way he stooped a little bit. (Fred was a big man). . . . He had a lace curtain over his head. . . . I couldn't tell what Fred was trying to do. I didn't think he was going to a costume party. . . . What Fred was getting ready to do was

to clean the wasps' nests out of his well house, and Fred wanted to know if I would help him. . . . So Fred and I went into his house. He took his window curtain off of him, puttered around, found a straw hat for me, found another one of these lace curtains that didn't have any holes in it . . . and a pair of gloves. The straw hat was to keep the curtain away from your face. Then you take the curtain and you shove it down into your pants . . . and then you put the gloves on. . . . This was a little well house. We opened the door and crawled, kind of hunched down, and reached up and got a hold of these wasps' nests and heave[d] 'em out the door. . . . I could see these wasps all around my face and making this sound zzzzzz noise. They were wild, flying and bumping into everything. But Fred was pretty smart. We tore down four or five of these nests, threw 'em out, and Fred and I said, "in the morning they'll all be gone." Well, after we got through doing this chore, we went in and Fred sang some songs for me.[64]

Hunter later said, "I done an awful lot of visiting with Fred High, probably spent more time with Fred High doing other things that I did [than] getting him to sing for me."[65] In the end, High sang thirteen songs for Hunter, which fit a variety of categories, many of them comedic, a prime example being the "morning after" song titled "In a Hog Pen:"[66]

> . . . Hog's bein' displeased
> They snuffled an' sneezed
> And they covered me up with their noses
> They chewed up my hat
> Both greasy and flat
> And tore up one-half of my shirt

High was unabashed when it came to sharing dirty songs—a rarity among balladeers, according to Hunter, who once told an audience "getting people to sing bawdy songs is real hard."[67] That said, Hunter once boasted to a university audience about his capture of "Bawdy Strawberry Roan" from contributor Glenn Ohrlin.[68] High shared several bawdy songs about unfaithful wives such as "Will the Weaver" (recited rather than sung), in which Will ends up literally and figuratively "up th' chimney," and "Shoot the Cat," which describes a sexual encounter between a milkmaid and a man named "Mr. Rogers."[69] In addition to some Civil War ballads like "Battle of Prairie Grove," High also sang a song he claims to have authored titled "O, Do Come Onc't More," which makes mention of the ephemeral beauty of young women.

In the same year that Hunter helped High with the wasps' nests, 1959, collector John Quincy Wolf Jr. came through and recorded High's unsentimental

Fred High with his dog. (Courtesy of Special Collections, University of Arkansas Libraries, Fayetteville)

autobiography. This narrative illustrates why High was locally famous for his status as a self-reliant (and at the same time gregarious) loner:

> I'm [with]in twelve foot of where I was born. I'm 81 years old. My Poppy and Mommy was poor folks and sickly, died when they was young . . . 60 and 66. . . . I never went to school but 207 days in my life. Couldn't go to school 'til I was 8 years old. There's so many at the school, why, they'd run over me. Then I had to work when I was 17, and never went to school any more after that. . . . But I've written three books. One of them was *Forty-Three Years for Uncle Sam*, 'cause . . . I was postmaster for 35. . . .

I sold goods 26.5 years and went broke at it, selling on the credit. All that hears this, think about it and not try to sell on the credit. But I finally got out of debt, and I've made three now. One of them's a song book, sells for 75 cents, I'll send it anywhere. And the others I sell them for $1 apiece, I'll send them anywhere for the pay, and I'll pay the postage on them. . . . My wife died two years and a half ago. I raised seven children; two of them's dead now. I'm a-living here at High by myself.[70]

One of the most interesting aspects of Hunter's relationship with High was the blurred line between contributor and collector. In 1969 Hunter recalled a field trip he made in the company of his singing companion Joan O'Bryant: "When we got there Fred sang for us, but Fred also had a recorder and he wanted us to sing for him. So between the three of us swapping songs back and forth we had a wonderful afternoon."[71] Folklorist Norm Cohen pondered, "Who is a songcatcher? When old Fred High of High, Arkansas, collects songs from his neighbors, and then Max Hunter collects from Fred High, and then Vance Randolph collects from Max Hunter, . . . which one is the song catcher? Ballad collectors Mary Parler and Randolph made this point in the brochure to an album of Hunter's recordings: 'Nearly all folksingers are collectors, in a sense.'"[72]

In *People Studying People: The Human Element in Fieldwork*, the authors put it this way: "The dichotomy between inquirer and subject is often drawn in the fieldwork literature. Yet . . . the distinction is neither clear-cut nor consistent. Fieldworkers not only observe and question informants, but they are studied and queried themselves in a continual reversal of roles."[73] Hunter innately understood the elliptical nature of this relationship and was open to the moments in which, in the straightforward and eye-opening words of Robert A. Georges and Michael A. Jones, "subjects are knowledgeable, and the fieldworkers are ignorant."[74]

Looking back on his time with High, Hunter later poked fun at himself for misperceiving this Arkansawyer's circumstances: "First time I went to see him I felt sorry for him. . . . I thought, this guy needs financial help. His only heat was a fireplace. Here was this old fellow living all alone in this old house, and he was making canes for 75 cents and I bought only four or five of them. . . . I come to find out Fred High had money loaned out all over Carroll County. . . . He didn't need no help!"[75] What Hunter was encountering was the frugal lifestyle of a father of seven children who had finally—thanks to his talents and resourcefulness—arrived at a moment of comparative economic stability.[76]

"This is where Fred High lived. In the winter Fred lived in the room on the right. Kept fire in the fireplace." (Photograph and caption by Hunter, courtesy of the Springfield–Greene County Library)

## Judgment Suspended

Indeed, one of the most important lessons Hunter learned during his journeys through the Ozarks was how easy it is to be fooled by appearances. Sometimes, as in High's case, the lifestyles encountered were dictated more by choice and temperament than economic necessity. Later in life, falling under the influence of close academically minded friends, Hunter reflected on his own efforts to withhold judgment—regardless of people's circumstances: "We have a discrimination system of enormous complexity. . . . We are suspicious of all outsiders, sometimes even to the point of resentment. We expect a behavior pattern from everyone as per our norm, yet we deny the existence of classism in our own community."[77] He then went on to list a number of labels that people put on one another, from "people who live like animals" to "people who live high on the hog."[78] Taking his point of open-mindedness a step further, Hunter wrote:

I have known of and know now of men and women living together who were never married by a preacher or any other person. . . . They don't see anything wrong with the arrangement as it is. One woman is a well-known and well liked business person in a small town. . . . I knew a very nice elderly lady . . . that was a pretty strict, religious person. She thought drinking of any kind of store-bought alcohol was a sure road to self-destruction. Yet, she and a younger man that lived with her made a batch of moonshine at least once a year. It was used as a body builder-upper, sort of tonic. *What right have you and I to pass judgment on these people?*[79]

Hunter savored the experiences that came along with his fieldwork, and sometimes the experiences themselves proved more rewarding than the song bounty. The aforementioned visit to Leander Witt is one case in point. Witt yielded Hunter but one song, "I Wish I Was a Little Bird," in which Witt played banjo accompaniment, but Hunter would never forget the warm sound of nylon strings and crickets during that late-night session.

In April 1958, Hunter recorded seven songs from Goldie Schott, of Mundell, Arkansas (a village now under the waters of Beaver Lake), but not before straddling twenty-one baby calves, which he held by the ears while she fed them from a nipple on a bucket.[80] Apparently she was in the habit of buying cheap baby calves that had been abandoned by their mothers.[81] Hunter described Schott (who was sixty-nine at the time) as "quite a character":

She loved jewelry. . . . She had several bracelets on each arm, and she had two or three sets of beads on. And probably her face [was] painted just a little too much for her age. She had a boyfriend too, and he came down to visit Springfield. He came down every weekend. He was a painter. When I drove up, it was kind of stormy, and I saw her out in the garden by her house. She had on a pair of men's rubber boots because it was kind of wet and damp. She hollered up, "Hello! I'll be up in a minute." And I went on into the house. And you can hear, on the tape, if you're listening, thunder, where it started to storm. . . . But seeing Goldie out there in the garden, with her rubber boots on and all that jewelry, it just didn't make sense."[82]

Not the least of Goldie's eccentricities was her occasional lapse into an Irish brogue, as can be heard on "Branigan's Pup." The stage Irish tradition (from whence such imitations came) influenced both the repertoire and vocal delivery of many other Ozark songsters, including Hunter contributor C.

Goldie Schott in Mundell, Arkansas, circa 1958. (Photograph by Hunter, courtesy of the Springfield–Greene County Library)

W. Ingenthron, whose renditions of both "My Kind Ole Husband" and "The Irish Wake" had their own comic strain, and the Ozark Folksong Collection has several examples of songs from this time period in which contributors did their best to imitate Irish accents.[83] But the manner of delivery remained of least concern to Hunter, who summed up his impression of Goldie Schott by saying, "She was living in that nice little house all by herself, and she was doing what she wanted to do."[84]

Not all recording sessions put Hunter at ease, and the discomforts that he experienced were sometimes more social than physical. He recalled one particularly awkward incident that occurred during a recording session with an unidentified woman:

> She said, "Do you mind if I chew?" I said, "I don't mind—you chew and I'll smoke." She got her chair . . . put her can down—was chewing and spittin', and leaned over a couple or three times and all at once she broke wind that would rattle the doors. . . . I know my face turned purple and red—really, I didn't know what to do. We just went right on talking. She

Fred Smith inside his Oriole Barbershop, Bentonville, Arkansas. (Photograph by Mary Celestia Parler, courtesy of Special Collections, University of Arkansas Libraries, Fayetteville)

didn't miss a word. Anyway, I told Vance about this and he said, "well, that's nothing unusual for older people like that. . . . The old-timers thought that that was an act of nature . . . and they wouldn't do it in front of people they didn't like. . . ." But if that's a compliment, it's a hell of a way to pay a compliment to anybody![85]

Despite his initial embarrassment, Hunter later described the bounty with which he came away: "She sang some of the oldest songs known and a few were very rare in America."[86]

Fred Smith of Bentonville, Arkansas—a contributor Hunter met through Mary Celestia Parler—also had a fondness for Irish songs, several of which he sang for Hunter during that marathon summer of '58.[87] The "Singing Barber," as Smith was dubbed by University of Arkansas students and faculty, was an enthusiastic songster who sang in a decidedly untraditional and histrionic style, much like that of the locally famous May Kennedy McCord,[88] with whom Smith would have been acquainted. When it came to songs, Smith was as prolific as he was emotive. "He claims that his memory is bad now, but he can still shut his eyes and sing from memory for hours and hours," reported Parler's student Georgine Cawood, who visited Smith six years after Hunter's initial recording session.[89] While Cawood mentioned that Smith played the "clatter bones,"[90] she neglected to mention that he was also a deft fiddle player, having learned the instrument early on from his father. Although Smith was also popular among collectors, he was hardly a native Ozarker. Born in Wisconsin in 1888, he learned much of his foundational repertoire from Chippewa River mill-workers and lumberjacks and later learned songs from as far west as Texas.[91] A seasoned performer who owned several instruments, Smith sometimes handed visitors homemade music tapes so as to allow more time for storytelling and the sharing of his wife Ruth's pastries.[92] If Hunter was concerned about the provenance of Smith's songs, there is no record of this.

In August of this same year, Hunter went in search of a singer by the name of Iva Haslett, who resided in West Plains, Missouri:

"Fred woos Ruth with an old love ballad," in fall 1963. (Photograph by folklore student Georgine Cawood for Professor Parler, courtesy of Special Collections, University of Arkansas Libraries, Fayetteville)

It was a real hot evening . . . about four-thirty, five o'clock. And at that time you had to ford a little stream. And I was in no hurry. In fact, I was enjoying the drive. Down this country road, and it begin to get a little narrow. And when I got down to this little stream, why it didn't look too bad. . . . Well, the rain from a few days before apparently had washed the larger rocks out and had left kind of a sand-silt [in the] small valve, and my car just went plunk! and went down. The tailpipe got down under the water. . . . It was the water in the tailpipe cut the motor off. I didn't know what to do. I was right in the middle of it. I guess normally you're supposed to get a little excited. Well, I didn't. I just took my shoes off, rolled up my pant legs above my knees, and just stepped out into the water. And I wasn't very far from a farm house . . . and walked up to the farm house and a very nice elderly couple there. I told 'em what had happened and wondered if they had a tractor and just wondered if they could pull me out. No, he didn't have a tractor, but he had a pick-up truck. He'd be glad to try. So, we took his truck, and he had a rope.

Iva and Sam Haslett, West Plains, Missouri, August 1958. (Photograph by Hunter. Courtesy of the Springfield–Greene County Library)

We went back down to where my car was. But the front end was not out of the water. . . . Had a very nice visit with him. Thanked him, went on down, got the songs I wanted. However, I told Mrs. Haslett what had happened and she said, "Well on the way out, go around this way. Take a little different road and you won't have to go across the road."[93]

As physically demanding as this visit to the Hasletts' farmstead had been, Hunter came home with almost a dozen songs, several of which featured Mrs. Haslett as an enthusiastic documentarian of local disasters such as the "Salem Cyclone" of January 1947 (in which her house remained untouched) and the "West Plains Explosion" of April 1928, which was covered across the nation. A newspaper as far away as New York gave a vivid recounting of the Bond Dance Hall explosion, which included approximately forty couples of "the West Plains younger set," a piano player named Dimples Martin (killed instantly), and her partner trombone player named Ball Allen (who was blown through a window but survived). "The floor of the dance hall above was lifted almost to the ceiling," the article said, with this macabre endnote about the catalyst himself: "[J. N.] Weiser was found not far from the wreckage, his hand grimly holding the doorknob of the shattered garage. Nobody seems to know what happened to the motorist. The common belief prevails that Weiser [the owner of the building] must have lighted a match into the fumes of escaping gasoline."[94]

Sometimes getting relative strangers to sing for him simply meant being a good listener, but more often than not, Hunter found himself helping with farm chores. Spending a day, or the greater part of an evening, with musical contacts was not an unusual occurrence, and if some collectors resented the amount of give-and-take that it took to get material, Hunter reveled in it.[95] In addition to being "handy," he had a high tolerance for physical discomfort, another quality that served him well in the field. According to Hunter, here's what it took to get songs out of Marshall, Arkansas, farmer Odis Bird in August 1958: "I helped a guy put up hay—drove an old truck—there was something wrong with it and he didn't have any cushions; the only thing that you sat on was the spring and he had a board—a 1 [by] 12, . . . and boy, if that board had of moved at least six inches I'd have been ruined for life one way or the other."[96] Hunter never tired of telling this story: "I was told, the truck only had one speed forward and reverse, as there was something wrong with the steering. There was, because it took 'one-half-of-a-city-block' to turn and went forward a little faster than the speed of a turtle. . . . We got done about 6:00 p.m. that evening."[97]

Back at a local motel room, the inexhaustible Odis Bird kept Hunter very busy that night: "When we got through [haying] and he got cleaned up he sang for me, sang some real good songs. . . . The only thing wrong with that guy was that when it come about midnight I was ready to quit and come back and see him another time, and he felt like he was just getting started."[98] He first sang a song about a gunman by the name of "John Henry." That evening Bird also sang "Little Billy," a variant of "Pretty Polly." Below the transcription of this song, Hunter made a brief but significant note: "Odis surprised me by singing a Child ballad."[99]

If Bird had sung no other, this ballad alone would have been worth Hunter's toil on that hot August day. Just as Hunter misperceived High's circumstances, he also thought, upon arrival, that the Bird family was in dire straits:

I drove up to this little cabin. . . . And when I got up on the porch there wasn't a screen door; there wasn't a screen on a window. The wasps and the June bugs and the flies and everything was just going in and out of that house. I knocked on the door and this lady came and I told her what I wanted; I wanted to see her son. Well, she said that it's about noon and they'll be in from the field in a minute to eat, then you could talk with him. . . . Just come on in and sit down. I did. . . . I could see in the kitchen. Now these people were from all appearances [poor]. . . . They could have lived better if they wanted to, but on that table was . . . you talk about garden vegetables (!) they wasn't going to go hungry and probably never will.[100]

Years later, Hunter entertained the Schroeders and their guests with more tales of his visit to Bird's place on that hot summer day: "If I hadn't gotten any songs out of Odis, his father would've well been worth the afternoon." Apparently the house had no electricity for fans, so Bird's father sat out on the porch in his underwear while his son got ready to go to the motel. Hunter went on to say, "He had a hanky tied around his neck and around his forehead to catch the perspiration. He was dirty. Well, come to find out he was a preacher."[101] According to Hunter, Bird Senior had a way with words: "He said something like this, 'I told Brother Jones that if he didn't get right with the Lord he was going to Hell. The old son of a bitch died unsaved and he's burning just as sure as shit.'"[102]

For many of his singers, a visit from Hunter presented an opportunity to share memories associated with their songs. Such was certainly the case with Lizzie McGuire: "Mrs. Lizzie McGuire is a very old lady, now living in a dilapidated house on the outskirts of Fayetteville, Arkansas. . . . When she sang 'Oh Miss, I Have a Very Fine Farm' for Hunter in June, 1959, she thoroughly enjoyed telling how, when she was a girl on Greasy Creek in Madison County, she had learned this song from a beau, and how they used to sing it to each other as they were going to play-parties or 'literaries.'"[103]

One of Hunter's favorite song bearers was Olive Coberley of Wheatland, Missouri. From 1958 to 1959, Hunter collected over twenty ballads from Coberley. In a rare interview recorded in October 1958, Coberley announced that she would soon turn ninety-one.[104] Even though she was blind and hard of hearing, her voice was still remarkably strong. Also apparent was the warm rapport that she shared with Hunter; he taped her at least five times. The first time he visited Coberley, she couldn't think of any songs to sing, but "on my next trip, she was loaded."[105] Coberley contributed some remarkable old ballads, some of which she had learned from her English husband.[106]

In describing the visit, Hunter said, "I had to sit down on the bed ... so she would know where I was. She got ahold of my shirt and all the time I was there, Mrs. Coberley hung on to my shirt just like this. . . . And she didn't enjoy my visiting her as much as I enjoyed visiting with her."[107] Hunter felt

Olive Coberley at ninety-one years. (Photograph by Hunter, courtesy of the Springfield–Greene County Library)

sure that if he had been too pushy with this informant, he would never have gotten "Bailiff's Daughter" (a rare Child ballad that also doubled as a broadside ballad during the seventeenth century).[108] The dozen songs that Coberley recalled for Hunter encompassed a startling variety of genres. In addition to the rejected-lover songs like "Lonesome Scenes of Winter" (first recorded by Henry Belden in 1901), there were popular parlor pieces like "Time Enough Yet" (recorded by Belden in 1905) and "Charley Brooks," as well as spiritual songs like "Tell Ye the Story." All were delivered with a vigor that belied her old age.

Sessions with Coberley taught Hunter another critical lesson. Looking back on his early recording techniques, he particularly regretted trying to "save tape": "Over the years gone by [I] have missed a lot of information because I . . . turned the tape off and it's the conversation *between* songs [that matters]. . . . You learn after a while [to] go ahead [and] leave the tape on."[109] Sessions with Coberley also made him realize how excited singers were to hear their own voices—often for the first time: "You play this tape back for them and watch their face, watch their eyes. . . . I don't remember a one that didn't thoroughly enjoy hearing themselves, good or bad."[110]

## Community Songsters

Among Hunter's most gifted Ozark singers was a man by the name of Raymond Sanders of Mountain View, a balladeer who had lived in Arkansas on and off since 1916. When Hunter recorded him on May 12, 1970, the eighty-one-year-old singer gave him a staggering seventeen well-oiled songs, this despite the fact that Sanders had suffered a stroke and claimed, "I sometimes have to ask my wife what my neighbors' name[s] are."[111] Age seems never to have diminished Sanders's voice nor his way with words. In addition to his artful song delivery, his broad repertoire and ability to accurately recall lyrics made him popular among other song gatherers, including Parler.

We know a great deal about Sanders, thanks to a series of in-depth interviews known as the Rackensack Folklore Collection, conducted by Arkansas folklorist Vaughn Brewer and his colleagues in 1969.[112] Born in Kentucky on September 28, 1889, Sanders was a man of many trades. Speaking about his parents, Sanders described his father (John Sanders) as "too good for his own good" and a man who signed paid bills for his neighbors when they couldn't afford to pay off a debt: "He signed a bunch of notes and they sat around there and came due. He had to sell everything that he had. You might say he left Kentucky afoot."[113] After moving to Arkansas, Sanders's father took a job at the Chess & Wyman Stave Mill in Richwood, where he died early as a result of an industrial accident involving a snapped belt. This event would have a profound impact on the younger Sanders.

Out of both economic necessity and innate ability, Ray Sanders, tall and powerfully built, made a living using his hands—first as a teamster, later as an overseer at a mill, then cutting timber and railroad ties, and finally growing apples in the state of Washington before returning to Arkansas to "retire."[114] Of all the things he had done in his life, the mill work seemed to have left the greatest mark on him. "I always thought that whoever invented the stave mill business knew just about what a man could stand because . . . I do not know of any harder work," Sanders said.[115] But there are indications that life at the mill had some pleasurable times as well. Being a mill hand meant living in a tent all year round. Sanders spoke fondly of the King heaters they used while camping, and he enjoyed staying up late and "visit[ing] around over town,"[116] during which he got to hear a lot of banjo and guitar music. Sanders himself was a guitar picker until he lost his pinky finger to a barrel saw in a mill accident.

Sanders had a prodigious memory for songs:

> You know, when I was just a boy, like a kid, I could hear a song sung and I did not have to hear it over twice. . . . I remember a cousin of mine come over, his name was Ward Blair. . . . He had a guitar and that was the first guitar I ever saw. He came over there and he sang a lot of songs. I kept on humming around on them until I mastered most of it.[117]

He learned a lot of songs from his father: "I was just around his knee, you know. He would sing to us and I don't know [how,] I just learned them some way." One of the most powerful and rare songs Sanders contributed to the collection was one he learned from his mother, who received it from her father, who fought in the Battle of Shiloh during the Civil War:[118] "Granddad got shot right over the hip . . . built him a scaffle across a little cool creek there. He tore up one of his blankets and he lay there. He poulticed that for three days before they ever picked him up. . . . So when they picked him up, he was [in] plumb good shape. . . . He brought one song back that I know of from the army. It was 'A Wounded Soldier,'" which Hunter recorded under the title "Dying Soldier Boy—Mill Spring" instead.[119] Sanders picked up several other songs from his mother, including "Silver Dagger" and "Three Leaves of Shamrock."

First recorded by Hunter in 1959, William "Harrison" Burnett is another Arkansas musician who rivaled Sanders in his singing prowess. He was also an excellent self-taught banjo and mandolin player. Born in Madison County in 1909, he would have been about fifty years old when Hunter first recorded him at his home in Fayetteville. Hunter, who also met Burnett through Parler and Randolph, called him "one of the finest singers I have ever visited and collected from. . . . Harrison has a quality that you very, very seldom run into."[120] This (and Burnett's wide repertoire) explains why Hunter visited him several times. Like Sanders, Burnett was admired by all who came into his presence.

There is an introspective quality to Burnett's singing that held listeners spellbound. This is best shown in his seven-stanza lamentation "Prisoner for Life," in which Burnett sings farewell to everything and everyone he has ever known—places, wild creatures, and people he has loved. In the wrong hands, the song would have sounded saccharine at best:

Fare you well green hills
  An' soft meadows adieu
  Your roads an' your mountains
  I now part with you
  No more your beauties
  My eyes shall be blessed
  No more of sweet bosom
Can sing me to rest

His artistry was heightened by an inclination toward songs of emotional intensity, such as the murder ballad "Little Omie,"[121] or the longing for home expressed by the prisoner in "Rome County." Author Ted Anthony was so taken with Hunter's Burnett recordings that he made a pilgrimage to Fayetteville to meet Burnett's daughter, Dortha Bradley.[122] Some of what we know about Burnett came from this meeting:

Harrison Burnett's mother, Mary Elizabeth Mattingly Burnett, . . . sang songs to him and his brothers when they were little, and he'd memorize them. Sometimes he'd forget them for years, but when he did his rounds as a night watchman around the university campus decades later, he'd review them in his mind and write them down the next morning. It wasn't uncommon for folks on the University of Arkansas campus in the late 1950s and early 1960s to see the gangly security guard making his rounds through the darkness, singing old songs as he walked.[123]

According to Anthony, one of Parler's students referred to Burnett as "Red, the singing night watchman."[124] Anthony learned how Burnett became a local music celebrity during the folk revival of the early sixties: "He was popular because most of the people who knew the old songs were extremely elderly and didn't have much voice to sing with anymore. Burnett's voice was nasal and strong, and he loved to oblige." In the words of Burnett's daughter, "'A few of the girls at church were getting pretty upset because there were all these boys coming over to our house. . . . But they weren't coming to see me. They were coming to see him.'"[125] At the time of the interview, Bradley had some cassette recordings that her father (who died in 1974) had left for her, but she was wary of playing them lest they wear out. Upon returning home, Anthony sent her "a CD of the songs her father sang for Max Hunter," complete with a picture of her parents.[126] Such was just one of the ripple effects of Hunter's earlier song gathering.

Like Burnett, Reba Dearmore was one of Hunter's younger contributors. When he visited with Dearmore on January 7, 1969, in Mountain View, Arkansas, she would have been forty-three years of age, although her bell-like soprano voice sounded much younger. In addition to a dual career as both a teacher and a businesswoman, Dearmore was a respected vocalist who sang for a variety of events, including some Washington, D.C., parties that were attended by public figures such as Ted Kennedy and journalist John Chancellor. Dearmore, among the most educated and culturally sophisticated of Hunter's contributors, provided invaluable information on the sources of her songs and what they meant to her family. She learned most of her repertoire from her father, David Byrd, a farmer and a stock man who, she said, "drove cattle back before they had cars. . . . There was a stock sale every day of the week. . . . He'd just buy hogs and sell them for a profit the next day, had a lot of fun all the time. But he was real strict."[127] Her father had also sung for John Quincy Wolf Jr.: "He [Wolf] went over there on June 18th or 20th, the night of the Mountain Home Folk Festival. He got there just as Dad was about to eat supper. (He didn't want to interrupt him, you know.) But he recorded some of his singing. . . . Dr. Wolf said he would send me a copy, but he got sick with arthritis and has been quite sick ever since."[128] David Byrd passed away just two months after Wolf's visit.

She also learned songs from her mother, Lucy (Hargreaves) Byrd. According to Dearmore, her parents "didn't even title their songs. They'd just start singing them." Dearmore was well aware that she had mislearned the lyrics of songs at the knees of her parents, who taught her to sing "Fy Foley" even though in later years she realized this must have been the words "fife slowly." Well connected in Arkansas, she and her husband, Thomas Dearmore, were friends with Jimmy Driftwood and his family as well as several of Hunter's other musical contacts.

During her recording session with Hunter in 1969, Dearmore shared several stories that highlighted the significance of her musical inheritance and showed how spontaneous music making easily comingled with the religious experiences of Baxter County residents:

> Back in revival . . . the preacher'd be preaching. My Dad would just start singing this and everybody would just stop and start singing, the preacher and everybody. And when he was in bed sick he would sing this song: [sings] "I Feel Like Traveling On" . . . and another [Dearmore sings] "I've Got Mother in the Promised Land." He was singing that one on Thursday before he died on Saturday. He regained consciousness and called all the kids in around his bed and talked to three of the boys . . . saying he wanted to meet them in Heaven . . . just sort of had a revival in his room. . . . He just came to long enough to do this.[129]

It seems unlikely that Hunter visited Dearmore in 1971, since this batch of songs is labeled under Gaithersburg, Maryland. Most likely she simply mailed him some tapes from her new home.[130] Dearmore contributed over forty songs to Hunter's collection, although in later years she, like other singers, came increasingly under the influence of artists whose songs were broadcast on radio and television. But at the close of his active collecting days, Hunter, like Randolph before him, noted that his focus on "traditional" material might have kept him from the equally important task of recording a person's complete repertoire.[131]

Dearmore stayed in touch with Hunter and his wife long after the singer and her journalist husband had relocated to the Washington, D.C., area. In her letters, Dearmore encouraged Hunter to record other individuals from the Mountain View area, including her own mother, Lucy Byrd.[132] In 1972 Dearmore wrote Max and Virginia Hunter a letter that sounded a note of sharpened urgency where the last ballad sweep was concerned: "Stop at Twin Lakes Nursing Home north of Mountain Home *soon* and talk to Mary Rost, 94. She can recite long songs to you in a speaking voice and can hum enough of them that you can tell the tunes."[133] And then, with a blend of humor and melancholy, Dearmore wrote, "I recorded her the day before I moved when I was trying to sweep out the house, sell the car and get the tar off the dog's feet so the truck driver would let him ride with him. So I was in quite a rush, but loved what I got of her."[134] Once Dearmore arrived in Washington, she wasted no time in getting to the Library of Congress: "I found several old folders of your collection and records, but apparently you never did get everything compiled on the project you were doing when you recorded me," she observed.[135]

Thanks to the efforts of longtime archivist and librarian Joseph ("Joe") Hickerson (who had been with the Library of Congress since 1963) and to Alan Jabbour (who would precede Hickerson as director of the Archive of American Folk Song, now the American Folklife Center, starting in 1969), some of Hunter's materials had already been copied for the library. Hickerson's interest in Hunter began as far back as the late 1950s while a graduate student deep into research on the variants of Child 274, "Our Goodman,"[136] and he is one of the individuals most responsible for bringing Hunter's collection into the light of day. But none of this concerned Dearmore, whose emotional investment in the success of Hunter's work did not diminish with her distance from Missouri; instead she remained concerned about the materials that had *not* yet made it to the nation's capital.

# 5

# SINGING GRANDMAS AND
# THE MUSICAL TRIBES
# OF STONE COUNTY

## Aunt Ollie Gilbert

Out of the approximately two hundred Ozarkers who sang for Hunter, roughly a third of them sang for other collectors as well, as evidenced in the University of Arkansas's Ozark Folksong Collection. This is not surprising given that folklorists of all kinds and archivists in general have always relied upon one another for leads. In addition, word naturally spread about the most prolific or skilled Ozark ballad bearers. Such was certainly the case with Ollie Gilbert. As Hunter himself acknowledged, "Many people from all over the country have collected from Mrs. Ollie Gilbert."[1] One of the most prominent persons to visit Gilbert ahead of Hunter was English professor and folklorist John Quincy Wolf Jr. of Southwestern at Memphis.[2] As described by Brooks Blevins, "Among his notable 'discoveries' were Gilbert, a Stone County grandmother whose phenomenal repertoire of British ballads was eventually displayed at the Smithsonian Folk Festival in Washington, D.C., and other festivals around the country."[3] Despite the enormous potential to cross paths, it is ironic that two of Gilbert's most devoted chroniclers, Hunter and Wolf, never *did* manage to meet each other, despite having corresponded on several occasions. Alan Lomax, working for the Library of Congress, was also among Gilbert's most renowned song catchers, and he included several of her songs in his 1959 *Southern Journey* collection and later in the 1977 compilation *The Gospel Ship*.[4]

Although Hunter didn't start recording Ollie Gilbert until 1959, she most likely came to his attention in the late 1950s when he first attended the Ozark

Folk Festival. Hunter would visit her again and again, both because he rec-ognized how important his visits were to Gilbert and because she almost never ran out of material: "The first time I saw Aunt Ollie we became very good friends. . . . She said, 'I'll sing 300 songs for you before I quit.' Well, after we got to 250 or 260 Ollie decided she was gonna raise that up to 400. But when we got near that number she decided she should sing about 500 songs. . . . It took me about three years."[5] Gilbert was also important to Hunter as a gateway to other contacts in her deeply musical community, not the least of whom was her longtime neighbor Jimmy Driftwood, as well as the afore-mentioned Raymond Sanders.

The eighth of thirteen children, Ollie Eva Woody was born at Hickory Grove, Arkansas, on October 17, 1892. Her parents, Mary Balentine and James Franklin Woody, came to Stone County from Tennessee, and both were fond of singing.[6] Mary lived to the age of 101 and was the source of Gilbert's earli-est songs and many a Civil War story. Gilbert once remarked of her mother, "Oh, she sang like everything! and she might have lived longer than that if she hadn't fell and broke her arm."[7] Balentine also knew several Child ballads, including "Two Sisters," "Lord Randall," "Barbara Allen," and "It Rained a Mist" (otherwise known as "The Jew's Garden"), among others.[8] In contrast to her mother, Gilbert's father was "an itty bitty little man," who played the fiddle for local dances.[9] Although Gilbert was never allowed to attend these events, she recalled him at the advanced age of 86 playing the tune "Sally Goodin": "I can hear that [now] and seems like I can't hardly keep from hit-ting the floor."[10] Memories of tunes ran that strongly in her.

Another influence in Gilbert's early life was that of an older brother (likely Benjamin Woody) who gave Gilbert her first banjo lessons. "Mother raised these long-handled gourds . . . and she would . . . bore them and use them for dippers, you know, to drink water. And my brothers, we would go to picnics and see no guitars. [Back] then they used banjos and fiddles. . . . And one day my brother decided that he was going to make him a banjo so that he could learn to pick," she told Hunter during their first recording session in 1969. This first instrument, which they shared between them, was made from a gourd and covered with squirrel hide (one of a plentiful supply brought home by their father). It had five hand-carved wooden keys and five strings. At the age of seventy-seven, Gilbert recalled this day as though it were yesterday: "We went to the barn and got hair out of the horse's tail and made strings. (You . . . make double strings for the bass). . . . He let me play 'Green Corn' that night. I was just a little, bitty thing."[11] As time went on and Gilbert learned more tunes, she would often spend evenings taking turns on the banjo.

Mary Balentine Woody, who lived 100 years (1858 to 1958). (Courtesy of photographer Susan Gilbert Kemp)

But life on a small Arkansas farm was not all about the music and folklore. As a child, Gilbert was never allowed to attend school, purportedly because she was blind in one eye. The cause of her blindness is unclear; by one account she was looking up at a chinquapin tree when a "burr" from the tree fell in her eye, resulting in a painful infection.[12] But during another interview with Hunter in 1971, Gilbert ascribed her loss of sight to a bad case of poison ivy.[13] Although she was a slow reader, Gilbert was inordinately fond of the one book she remembers her father bringing home—*Three Years in Arkansas*,[14] by Marion Hughes and published in 1904—a book that she knew cover to cover.[15] Her life away from the schoolhouse, in combination with her visual impairment, also helps to explain why Gilbert became such a rich repository of songs and stories; she did a lot of learning by ear and in the company of her parents.

Like most of her brothers and sisters, Gilbert was expected to help on the farm. She recalled one particularly gruesome instance of her father trying to slaughter a sheep: "The last sheep that Daddy ever bought. . . . Nobody would hold its head down while he cut its head off. I thought I was a big one and I would go and hold it myself." When the ax blade proved too dull, things did not go smoothly, and the animal suffered. "I said, 'Daddy, don't you ever ask me to do another one.'"[16]

In speaking with Gilbert between songs, one of the things that Hunter found most interesting about her early life was the absence of funerals. When he questioned her about this, she replied, "No, it was as if nobody died. . . . Only my sister, and I didn't get to see her. . . . There was no funerals. . . . It's funny, ain't it? You never hear nobody died. . . . They just then buried them, and that'd be it, I reckon. I was never at a burying that I remember of."[17]

Music followed Gilbert into her adult life. On July 29, 1909, a few months shy of her sixteenth birthday, she married a twenty-four-year-old banjo-picking farmer by the name of Ewell "Oscar" Gilbert. They started married life in Alco, Arkansas, but after a few years of moving from house to house, the couple eventually put down permanent roots in the town of Timbo, where they raised six sons and two daughters. They did so in what Ollie Gilbert's granddaughter Susan Kemp described as a "dogtrot" house, meaning it was two cabins adjoined by a breezeway.

Similar to Ollie Gilbert's parents, Oscar was also known for being a fine singer, and, indeed, the few samples of his sonorous vocals in the John Quincy Wolf Collection attest to his skill. One of the most extensive sources of information on Gilbert comes from an interview with Willadean Barnes, who was five when she lost her mother and was taken in by Oscar and Ollie Gilbert. Speaking of "Uncle Oscar," she said, "He had the most beautiful voice, and he could make up songs—just sit around and make them up on people, and they were outstanding."[18] He particularly enjoyed writing songs based on local events, and this led him into a habit that sometimes proved distressing to his family. Barnes explained this habit, saying, "We called them tramps. It would be hobos, I guess; but if he sees one a coming he would be sitting out there on the porch. He would go to hollering for him [the stranger] to come by and spend the night. That way he knowed he would learn the news from different places."[19]

Despite both Ollie and Oscar Gilbert being musicians, there is little evidence that they enjoyed this pastime with each other. Ollie's music was more a bone of contention, as she was expected to focus on her domestic duties. As indicated in the 1971 interview with Hunter and Neal Morris, Gilbert's domestic duties extended well beyond caring for the children. "We was always workin' out in the fields," she said. "We killed hogs, and we had plenty to eat too. He laid it out and I planted the corn or crops of seeds."[20]

Likely the person who traveled the greatest distance to visit with both Ollie Gilbert and her husband was British folk singer Shirley Collins, who made a field recording trip to the South with Alan Lomax in 1959. Her account of this meeting, while partially apocryphal, illustrates some aspects of Oscar Gilbert's character: "Oscar was reputed to be 'the fightingest man in Arkansas,' having killed seven men, mostly 'over women and moonshine.' After dinner Oscar told me to 'go join the womenfolk' while the men drank whiskey. I didn't protest—and Ollie and I had a splendid evening swapping stories."[21]

This scene took place a year before Oscar Gilbert's death, and it is important for several reasons: it suggests a hardscrabble life, a husband with a quick temper, and—perhaps most significantly—a suppression of Gilbert's musical life, which took place in a back room separate from that of her musical husband. Gilbert once shared vivid memories of that evening with Hunter, an evening when Morris (Driftwood's father) was also purportedly present: "Oscar was there, and he was telling Alan Lomax that I could sing songs he'd never heard, and he [Lomax] said, 'Oh, no, she can't.' . . . I sang him four, he'd never heard 'em in his life, I reckon." Hunter asked Gilbert whether Collins had asked her to sing bawdy songs, to which Gilbert replied, "Yes . . . and *he* [Lomax] did. And I looked over and I said, 'No, Mr. Lomax. I don't do that. . . . I'd get more money out of it. But what's money?'"[22]

Willadean Barnes gave a detailed and poignant account of Gilbert's early years of marriage. After being asked by Brewer whether Gilbert was ever allowed to sing in public, she answered without hesitation, "Definitely not."[23] She added, "She sang all the time, just going around with her work, like washing dishes." The way Barnes remembered it, Gilbert carried out her domestic duties with great deliberation, possibly in reaction to a tightly controlled environment: "She went about her work real slow. . . . She never got in a hurry about anything. . . . It would take her all day to do the laundry, sometimes two or three days. . . . Done it on the washboards and sit right down and play [the washboard] and boy, he would catch her and he would give her hell."[24] As time went on, it became more apparent that Gilbert's marital life, which had begun when she was (by today's standards) still a child, was more than she could psychologically handle. Barnes explained, "All of her children was close to the same age. You know there was one right after the other."[25]

Although her childbearing days were far from over, Gilbert reached a breaking point after the birth of her third son, Colley: "She completely lost her mind. . . . She was just crazy as a lunatic," said Barnes.[26] "She did not even know her baby. She would have nothing in the world to do with it. A neighbor woman had to take the baby until she got well."[27]

Once her children were mostly grown, Gilbert had to endure other anxieties in connection with World War II: "Six boys and two girls. I had five of them in service at one time. . . . Lord, I worried about it. . . . I dreamed

Oscar and Ollie Gilbert, 1950s. (Courtesy of photographer Susan Gilbert Kemp)

them coming home of a night. . . . I would just catch them when they come in the hallway and go to screaming. That would wake me up." According to her granddaughter, Gilbert always associated the "Three Little Babes" Child ballad with that time in her life. Much to her relief, all of her sons survived the war: "But the Lord, I thank Him yet. He watched over them and sent them all home."[28]

Throughout her life, Gilbert often made mention of her dreams, which wove themselves into the fabric of her daily existence:

> I ought to tell you my dream before I sing ["Angel Band"]. I dreamed me and the two baby boys went somewhere . . . and we got started back home and come to that creek, and Lord, it was just rolling plumb off. I said, "Lord, what can we do to cross it?" I thought that, I just fell on my knees and prayed and prayed. When I raised me up . . . them two kids crossed over. Them rocks are just as plain where we crossed over and just a little ways—about as far from here to the window—I looked and Jesus was sitting at the root of the tree. I went to him singing "Angel

Band." My husband waked me up. I said, "Why didn't you leave me alone. I was dreaming the best dream that I ever did dream". . . . That is what I told them[—]I want them to sing out over me when I die.[29]

Because she was such a rich source of traditional song, Hunter would make a habit of visiting Gilbert whenever he came through Timbo territory. He stopped by so often, in fact, that by October 1969 Hunter declared that he had indeed lost count of his visits with Gilbert, settling on "this was the *umpteenth* time I have been here."[30] It was during this session that Gilbert opined, "We never will get them all done," meaning she had far too much material for anyone to capture. While there was some truth to this statement, there came a time (in her eighties) when Hunter noticed that Gilbert was going to almost heroic measures to come up with new "old" songs, and this behavior proved both amusing and mildly problematic for her collector, who remained interested only in authentic, orally transmitted material.

The reasons for Gilbert's fecundity are several; chief among them is the fact that songs and music in general served as a life raft for her. Hunter was certainly aware of her troubled history. "Ollie had an awful hard life . . . and when her children were grown and her husband had died all of these [songs] came back to her," he once commented.[31] While these words conjure up the rather romantic notion that Gilbert's amazing recall for lyrics was triggered largely as a result of social losses incurred in old age, it is more likely that she had this uncanny ability from day one. As Driftwood commented in the liner notes to one of her albums, "Aunt Ollie has a mind like I have never known. If she hears a song, and likes it, she remembers it." Then, clearly referring to Hunter without naming him, "We have taped over five-hundred songs as she sang by oral tradition, never looking at a book or list, and never repeating the same song in one sitting."[32]

By the time Hunter recorded "Aunt Ollie" in the mid-sixties and early seventies, she was already a national celebrity. She had made repeat appearances at the nearby Arkansas Folk Festival in addition to the Ozark Folk Festival in Eureka Springs. She had sung and given banjo performances at the Cow Palace in San Francisco (May 1965), the Newport Folk Festival (1964), the University of California at Los Angeles Folk Festival (May 1965), the Grand Ole Opry in Nashville, and Madison Square Garden in New York. In July 1970 she was featured—alongside her Arkansas neighbors—at the Festival of American Folklife (later renamed the Smithsonian Folklife Festival) on the National Mall in Washington, D.C. These were some big, late-life gigs for a singing grandma from Arkansas.[33]

Interviews with Gilbert's granddaughter Susan Kemp and others strongly suggest that this public recognition, and the travel that went with it, meant little to Gilbert in comparison with life at home. "It was not prestige for her. She was just ready to go whenever somebody . . . would come by and pick her up," said Kemp. Gregarious by nature, there is no doubt that Gilbert looked forward to travels with her musical friends, chief among them Jimmy Driftwood, whose multifaceted life as an educator, rancher, cultural preservationist, and Nashville star has been well documented. Driftwood and his wife, Cleda, owned a 150-acre farm near the Gilberts and were among Gilbert's most reliable friends throughout her life. Although he contributed just a handful of songs to Hunter during one visit in 1969, Driftwood was important to the Ozark ballad collector because he sometimes helped facilitate interviews with Gilbert, drawing her out in ways that were unavailable to Hunter.[34] Driftwood also created opportunities for Gilbert to share her music—a music that had been muted during the many years of an arduous marriage and onerous domestic life. When illness in her eighties landed Gilbert in the Mountain View Nursing Home, she repeatedly told her granddaughter Susan, "Now, as soon as I get better, I want you to take me out to Jimmy and Cleda's so that we can visit."[35]

Like Driftwood, Glenn Ohrlin also accompanied "Aunt Ollie" on festival trips—most specifically, California and Newport, Rhode Island.[36] However, despite the long reach of Washington-based talent scouts such as Ralph Rinzler or Alan Lomax (at the Library of Congress), and John Quincy Wolf Jr. out of Batesville, national fame seemed to have only a fleeting effect on Gilbert, who remained far more focused on her domestic life. Gilbert's musical identity, like those of her closest friends, was deeply rooted in porch jams, church services, and Friday night hootenannies at the Stone County Courthouse Square in Timbo.[37] Hunter often chose Friday mornings for visits to her house so that he and his wife, Virginia, could stay and attend the evening gatherings of the "Timbo Tribe," as they came to be known. The Courthouse Square gatherings provided rich fodder for Hunter.

In 1969 Hunter provided a rare taped narrative of the setting in which he recorded Gilbert: "The divan she is sitting on is covered almost completely with her handwritten ballad songs [and] individual sheets of papers. This is where she is getting the ideas of the songs that she wants to sing. Occasionally, she will look down to kindly jog her memory for what the next line or word is. . . . For the most part Ollie is still singing these songs from *memory,* . . . and from the looks of what she's got laid out we've just made a small dent."[38] A year later, the divan papers were "to a depth of about two foot high."[39] She loved nothing more than to quiz Hunter on how many songs she'd sung for

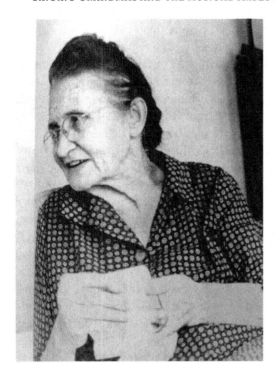

Ollie Gilbert, 1960s. (Courtesy of photographer Susan Gilbert Kemp)

him, and during his visits she would often direct him to scavenge for the song lists that seemed to occupy every corner drawer.[40]

Hunter knew that if he arrived early in the morning, Gilbert would keep him busy until evening. This is partly because she had a repertoire that extended well beyond the ballads themselves. Gilbert's infrequent (and often reluctant) breaks from singing sometimes took the form of banjo interludes, during which she would chat her way through multiple key changes, retuning the instrument before every other song with apparent ease. During one recording session, when Gilbert complained about her throat, Hunter offered to run to the local drugstore for a Coke, but she didn't take him up on it, instead launching into a set of lively dance tunes, from "Sugar Hill" and "Green Corn" to "Buffalo Girls" and "Battle of New Orleans." Then the indefatigable seventy-seven-year-old grandmother invited Hunter to accompany her on his guitar, at which point Hunter responded soberly, "I'm a collector. Not an entertainer."[41]

Indeed, it wasn't unusual for Gilbert to try switching into jam mode with Hunter. Once she tried handing him her banjo: "You wanna thump on it a little?" But he declined. The banjo she played was from Driftwood's father, Neal

Morris. "I took it everywhere. When I played, them kids gathered around me like everything," she once commented.[42]

When Gilbert wasn't singing or playing the banjo, she showered Hunter with jokes or stories, many of which were from newspaper clippings that she had squirreled away all over the house. Hunter's collection includes about fifteen hours of jokes, several of them from Gilbert.[43] Addressing a university audience, Hunter once had this to say about the sideline activity: "You can tell . . . so many things about jokes. During our political elections we hit these political jokes. . . . And then after that election, these jokes you don't hear any more. . . . And ladies . . . tell sometimes dirtier jokes than men do."[44] The latter comment referred mostly to Gilbert. "She told these whopper jokes, but only in the company of other women," commented Cathy Barton, who spent a great deal of time offstage with Gilbert during concert events.[45] Similarly, Barnes claimed that Gilbert "knowed more dirty stories than any person alive."[46]

Gilbert was very busy in 1969. Just a few months after Hunter started recording her songs, Fred Danker, an American Studies professor at the University of Massachusetts, teamed up with Arkansas folklorist Vaughn Brewer and landed on her doorstep to conduct interviews.[47] Danker and Brewer soon learned that Gilbert could recite whole chapters of the New Testament verbatim and that she had learned them by ear long before her son gave her a physical copy of the Bible. In addition to a strong auditory memory, she seemed to have a photographic memory to match, something Hunter had made note of earlier that year: "We just went through a list of songs that Mrs. Gilbert knows, and I'll tell you for sure, there's about 500 songs on that list and there isn't anybody else that I know of . . . that knows that many songs."[48] Both Brewer and Danker were nothing less than awestruck.[49]

It is unclear whether Gilbert was totally at ease with the nonstop activity of her own mind. Once during an interview with Barton, Gilbert was about to sing "In the Garden" (one of many songs passed down to her by her mother) when she remarked, "No wonder of a night when I am laying there that is going in my mind, over and over, you know, different songs. Sometimes I will sing over a dozen before I go to sleep. . . . Sing yourself to sleep. That is all right, ain't it?" she asked her guests, as if for reassurance.[50]

Indeed, when it came to music, Gilbert appeared to have no "off" switch. Even when Hunter was ready to call it a day and was in the midst of packing up, Gilbert would ask, "Have I sung this one for you yet?" or "What about . . . ?" Gilbert appeared undeterred by the constant stream of children, grandchildren, and even occasional stinging insects that milled in and out of her house. Since Hunter was in the habit of recording whatever Gilbert came up with, and because she gave him so much material, he had a lot of weeding out to do post-session. This was particularly true toward the end of her life: "By the time I went to see her she began to pull some 'sneakies' on me," Hunter explained to the Schroeders, "and she was running out. She knew it, but she didn't wanna quit."[51]

By "sneakies" Hunter meant that she was giving him songs that came off the television or the radio—not ones that she had come by organically[52]—songs such as "Daddy Sang Bass," "Hound Dog," and "Last Thing on My Mind,"[53] in addition to several songs she would have heard from Carter Family broadcasts.[54] The provenance of "traditional" material, the oral tradition itself, was now irrevocably altered, the lines of transmission no longer clear.[55]

But as biographer Robert Cochran reminds us, Gilbert was probably singing popular songs long before she ran out of traditional material; such numbers were simply part of her larger repertoire. He recounted, "When collector D. K. Wilgus visited Ollie Gilbert in Stone County in 1965, the famous ballad singer treated him to a sprightly version of 'Blue Suede Shoes.' Songs in family tradition are treasured, and many factors encourage their faithful preservation. But they are above all used, employed in the business of living, not tucked away in some scrapbook as mere relics of a revered though vanished past."[56] But the ballad chaser's impulse to freeze individuals in both time and repertoire was a strong one.

Toward the close of her life, when failing health necessitated her move to a nursing home, Gilbert insisted on taking her lyrics and "song rolls" along with her. According to Vaughn Brewer, who had seen them firsthand, these rolls consisted of adding machine paper estimated to be anywhere from fifty feet to three hundred feet in length, and they contained song titles written "on *both* sides."[57] It was estimated that the rolls contained over nine hundred songs.[58] Over the years, many visitors had commented on Gilbert's habit of displaying the rolls in order to show how many songs she knew. Brewer described visiting Gilbert at the nursing home after she had lent him these precious documents. He took some time to return them, and, the folklorist recalled, "When she thought that they *might* have been lost, she immediately started rewriting new rolls with titles."[59] It was hard to escape the idea that there was a compulsive quality to her list-making activities.

As trying—and at times tedious—as some of those "umpteen" hours in her company might have been, the friendship Hunter formed with Gilbert was among his most prized. In 1971, while visiting her, the opening statement on the session tape showed Hunter's protective attitude toward his friend: "I want her to know that if I ever make any money off of her songs, I'm gonna give her fifty percent of whatever we make."[60] Unlike Alan Lomax, who periodically sent money to Gilbert after recording sessions,[61] Hunter was not in the habit of paying his contributors. In Gilbert's case, he took great pride in being the first collector to give her personal cassette copies of the over four hundred songs that she had bestowed upon him: "Nobody has ever taken time to do anything for her as much as she has done for other people," Hunter commented during a taping session at Mountain View.[62]

Hunter's recording sessions with Gilbert ended just about the time that a dramatic cultural shift was taking shape in Stone County: the building of the Ozark Folk Center. Gilbert's devotion to the Driftwood family remained unwavering, even when community rumblings arose over the economically bedeviled folk music center, of which Jimmy Driftwood was both a founder and director. Although Hunter himself never became directly involved with Arkansas's Ozark Folk Center or with its associated Arkansas Folk Festival, their story had much to do with the era when he was doing his collecting. Built in fits and starts between 1971 and 1973, it has been said that the Ozark Folk Center (which Dave Para once described as looking like a spaceship[63]) "put Stone County on the map."[64] However, the music center's divisive history created a culturally complex backdrop that epitomized the love/hate relationship that Ozarkers had with the economic need for tourism.

But none of these rifts came between Gilbert and Driftwood. As related by Barton, "I heard when she went to church one time, they started criticizing Jimmy and the folk center and all that kind of stuff, and she got furious. . . . And she stood up and said, 'You all don't know what you're talking about, and I'm never coming back here again,' and she walked out and has never been back."[65] Such was the backdrop to Gilbert's musical life during the years when she shared her songs with Hunter.

## Almeda Riddle

Twice while visiting with Gilbert, Hunter also left time to see the other "singing grandma" of Arkansas, Almeda Riddle of Cleburne County, who happened to be close friends with Gilbert and often toured with her.[66] Riddle had been a touring artist for many years by the time Hunter started recording her, so catching her at her homestead was not always an easy matter. Sessions with Riddle, who was conscious of herself both as an artist and as a conveyer of tradition, would have served as a welcome contrast to Gilbert's

Ollie Gilbert in 1979. Kemp made a painting of this portrait, which is on permanent display at the Ozark Folk Center. (Courtesy of photographer Susan Gilbert Kemp)

less artful approach. But the same qualities that made Riddle famous for her stage presence also made her problematic when it came to provenance, largely because of her tendency to pick up song lyrics from a multitude of sources. It is Riddle whom Wolf ultimately identifies as employing artistic license. "More than any other singer I know, Mrs. Riddle tends to create as she sings—and no songs are completely exempt from change, not even the Child Ballads," he once observed.[67]

Both women were known for their ability to retain songs, although Riddle probably worked harder at it. Unlike Gilbert, whose repertoire was wide-ranging to an indiscriminate degree, Riddle chose or altered material to fit her persona and match her quietly emotive vocal style. In contrast to Gilbert, who approached recording sessions as something of a marathon, Riddle often expressed strong feelings and opinions about each ballad.

When Hunter first recorded Riddle, in October 1965, the sixty-seven-year-old Arkansawyer sang Child ballads such as "Four Marys," "Lady Margaret," "Barbara Allen" and "Orphan Child" (a particular favorite of hers). For Riddle, songs were all about the narrative: "Nearly all the songs I sing have stories to them. I don't care a thing in this world—or hardly a thing—for a song that doesn't tell a story or teach a lesson."[68] "Fair Willie Drowned in Yarrow" (Child 215) was one of the rarest ballads she bestowed upon Hunter. He would have heard it sung just twice before: a hauntingly modal version by Lola Stanley of Fayetteville, Arkansas, back in 1956 called "The Derry Dems of Arrow," and then a rendition by the elusive Herbert Philbrick, which Hunter never managed to get on tape because Philbrick was too busy living the life of "a booze hound," as Hunter colorfully expressed it.[69] The melodies for the three "Yarrow" variants in his collection are very different.

Hunter made another visit to Riddle five years later, in February of 1970, when, even at the age of seventy-two, her voice remained remarkably resonant. On this occasion, Riddle sang songs about local history such as the "unpublished" ballad of George Poole titled "The Drown'd Boy." Riddle commented, "It took George Harmon and I from about '65 to '67 to get this together. I heard it many times in my youth as he did. The boy was drowned in 19 and 1 [1901] and the minister sang this song at his funeral. . . . He was buried in a little cemetery called Pleasant Ridge here in Cleburne County near my home."[70] Riddle's reference to constructing this (likely incomplete) song goes a long way toward describing why Hunter approached this ballad bearer with some caution. In fact, it is this 1970 session that led to one of his greatest disappointments as a collector: Riddle's magnificent rendition of "The Maid of Dundee," which he promptly erased after their session. Hunter was so upset by this episode that he quickly committed this experience to tape, starting with the pained preamble: "What I'm going to say here, I know I'm going to have to be careful with" (undoubtedly a reference to her standing in the traditional ballad community). "Almeda has a tape recorder and has done some collecting. She's quite honest about it," after which he related her lyric gathering from a variety of geographically far-flung sources. [71] Regardless of Riddle's fame and underlying worldliness, and in part because of these circumstances, she presented a unique hazard to the Missouri collector.

But the song that carried the most emotion for Riddle was one written by her father, J. L. James, and neighbor Ruby Dylan. "Heber Springs Tornado" tells the story of this devastating weather event on Thanksgiving 1926. [72] A full forty-four years after this event, the loss was still fresh: "This is the tornado in which my husband [of nine years] and youngest son was killed. I'll do the best I can to sing it, sometimes I can sing it. I have it here on old tablets hand written by my father. While I had heard him sing it a few times, and knew that he had written it, he never published a lot of things that he wrote. . . . *But this is not to be published.*"[73] Riddle's latter comment is interesting in light of the fact that Hunter *did* publish it insofar as it became part of his collection. Riddle then began to sing with her straight-arrow voice, stopping just one moment to say, "Now, Max, I want to skip one verse. It's about me personally and for some reason, I choke up on that one."[74] After singing the song, Riddle commented on the religious ideas embedded particularly in verse four:

Some people in that city
Declared it was God's word
To cause th[e] great tornado
To do its awful work
They pointed to our churches
Where they'd refuse to go
To pay to their Redeemer
Th[e] debt of thanks, they owed

Riddle added:

I had been to a Thanksgiving meeting that the company had given that my husband was working for: We had been there all day for meeting and Thanksgiving dinner from 10 'til about 5 and ——— [inaudible] went back home. . . . Many people thought that because of these big feasts that we had instead of going to the church, and that was why [the tornado happened]. . . . There was not a church in town that wasn't either demolished or unroofed and damaged. I don't think God's in these things. No indeed.[75]

According to Riddle, the tornado struck at 5:00 p.m., just as they arrived home. After singing this emotionally laden piece, Riddle—a distant cousin of Frank and Jesse James—then shared what she described as a "family version" of the ballad "Jesse James."

Regardless of the challenges she presented to Hunter as a collector, he and his wife, Virginia, stayed in touch with Riddle for many years. In 1972 they hosted her in Springfield when she was on the program at a local folk festival, and in May 1974 she wrote a detailed letter to the Hunters apologizing for her slow reply and updating them on her activities, which included nothing less than the Mariposa Folk Festival in Toronto, Canada; a presentation at the International Congress of Anthropology in Chicago; and a concert stop in Bardstown, Kentucky—all of this at the age of seventy-six. Her letter was mailed with a copy of her book, which she described as "like me, a little old and outdated, but use what you need or wish."[76] Her fondness for Hunter was apparent. "But [I] do wish you could come down and we would *talk*," she wrote. "Call or write me first if you can then [I] will try to be home. I can stay home for months—no one comes—then go for a day or so—my one drop by. Am glad your business has been good but hope it lets up enough for you to take time to come down. Here is my phone no. and if you would call after 10 PM, [I] will be inside. Otherwise [I] may be in my garden and not hear the phone ring. . . . Must stop now. It is mail time."[77] Given his experiences with Riddle, another recording session would have been complicated at best.

# 6

# CIRCLE OF FRIENDS

## Mentors and Collaborators

So much of the work Hunter did in Stone County and other Ozark regions would never have taken place if it hadn't been for the guidance and support he received from both Mary Celestia Parler and Vance Randolph. Hunter took up collecting just when Randolph's field days were coming to an end, thus giving their friendship all the more significance.[1] As the years went by, their connection extended well beyond the Ozark Folk Festival, and he got to know these folklorists on a level to which only a few were privy.[2] Before marrying Parler, Randolph went to great lengths to be inaccessible to the general public because, according to Hunter, "Vance had been taken advantage of many, many times. . . . People would come to visit with him and go back and the first thing you know he would read a quote from Vance Randolph that he did not say or it was misquoted."[3] As described by Hunter:

> A lot of people came in to visit with Vance just to waste his time. And he got to be pretty sharp about being able to tell the difference. . . . Some students of Mary's . . . that was doing a project, would come and see him and . . . was wanting some advice from him. Why, he just did everything he could to help these students. If you call him on the phone, say "I'm in Fayetteville and I'd like to come by and see you," forget it! . . . And I know some big name people . . . that never got to talk with him.[4]

As a fledgling collector who came from an unassuming background, Hunter was able to gain a unique perspective on his friend as both a public and private figure. Looking back on this friendship, Hunter described how

early on he would visit his Arkansas friends at their separate residences—
Randolph in Eureka Springs and Parler in Fayetteville. Hunter was particularly interested in the couple's homegrown method of collaboration:

> Even though they weren't married at the time, Vance slept at his own
> apartment but he usually spent the whole day at Mary's house. . . . She
> required her students taking folklore to turn in cards of some folklore
> item—a song, a tale, a story, a joke, remedy, recipe, or something—on
> a little 6x8 card, and each day she would collect those and bring them
> home and Vance would go through them. . . . If they got six cards . . .
> with the song "Barbara Allen"—why, those were discarded. They didn't
> need six more "Barbara Allen's" when they probably had 600.[5]

Since Virginia Hunter was primarily a homemaker and only marginally
involved with Hunter's ballad-collecting activities, this level of collaboration
between the two folklorists certainly caught his attention, and he would soon
take pride in being a part of it. To start with, Hunter's serendipitous acquisition of his treasured Child ballad books had much to do with his friendship
with Randolph, who kept two sets of his own in a special hiding place in the
attic and lent him four volumes "in the original cardboard binding."[6] Shortly
after that, Hunter made the acquaintance of song scholar Irene (Jones) Carlisle, who often visited with Randolph and Parler in Fayetteville:[7]

> And I was down there one day and she [Carlisle] knew that I was inter-
> ested in this stuff, and her husband had died and she was beginning to
> break up housekeeping to go to California. So she said, "I've got some
> books that I'd sell to you. . . . I'm going [to] run home and get 'em." She
> did and came back in a few minutes and she had these big, beautiful
> bound books of Child's and I opened 'em up and it said "first edition."
> And I thought . . . (I could see dollar signs running through my eye-
> balls) that I could no more afford these books than the Man in the
> Moon. And she wasn't no dummy; she knew what they was. Oh I got up
> enough courage to ask her, "Awright, how much do you want for 'em?"
> She went, "I'll sell 'em to you exactly what I give for 'em years ago." She
> said, "I'll take $35." So I bought those real quick before she changed her
> mind. . . . I bought me a reprint cause on those books I was just afraid
> to use them. Period. . . . So after you do this a little while and you read a
> lot of songs, stories, why you begin to know what they are.[8]

Hunter's sudden awareness of the ancient British ballads gave his collecting efforts a new impetus, while Randolph's fieldwork was already finished.

In fact, by the time Hunter met the sixty-five-year-old folklorist, Randolph was already in questionable health: "Vance was told by a doctor several years ago . . . that his heart was very bad and for him to finish his work . . . because he may not last that long."[9] According to Hunter, Randolph managed to follow his doctor's advice for many years until he eventually fell off the wagon:

> I took him downtown and there was a little tavern down there. . . .
> Vance said he wanted to go in there to see Paul [Eddy]. So, we went in
> and rather than see Paul, Vance sat down at the bar and ordered a beer.
> Come to find out this was the first beer that Vance had had in twenty
> years. But he believed he had done his work now and if he was gonna
> die he was gonna enjoy it. But he lived a few years after that. He drank
> more beers too. And stronger stuff.[10]

As Hunter liked to tell it, drinking also played a part in Randolph and Parler's nuptials in 1962:

> One time I was down there and Joan O'Bryant was there, and he and
> Mary told us they were planning on getting married. . . . Of course, he'd
> been livin' there anyway. However, he didn't spend the nights yet. He'd
> go home, but the next morning he'd go right back to Mary's house and
> spend all day. They took two attempts to get married. The first time,
> they went they got drunk. . . . They went up to the courthouse, and I
> think it was April Fool's Day. And Vance said no way was he gonna get
> married on that.[11]

While these drinking episodes no doubt made for entertaining stories, Randolph's lifelong battle with alcohol is well documented, including the time he went down to Illinois for the much touted "Keeley Cure."[12]

Hunter was proud of the modest role he played in bringing Parler and Randolph together: "He [Vance] moved on a Saturday; I took my pickup truck down and moved him—from his apartment in Eureka over to Fayetteville. In fact he gave me that oxbow hanging [over my] . . . fireplace—said every man should have one of those over the head of his bed so that when he wakes up in the morning . . . he'll remember the situation."[13]

While Randolph's first marriage was known to be difficult, Hunter said that his second alliance, with Parler, was the charm: "It was a good thing for them. . . . Their heads was mutual. . . . Sometimes they didn't agree, but at least even that made their conversations longer because they would change each other's view."[14]

Because Hunter looked up to Parler and Randolph as mentors, he gave considerable weight to any comments or judgments the experienced folklorists sent his way: "He [Randolph] was very interested in every [song] that I played for him. . . . He made comments and there was very few songs that he didn't recognize when he heard the tape. . . . He was very interested in where I got them, who from, and a little bit about where they lived, how they lived. And he made a lot of mental notes on all this stuff. Vance was a friend, and I let him hear as much as I possibly could."[15] In short, Hunter did not hold back material and appears to have welcomed suggestions or corrections on the part of Randolph.[16] In a tandem letter dated November 21, 1965, Parler and Randolph sent Hunter advice about an upcoming musical presentation he would be giving, most likely for Parler's students at the University of Arkansas.[17]

But at the same time that Hunter looked to Randolph for guidance and advice, he also recognized the older folklorist's limitations. Despite Randolph's fame as Cochran and others coined him "the greatest living authority on the Ozarks,"[18] his output was limited by the time period in which he had done most of his song work. Hunter observed, "The way he had to travel around: horse and wagon, buggy, model-T, no pavement, all rough roads or cattle trails or something like that. . . . If Vance had had the conveniences we have, he might have had a collection that would be ten times as big as it was."[19]

Although there are no indications that Hunter took the time to read Randolph's books, the younger ballad collector would certainly have heard stories about his friend's early struggles with song documentation. A master of hyperbole, Randolph frequently blurred the lines between fact and fiction, as in this portrayal of early forays into song gathering:[20] "The ground all about me was littered with scrawled sheets of paper, which must be numbered and corrected and set in order before I could proceed farther, and the fingers of my right hand were well-nigh paralyzed. One of the most serious mechanical difficulties of this folk-song collecting is the necessity to write so rapidly."[21] But the picture Randolph painted may not have been far from the truth.

Hunter, who had earned a steady middle-class income for most of his life, was also aware of Randolph's constant state of economic insecurity: "He got very little money from the government. Very little from time to time. But he wrote articles for magazines under all sorts of different names. He even wrote articles for magazines like *True Romance*. . . . He wrote about things that he didn't know anything about, too. He would study up on them and wrote an article and think he was an expert."[22] In short, being a freelance writer did not make for an easy life, and while Randolph authored many books, it took him decades to win the praise and acceptance of the scholarly community. Nor would he get to enjoy the economic fruits of his most popular title, *Pissing in the Snow and Other Ozark Folktales*,[23] since at eighty-four years of age, he was well into declining health and spirits when it was published.

In Hunter's estimation, Parler and Randolph were on par with each other when it came to their levels of accomplishment: "She done some field collecting, some *good* field collecting. Not as much [as her husband]. But what she's left and the way she left it, at the University [library] for anybody to take over, is just exceptionally good. . . . Sometimes, she would ask him about something, but many times he also asked her."[24] The couple's exchange of ideas greatly influenced how Hunter went about his own song chasing and documentation.

Twelve years younger than Randolph, Parler had an immense store of well-directed creative energy and was particularly generous with her contacts, often telling Hunter how to get ahold of them: "Mrs. Gladys McChristian . . . lives at Huntsville, Route 6, and teaches in a wing [of] school at Japton. The best way for you to find her would be to find her at school. Mrs. Donna Everett teaches right in Huntsville and also lives right in the town. . . . Get Mrs. E. to tell you how to find Mr. Johnson who knows 'How Come that Blood on your Coat Sleeve.'"[25] The level of collaboration Hunter enjoyed with Parler cannot be overestimated. Parler had collecting experience and contacts, all of which proved invaluable to Hunter, and he, in turn, was a personable and entertaining presenter who enriched her curriculum.

An undated note that was later attached to Hunter's 1959 interview with Herbert Philbrick spoke of the pride Parler took in mentoring the younger collector:

> I met Max Hunter during the Eureka Springs Folk Festival in October 1957, and in December of that year he sang for my class in Arkansas Folklore. It was then I first heard him sing "The Dewy Dens of Yarrow," which he had learned from Mr. Philbrick. It was my insistence on hearing his tape of the old man's singing of the song that made Max realize that collecting for its own sake was important, and that it was not enough to learn a song himself. Since that time, he has become, in my opinion, the best field collector of folk songs active today.[26]

And while Parler championed his efforts early on, Hunter would return the favor by allowing her to dub his tapes for the University of Arkansas Folklore Research Project.

From 1958 onward, Hunter and Parler were of immense use to each other and were part of a growing community of Ozark folklorists, collectors, and

808 Cleveland
Fayetteville, Ark.
Nov. 21, 1965

Dear Max:

We have just played the last part of your tape, where you ask for suggestions.

Well, since you asked for it, here she is:

1. Cut out the business of costumes
2. Shorten the whole business to 1 hour, no intermission
3. Cut out Fred High's song about the man who fell into the pig pen
4. Try to put in at least one Civil War song. If you've got "I'm a Good Old Rebel" use it
5. Put more emphasis on the age of the songs. Say "Nobody knows how old this song is. But it was printed in London in 1774, and may have been sung a hundred years earlier." Or Professor So-and-so has proved that this piece was known in England, a hundred years before Goerge Washington was born" etc. etc.

Sincerely,

VANCE

Dear Max:

I agree with all the above. Why not include The Drunken Fool?

I stole your Nightman to put on my Child ballad tape. Somehow I didn't have it on there.

You have plenty of stuff, and I know you'll do a wonderful job. When you get ready for that meeting in your stable, let me know.

I hope you'll be down to see us before long. I'll mail your tape tomorrow.

As ever ,

Mary

Correspondence courtesy of the Springfield–Greene County Library.

musical performers who shared a variety of ideas and resources. This exchange included a lot of guitar swapping as well. At one time Parler wrote to Hunter, saying, "Remember, you promised to lend me a guitar you're not using? Well, Joanie brought me her grandfather's guitar which I have practiced on religiously for nearly two weeks (very little progress, but I'm still trying), and now I feel like a dog not letting Fran Majors use it."[27] Parler then made mention of the impact a Child ballad had had on this particular student: "She learned 'The Lady from the West Countree' from hearing me sing it that night, and cried when she sang it for me. Anyway, will you lend me that guitar, so I can let her use Joanie's?"[28] Hunter, who had an open invitation to attend Parler's folklore classes, was already well acquainted with Majors, one of Parler's most devoted and talented students.

There was a regular swapping of favors during this time, and indeed Parler had big plans for Hunter on the University of Arkansas campus: "I've hired a hall for Oct. 14 and will start the publicity rolling next week. You're going to miss my class with this schedule, so will try to plan things better after this."[29] According to a letter sent by Loman Cansler shortly after Hunter's presentation, Randolph said the event was a great success.[30] Indeed, the Missouri collector's natural ability to strum a guitar and sing the songs he collected made him a valuable resource for Parler, who was devoid of musical talent. As Hunter recollected, "I was down at her house and Vance was there at the same time, and of course he'd knew what she was doing, and he just told her that 'Mary, you don't play the guitar any better than you sing.' So she quit."[31]

## A Singing Partner

If Randolph necessarily exerted a fair amount of energy in keeping the public at bay, it was part of Parler's job as a university professor to make herself accessible. Early on in their acquaintance, Parler wrote a positively gleeful letter to both Hunter and Joan O'Bryant describing what her University of Arkansas folklore students had to endure when they received a classroom visit from a man calling himself "Antone, the Professional Folk Singer," who was anything *but* professional.[32] The detailed letter, carbon copied and addressed to both "Joanie and Max," was intended to both entertain and cajole her new friends into making another visit to her students at the University of Arkansas. Parler wrote, "I want you to know that your stock was never higher—at least with 85 students at the University of Arkansas, who compared 'Antone' with 'Max and Joanie.' . . . Max, you must make it to sing for them before their Xmas holidays begin on December 19. They are hungry to hear someone sing folksongs RIGHT. Again. They'll never forget yours and Joanie's concert last October."[33] Parler was extending the collaboration she enjoyed with Randolph to both Hunter and O'Bryant, and this was both flattering and motivating for her young friends.

There is no doubt that Hunter and O'Bryant, who returned Parler's favors by making impromptu appearances at the university, made an attractive duo on stage; like her Missouri counterpart, O'Bryant had a ready sense of humor and was quick to make friends.[34] Along with her oft-documented glamour and charisma, O'Bryant shared Hunter's straight-ahead singing style and unadorned guitar accompaniment, all of which made her music particularly accessible.

O'Bryant, whose academic and musical career was cut short at age forty by a fatal automobile accident, comes down to us like a bright and shooting star that was extinguished too soon. She was on her way to a new academic position in Durango, Colorado, when she drove her jeep off a deserted mountain road in Ouray. Twenty-three years after her death, Hunter would speak of this accident in the muted and sorrowful tones of a man who was still in mourning: "Vance and Mary thought the world of Joanie and there [were some who] were certainly trying to replace her after she got killed. [But] you just couldn't replace Joanie with Vance and Mary."[35] This was also the case for Max Hunter.

At the time of her death in 1964, O'Bryant had already done a prodigious amount of work in various branches of folklore, as evidenced by the Joan O'Bryant Folklore Collection, which is housed at Wichita State University. Unlike Hunter, O'Bryant had far fewer rules and strictures around the materials she was seeking. Indeed, the approximately fifteen hundred ballads in her collection are marked by their geographic and ethnic diversity rather than their commonality of origin.[36] This is largely due to the fact that, according to O'Bryant, ballads were hard to find in Kansas, in contrast to other materials such as folktales and customs. O'Bryant once remarked, "Kansas isn't a singin' state as is Arkansas,"[37] hence her search for ballads in neighboring states. The eclectic and wide-ranging contents of the O'Bryant Collection are also the product of students who were kept endlessly busy gathering oral histories, local beliefs, quilt patterns, rhymes, children's games, and medicinal cures, among other items.[38]

O'Bryant's educational background was markedly different from Hunter's, and there are indications that she did some deliberate dumbing down in order to connect with her contributors. According to some Wichita sources, "She called herself a 'school teacher' and not a 'university professor' when talking to her singers." But since these remarks were penned nearly two decades after O'Bryant's death, likely by individuals who didn't know her well (if at all), they are conjectures at best.[39] These same sources portrayed her as an "enthusiastic outdoor woman" who "could ride like a seasoned cavalryman" and was capable with a Colt .45.[40] Regardless of their veracity, such colorful accounts tended to obscure the realities of her life as a working folklorist.

What we do know is that, like Hunter, there were times when O'Bryant had to get her hands dirty in order to get the results she wanted. In the vivid words of her friend Mary Jabara, who accompanied her to High, Arkansas:

> We wanted Fred High to record a particular song we had been trying to collect from him. When we got there, Fred was pulling clapboards from the south side of his house. We asked what he was doing, and he said, "When I built this I had a gun. And my wife afeard them, and she made me throw it away, and I threw it in the wall and then I just boarded it up. Well, a feller told me that it was worth a lot of money, maybe even five dollars' worth. I'm a lookin fer it." So he was tearing the side of his house down. . . . Pretty soon . . . he made us two black molasses sandwiches, and I'm telling you there has been nothing that I've ever put in my mouth like that, that I could *not* swallow. It was awful, and we were kind of gagging a little bit and so we said what we needed was a little something to drink, so he went in and we disposed of most of the sandwiches. . . . He did find his gun. It was all rusted up and everything. And then we spent quite a bit of time putting boards back on the side and Joan finally got him around to trying to sing while he was doing it.[41]

O'Bryant, like her Missouri friend, certainly collected more than the song that had prompted her visit to High, and both she and Hunter had an enthusiasm for the relationship building and adventures that came along with ballad hunting. Add to these the pleasures of musical performance. Hunter had fond memories of rendezvousing with O'Bryant and Parler at a park in Fayetteville where they held musical events: "[There was] this little outdoor pavilion thing which was real nice, and we'd put on an afternoon program there, between Mary's class and Joanie's classes, . . . and then Joanie and I'd sing a song."[42]

In addition to the sharing of names and locations, Hunter, Parler, and O'Bryant occasionally went on field trips together. In a letter written to Hunter, Parler described a time when O'Bryant brought several students over to Fred High's place ("High Community Center," as Hunter referred to it). High was a favorite of them all, not the least all of Parler's students, who sometimes enjoyed having him as a guest: "He proceeded to charm one class after another. . . . He sang and sang, one good one after another. . . . He sold them books, and whups,[43] and walking sticks, and walnut 'goodies,' and generally was FRED. They all loved him, and knew that this was IT."[44]

Hunter, Parler, and O'Bryant also visited with Fred Smith of Bentonville, Arkansas. (Thanks to the work of one of Parler's folklore students, we know a lot about Smith. He was a bit fussy about wearing out his voice and liked short recording sessions, so Hunter ended up visiting him several times, from 1960 to 1969.[45]) "Him and Joanie had a ball together," Hunter recalled. "She called him 'the sweet-scented barber' (that's a song); he'd kid her and she'd accuse him of using some kind of hair oil—rose, or something you could buy at FW Woolworth's. . . . He thought the world of her too, and he was a mighty mighty fine man."[46] But times with O'Bryant were mostly few and far between, because she had a busy performance schedule and was frequently in the midst of collaborations with a broad network of folk music enthusiasts and folklorists from all across the Midwest.[47] Hunter was fortunate to get the songs he did from O'Bryant—all in all a dozen ballads between the years 1959 and 1961, but several of these were "live" recordings from their university appearances; other contributions go undated and without further annotation. Their favorite song to do together was the satirical "O Miss, You Have a Very Fine Farm," which was captured on tape at a University of Arkansas concert in July 1960. The pleasure they took in throwing insults at each other and the enjoyment the audience got from their performance are evident on the recording.

In 1961 Hunter audiotaped his thoughts regarding the album he hoped to record with O'Bryant. This ponderous letter sent to her on a cassette tape provides a rare window into Hunter's workaday life: "When the phone's not ringing and the customers aren't here, and the hired help isn't runnin' in asking silly questions, . . . I can get more done in 30 minutes than I can in two hours during the weekdays."[48] Hunter detailed his plan to make an album with O'Bryant and included an exhaustive discussion of his correspondence with the record companies RCA and Opportune Records. After listing the pros and cons of record labels and recording technologies, he concluded:[49]

I don't think we ought to let it drop. . . . Even if the University of Arkansas doesn't go ahead with their book part of this thing, I'm going to go ahead with this record end of it and cut you in on it, and put us out 100 records. If we only sell two, we'll have 98 to give to our friends—but I don't think that'll happen. We can take some down to Crescent [Hotel in Eureka Springs,] and stick 'em on the counter and have Nick play 'em,[50] and put some over the countryside in some of the motels and get some of the record companies I know here in Springfield, and we can get rid of 100 very, very easy, I'm sure. Maybe more.[51]

But since she had already put out two albums of her own with Folkways Records,[52] it is unclear how interested O'Bryant would have been in taking on yet another recording project.

Partway through this long-winded letter, Hunter switched gears entirely to relate his experience of the annual Crescent Hotel gathering during the Ozark Folk Festival in Eureka Springs. Dwight Nichols ("Nick"), the owner of the hotel, had a basement room next to the bar reserved for organizers like Hunter, and this became a popular watering spot for festival performers and folklorists. This occasion, from which O'Bryant was absent, included such Ozark notables as journalist Ernie Deane and May Kennedy McCord, and Hunter was eager to share the experience with O'Bryant: "The only thing I didn't like about it—it got a little out of hand." Hunter then went on to describe the exchange of liquor bottles that took place and gave a running account of the attendees (most of whom O'Bryant would have been familiar with). Mrs. Hunter was there as well but appeared less than comfortable with the company that night. In the words of her husband, "Virginia enjoyed it to a point."

Joan O'Bryant and Max Hunter with singer Norma Kisner, November 25, 1960. (Courtesy of the Springfield–Greene County Library)

But after the passage of two decades, it was mostly the pleasurable memories that remained, and Hunter would look back on other festival weekends in Eureka Springs as high points in his life as a collector:

> Everyone at the hotel knew that the boss said we could have that room. . . . We'd go in there and sit in a circle. . . . Well, one time we had Dr. Halpert and May McCord,[53] and me and . . . Mary and Joanie and I don't know how many people. And we just sat in a big circle and the other people would sit around behind us. It was kind of a swap thing, you sang a song and just go around in a circle. . . . You could either bring your bottle in, or walk right through the door to the bar. Luckily it was good for business.[54]

In addition to cementing Hunter's friendship with Randolph, Parler, and O'Bryant, these events brought him into contact with a number of other folklorists. These were exciting times for Hunter the traveling salesman, who suddenly found himself in the company of song chasers and academics from across the country. It was Virginia Hunter's unstated job to keep things from spinning out of control, and she often accompanied her husband to the musical evenings, recalling one particular night when she had to put Mary Celestia Parler to bed: "She couldn't find her socks the next morning! . . . She'd get drunker than a skunk," a fact corroborated by Hunter on several occasions.[55]

While Virginia Hunter had warm memories of spending time with Randolph and Parler, there are indications that she was not totally at ease with her husband's admiration for O'Bryant. Years later, during a folklore discussion with their friends in Columbia, Missouri, Virginia verbally checked her husband when he talked about how "smart" O'Bryant was: "Smart in some ways" and far less so in others, she commented.[56] But their daughter Linda Bangs understood that such musical connections were cherished and rare, and she fondly recalled having met O'Bryant during a family vacation outside of Branson:

> Joanie had a stopover and she and Dad did an impromptu sing-along down at this motel. (And there were some of Dad's friends from Silver Dollar City.) She was a lovely person. Just as sweet as she could be. And she was crazy about Daddy. I think if Daddy said, "Joanie, go down there and jump in the lake," I think she would have done that. And he felt the same way about her. They just were the best of friends.[57]

In 1962, a year after the audio letter had been sent, Hunter and Parler did make a cassette recording of O'Bryant and himself singing together. Sadly, two years later, the tape would include the reading of O'Bryant's obituary.[58]

## A Sense of Abandonment

Not surprisingly, O'Bryant's death cast a long shadow on Hunter's relationship with Randolph and Parler, and it would be misleading to imply that the younger collector enjoyed a seamless friendship with his Arkansas mentors. As Randolph grew older and increasingly infirm, and as Hunter became less active in collecting and more involved in emceeing festivals such as Silver Dollar City and the Ozark Folk Festival, they visited each other less frequently. A letter Randolph wrote in 1971, though affectionate in tone, also revealed a sense of abandonment:

> Dear Max:
> It has been a very long time since we have seen you. Ain't Fayetteville on your route anymore?
> My wife went into a kind of decline for no good reason. I figger your long absence might have something to do with it.
> All joking aside, we are really concerned—my love to Virginia,
> Vance[59]

In a letter from July 1974, Randolph sent his usual open invitation: "Mrs. Randolph and I will be glad to see you any time, but don't tell no Yankee newspaper boys about it."[60] Indeed, at the age of eighty-two he was still trying to keep the public at bay.

As time went on, and more and more people tried to contact him, Randolph would often play sick just to avoid visitors. There was some basis for his infirmity, however, given that he suffered from arthritis.[61] One day he tried this on Hunter, who remembered the conversation this way: "'Max,' he [Randolph] says, 'I think I'm dying.' And I said, 'you mean right now?' And he said, 'no, you damned fool. Not right now!' I go, 'Well, I didn't know. I thought I oughta check.' And he said, 'Hell, you ain't got no brains.'"[62]

In July 1974 Randolph sent Hunter another letter requesting an odd assortment of favors, chief among them was this: "If you can find any Anchovies I could sure use a couple of small cans next time you come down here. . . . God bless you, Max, and all your kinfolks and connection!"[63] The last word is particularly telling in that it speaks to Randolph's obvious sense of growing isolation.

Randolph's economic difficulties also created pressure points in his relationship with Hunter. According to Cochran, Hunter was not the only recipient of these special requests: "Randolph, for all his wheedling and complaining via the mails when money and whiskey were his goals, found it easier to ask for favors than for company. 'Come see us when you can,' was his traditional last word for . . . all friends who called regularly."[64] In November 1974 Randolph wrote Virginia Hunter a letter indicating that her husband had failed to carry through on a promise he had made:

> Dear Virginia,
>
> I come to ask a favor. My wife has a portable tape recorder. It's a good one, and she is very proud of it. For a Xmas present, I want to give her a nice leather case to carry it in. It is a Panasonic; you don't load it [with] a reel of tape, but with a flat sealed packet called a cassette. Max knows about all this. I asked Max to buy this case and send me the bill. He knows I am bedfast and cannot get out to buy anything for myself. He gave me the old brush-off. He thinks I am too old and crazy and drunk to know what I want. Well, maybe he thinks I haven't got money enough nowadays to pay for my wife's Xmas present, but that case shouldn't cost more than $73 or $100 at most, and I still have money enough for things like that. I am disappointed in Max. I always counted him as one of my best and oldest friends, much nearer to my heart than these university people. I could have pointed out favors that Mary Celestia and I have tried to show him in the past, but I could not bring myself to talk like that to Max. God bless you anyway, Virginia, no matter what happens. Vance[65]

While the Hunters' response to this bitter communication is undocumented, four years later Randolph was still writing to Hunter, albeit in a broken script: "When your down this way, go see Harry McDaniels, Route 7, Fayetteville, Ark. He knows a lot of rare songs that have never been recorded." And he added, "Ask him to sing 'no balls at all.'"[66] But alongside the humor was a note of pathos that mirrored Randolph's decline: "It is very hard for me to write now. But Mary and I wish you a Merry Xmas. Come see us when you can. Our best to Virginia and Jenny. Vance."[67]

The utilitarian aspect of the two men's relationship happened on both sides of the fence. At the same time that the aging and infirm Randolph made requests of his Missouri friend, Hunter sometimes used Randolph's name as a calling card, as evidenced in a letter he wrote to California folklorist D. K. Wilgus: "Though I have never met you I am familiar with some of your work through my very personal and dear friend, Vance Randolph. Vance is quite feeble but he is still mentally alert. . . . Should you care to write to him about me or any other reason his address is Sunrise Nursing Home. . . . I might warn you not to call him on the telephone because he would let it

Virginia Hunter at the Westfield Road house in Springfield, Christmas 1993. (Courtesy of the Hunter family)

'ring off the wall' and still wouldn't answer it. I will be waiting to hear from you."[68]

But regardless of any accumulation of resentments between Hunter and Randolph, the Arkansas couple's affection for Virginia Hunter never wavered: "They just took to her like glue," observed Hunter years later. "Vance told her to get rid of me and he'd marry her. I don't know whether she ever give that any serious thought or not."[69] In later years, Virginia Hunter would enjoy reminiscing about her interactions with Randolph, who was often described as "a ladies' man":[70] "First time I ever met him, he gave me one of his autographed books and brought me lots of candy. And we went down to a little club and we danced around. And I tell you, he was damned dapper."[71]

# 7

# THE IMPORTANCE
# OF COLUMBIA

## The Schroeders

Almost a decade after O'Bryant's passing, Eureka Springs provided yet another life-altering connection for Hunter. Although the exact date is unclear, he met Dolf and Becky Schroeder at the Ozark Folk Festival sometime in the early seventies. The Schroeders were founding members of the revitalized Missouri Folklore Society, and they quickly became Hunter's biggest supporters and promoters. Early on, Hunter arranged a meeting between the Schroeders and the Randolphs.[1] Becky Schroeder, a volunteer editor for the University of Missouri Press's Heritage Series, intended to write a book on the history of ballad collecting in Missouri. Hunter's favor started a flow of introductions and opportunities on both sides. Shortly after meeting Hunter, the Schroeders enthusiastically began to make plans that would increase the visibility of both Hunter and his song collection. In 1973 Becky Schroeder wrote:

> Dolf discussed your work, Max, with the Honors College Director at the University of Missouri here in Columbia, and he is very much interested in having you come up for a concert sponsored by the Honors College. . . . We had no idea what your fee usually is, but we hope very much you can come. We would like you to stay with us (and we hope you both can come). And if the children who are still at home can come, we would be delighted to have the whole Hunter family. . . . We are delighted at this prospective breakthrough at UMC—as you know

there hasn't been much interest in folksong or folksong scholarship here, but if they have a chance to hear you it will show them how much they are missing and how much they don't know.[2]

After their initial meeting, the Schroeders often hosted the traveling salesman for song sessions and discussions both at the university and at their home in Columbia, and despite Hunter's distance from the ivory tower, he and Dolf Schroeder became close friends and collaborators. Schroeder's passion for German folksongs carried over into American balladry, and a letter he sent to the Hunters in 1976 indicates that the Schroeders viewed themselves as potential patrons:

> Dear Max and Virginia,
>    Joe Hickerson is going to be in Columbia next week, and we would very much like to have you for a visit during his stay here if you can arrange it. I know Max does not accept honoraria for his singing, but if you can come I would be able to contribute to your travel expenses. I am teaching a German Folklore Course this summer and have received some funds to have lectures, field trips and performances.

And then he put forth his rationale:

> Since folklore is international in nature and since Max is one of the most successful collectors of our time, I would like very much to have him talk to my class and other interested people about his experience.

This letter ended with an addendum: "P.S. Your Ozark songs were very popular in Germany."[3]

More than any other friends or acquaintances, the Schroeders encouraged Hunter to step into a world largely unknown to him—that of academia. They invited him not only to sing but to give lectures as well. Such activities provided a new and welcome focus, given that Hunter was now at the close of his own active collecting days. Thanks to collaboration with Dolf and Becky Schroeder, he could now turn his attention to safeguarding his ballads and making appearances that would publicize their existence. In 1974 Hunter addressed upward of fifty teachers during a weeklong training course on "Folklore in the Ozarks."[4] "Get involved," he told his audience. "Visit with the old-timers, let them sing to you, and sit on their front porches and chew tobacco if you have to. The monkey is on your back to tell our young people about their Ozarks heritage."[5] And in 1976 he started a monthly, albeit short-lived, folk music series for the Springfield Art Museum in addition to giving talks and music presentations to (now senator) Roy Blunt's history students at Drury University in Springfield.[6] A letter from Becky Schroeder in May 1977 detailed upcoming plans for Dr. Adolf Schroeder's Festival of Missouri Folk Music, including everything from the order of presenters (which included both Cathy Barton and her mother, Ruth) to a request for copies of Hunter's Folk-Legacy albums, which would be for sale at the event.

Hunter's Columbia friends were encouraging without fail; in this same communication, Becky Schroeder commented, "Your autograph will be a collectors item one of these days!"[7] The Schroeders, who recalled times with Hunter and his songs as some of the happiest of their lives,[8] acquired copies of his tapes and related materials for their private collection, which would eventually be housed in the State Historical Society of Missouri in Columbia.

In addition to how the Schroeders changed Hunter's concept of himself and his work, the warmth of their friendship helped him gain perspective on the loss of O'Bryant, a topic on which he rarely spoke. In 1987 the Schroeders brought all of their O'Bryant Collection materials to Springfield, and they deliberately kept the tape rolling while Hunter pored through the pages of the booklet, during which he offered several corrections, comments, and general recollections of his time with O'Bryant. Regarding her acquisition of the Child ballad "Charming Beauty Bright" from Laura McDonald of Springdale, Arkansas, Hunter described how O'Bryant often approached her contacts as both collector and singer. She learned this Child ballad "line for line" from the exacting McDonald, something that pleased O'Bryant immensely.[9] Hunter also spoke of O'Bryant's relationship with Springfield musical celebrity May Kennedy McCord. O'Bryant and McCord often shared the stage at Eureka Springs, and according to Hunter, "Joanie and May always got along real good. . . . Even though May was a little bit hard to handle, Joanie would just make the effort to work with her."[10]

Often the things most remembered about people's lives are the missing links that cannot be found. In addition to O'Bryant's early death and the lack of documentation regarding her personal life, there was the added conundrum of her missing RCA recording. According to Hunter, the master for this album was destroyed, and he knew of only one hundred copies of the recording, "and what happened to them nobody knows."[11] This was also a topic of discussion during the Schroeders' visit.

Twenty-three years after O'Bryant's death, both Hunter and the Schroeders expressed their mutual disappointment at never having made it to Wichita to view her collection: "Over 250 miles," said Dolf Schroeder. "And there's no short way to get there," added Hunter.[12] They particularly lamented the publication of a ninety-one-page booklet about her collection, which, according to the Schroeders, was rife with inaccuracies. Titled *The Unburnished Mirror: An Interpretive Study of Folklore and Content Description of the Joan O'Bryant Collection*, the 1984 booklet included many contributors.[13] Upon reading the booklet three years after its publication, Dolf Schroeder commented, "None of these people knew her personally. . . . They're only deducing from these tapes." Becky Schroeder expressed her regret that Wichita State University hadn't used Hunter as a resource during the writing of the booklet.[14] The scholarly perspective they imparted to Hunter's memories of O'Bryant, in combination with their boundless empathy, gave him room to connect her life and work more meaningfully to his own achievements as a ballad collector.

## Loman Cansler

During the same years that the Schroeders encouraged Hunter in his work and welcomed him and his wife into their personal and professional worlds, they also befriended Loman Cansler. Like Hunter, Cansler grew up in a family where ballad singing was part of everyday life.[15] But in contrast to Hunter, who never attended college, Cansler became interested in song collecting while "browsing in the University of Missouri library as a student."[16] As reflected in their eventual collections, Hunter and Cansler had very different relationships with the material they gathered. While Hunter certainly enjoyed singing, he did not think of himself as a professional performer, or anything close to it. In his view, the ballads he recorded belonged strictly to the singers who chose to share them. Cansler, on the other hand, was a skilled musical performer who concertized around the edges of his school job.

Early in their acquaintance, Cansler wrote to Hunter about his disappointment at not seeing him or Joan O'Bryant on the 1958 program of the Ozark Folk Festival. Nor, he noted, was he himself included in the lineup that year: "Frankly, I wasn't much surprised myself (perhaps ambiguously disappointed) to fail to receive an invitation to participate." Cansler then went on to ruminate on the increasing commercialism of the folk festival industry: "I'm beginning to wonder if the Duncans selected the participants or the Chamber of Commerce?" he wrote with marked sarcasm. "Since attending the Ozark festival I've fallen to wondering why some organizations in Kansas City . . . couldn't support a folk festival without all the drum beating, etc. . . . It might be that a folk festival couldn't pay its way without being hamstrung commercially, I don't know."[17]

If the tone of Cansler's communications was less than warm and bordered on cynical,[18] this was likely a reflection of his frustration at having insufficient time to pursue one of his most beloved activities. His letter to Hunter closed with this lament: "I wish time permitted more time for my folklore collecting, etc. but since I need to eat to live I have to work so must use my spare moments."[19] The same note was sounded in 1963: "It seems I'm doing little collecting any more. School will soon be open and that will take all my energies," a refrain that would come up repeatedly in his correspondence with Hunter.[20]

Regardless of time limitations, Cansler—whose scholarly and artistic interests involved him in a multitude of projects—did succeed in producing two Smithsonian Folkways recordings, one in 1959 and the second one in 1973, the latter of which included songs from well beyond Missouri. Similar to that of Joan O'Bryant, Cansler's collection is notable not only for its geographic diversity but also for its broad array of contents. It includes everything from field notes and family photos to large numbers of newspaper clippings, journal entries, and approximately seventy folders of song transcriptions, in addition to audio and audiovisual materials.

Due to his active interest in performing the songs he collected, Cansler was more guarded with his materials, and there are indications that he was reluctant to make his song archive universally accessible. When he first donated his papers and audiotapes to what was then known as the Western Historical Manuscript Collection (now the State Historical Society of Missouri Research Center–Columbia), he placed restrictions on the usage of his materials, requiring that patrons write him directly if they wished to use his songs for performance purposes.[21] Although Cansler made two recordings of Missouri and Midwest material for Smithsonian Folkways, he failed to identify his sources in his first album, an omission that emphasized Cansler as an artist rather than as a collector.[22]

Cansler's disposition toward his own song work stood in contrast to that of Hunter, who welcomed public access to his materials and had a far more insouciant attitude toward those who might profit from his archival work. As Hunter once put it, "My mouth to your ear—that's the best explanation I can give of folklore. Folk songs are in the oral tradition and the real ones can't be written down or copyrighted because they're everyone's domain."[23]

Although there's nothing to suggest that Hunter and Cansler viewed each other as competitors, Cansler's letters are constrained and somewhat perfunctory in tone, indicating that, temperamentally speaking, the two men had little in common. "Thanks for the tip about Mrs. Coberley in Hickory,

County," Cansler wrote about a year after he met Hunter, "but since you've gotten her I'll make hay with new material. There are so many songs dying out with the deaths of old timers that we must not duplicate too much these days."[24] Nor did he respond with enthusiasm to another of Hunter's invitations: "As to the Amalgamated Folksong Collectors Union, . . . I would need to know more about the purposes and the like before signing my name in blood."[25] And while Hunter and Cansler sporadically continued to consult with each other, they never became close collaborators.

# 8

## MORE THAN A HOBBY

### Talking to Washington

One of the most concrete outcomes of Hunter's friendships with both Randolph and Parler and the Schroeders was the ongoing (if incomplete) inclusion of his ballad collection in the Archive of American Folk Song in Washington, D.C.[1] This process began when Mary Celestia Parler, who had dubbed several of Hunter's tapes over the years, sent some of his recordings to the archive under the University of Arkansas umbrella, which included other Ozark sessions as well. It was March 1970 when Hunter sent a lengthy letter simply addressed to the "Folklore Division" at the Library of Congress. Hunter was concerned that the institution had received incomplete copies of his ballad materials via Parler at the University of Arkansas: "I believe to date you may have as many as 300 to 400 songs from my collection. However[,] I have perhaps 500 to 600 more that I don't believe that are in the Library of Congress. . . . If you are interested in what I have now plus what I may in the future find, please send me the details."[2]

In typical Hunter fashion, he made specific mention of his rule never to loan out original tapes. He then listed individuals for whom he *would* make copies, Randolph and Bertrand Harris Bronson among them:[3] "Anything I have collected is available to them. Others, without any credits in their behalf, I take a long look at their requests."[4] Hunter was interested in placing not only his ballads at the Library of Congress but his jokes as well: "[I] have 4 7" tapes—3³/₄—both sides full. They are all types—funny, good, bad, vulgar. I do not draw any line." And lest he be misconstrued as an academic himself, he concluded the letter on a note that emphasized the uniqueness of his position: "I am a traveling salesman and since 1957 this has been a hobby collecting."[5]

Two months later, Hunter received a response from Alan Jabbour, who was serving as head of the Archive of American Folk Song. Jabbour had already started his homework regarding the "evidently large gaps" in the archive's accrual of Hunter tapes,[6] and he opened the door for the Missouri collector to send as many materials as possible: "We are prepared to send you franked mailing labels which will enable you to send the tapes at no postage, handling, or insurance cost to yourself. We would also appreciate whatever lists or notes you might have in connection with the tapes, which we can photocopy for our files." Then came this much-needed reassurance: "After we have copies of the tapes and lists, we will return the originals to you."[7]

Receiving this letter, full as it was of procedural information, was an elevating and motivating moment for Hunter, who now understood that his "hobby" could have a much broader cultural impact. Despite degrees of feigned nonchalance, he soon made it clear that he was ready to go to considerable lengths to work with the national song archive: "I am getting ready to re-type my songs, from the beginning," he wrote Jabbour. "It may take several months but I believe I would like to send my entire collection for you to copy. . . . I think it is very important that a copy of my collection, in its entirety, be put some where for safe keeping. It may not be the best and the biggest but quite a bit of it will never be collected from the same people that I have." He punctuated this point by adding, "They are dead." Hunter then made mention of the newly organized Ozark Folklore Society: "We are collecting material from all over the Ozark region, songs, rhymes, recipes, jokes, remedies, etc." Then in full sail, he added, "I am the President (naturally)."[8] But Jabbour, insightful and courteous without fail, had no need to respond to such flourishes and efficiently facilitated the start of what would officially be known as the Max Hunter Duplication Project; fortunately for Hunter, it was the Library of Congress that would pick up the tab.

## Visits With Tapes

Modeling himself on the company he was now keeping, Hunter had begun to think of himself as more than a businessman who collected ballads; he

-- TO --

My wife, Virginia Louise and my children, Linda
Lou, Donna Sue, David E., Jenny Lynn for having
put up with a husband and father, who having been
a traveling man, has been gone from home nearly
as much as he was home. For trying to understand
me, as hopeless as it sometimes may seem. May the
rewards and credits, if any, go to them.

Max F. Hunter

Dedication to Virginia Hunter and the Hunter Children (Courtesy of the
Springfield–Greene County Library)

was a folklorist as well. In addition to collecting songs, he consciously went
about capturing a broader array of folkloric materials for his *Visits from the
Ozarks* tapes, and sometimes the folkways and stories he collected were of
more interest than the songs themselves. As diligent as Hunter was in the
elicitation, recording, and transcription of "old gems" (as he often referred
to them), these interviews, while rich in content, took place sporadically and
unsystematically throughout Hunter's many years of collecting. This seems
to have been more a lack of enthusiasm on his part rather than any lack of
training. And while Hunter always noted the time and place for each of his
recording sessions, he once expressed a disinclination toward the background
work: "I know it's important that studies be made of our folk heritage, but
to me it's not necessary to study some of the people I have visited with. . . .
Personal contact with people far exceeds any book that was ever written."[9]
This statement reflects Hunter's emphasis on the fun and social aspects of
collecting, something he often reiterated years later. Photographs were equally
rare, something he later regretted: "I think it would help if you could see the
person and the location and situation as it was."[10] Indeed, one look at the
primitive shelters in which some of Hunter's musical contacts lived belied
their elaborate descriptions of their circumstances.

While the majority of persons taped also contributed ballads to Hunter's
collection, there are also interviews with friends, acquaintances, and rela-
tives. Hunter was aware that not all future researchers would easily stumble

The Hunter Family at the Brentwood house in Springfield, Thanksgiving 1970 (l. to r.) Max Hunter, Linda, David, Jenny, Donna Sue, and Virginia Hunter. (Courtesy of the Hunter family)

upon this Holy Grail of biographical material, which even today took considerable time to unearth at the Springfield–Greene County Library:

> Buried in my song collection is quite a bit of information pertaining to the singer, or the singer's life, or the singer's family or some bits of folklore and history . . . just like this Mrs. Dearmore. She sang many, many songs for me. But along with the songs she put this very interesting information about her father. . . . While I'll have it in two different places, the "Visits With" and also in my song collection, there's a chance that people who might want to study the "Visits With" people collection would never think to look in my song collection for it.[11]

In 1970 he recorded an introduction to almost two decades' worth of *Visits With* material, which articulated his holistic approach. As part of this broader

VISITS

INTRODUCTION

SIDE 1.

I have been primarily interested in collecting Songs
that have been and were being sung in the Ozarks.
I have picked up other bits of folk information, on
tape, but I have not made a special effort to do so.

In playing back my Song Tapes, I became more interested
to the other information and begin to see where I could
add to my collection. I knew that what I had was
important and decided to try and collect more. However,
this Visit Collection will not be as big as the Song
Collection.

Many times, while my recorder was turned off, I have
heard, some jewels. Where I could, I went back to see
if I could recapture the "jewel".

You will find stories like:

a.  A twelve year old boy, that was hung up and gutted.

b.  Why Oxen are used instead of Mules

c.  How brooms are made.

d.  A lady telling about, a man getting his toes burned
    off because he would not tell where or if, he had hid
    his money.

e.  When a lady needed wood for the stove and her husband
    or boys had not cut and stacked any, she went out and
    brought in rails from the fence and used them.

f.  People being turned into horses, at night, and rode.

g.  Remedies that got good results, according to the teller.

h.  A lady that don't remember people dying, when she was
    a child.

With only a few leading questions, I tried to get the
people to carry on with whatever they wanted to talk
about.  In most instances, after a few minutes, the
person begin to relax and overcome the fear of being "taped".

I think this may be the most important part of my years
of collecting in the Ozarks.  However, don't ask me
about the other parts or I may tell you the same about
them.

Max Hunter

collecting effort, Hunter placed advertisements in the local paper urging Springfield residents to contact him if they wished to be interviewed. One of these respondents was Audrey Barclay of 1951 East High Street. The daughter of a caboose builder, she and her family moved to Springfield in 1915, three years before the influenza epidemic of 1918. In addition to recording several satirical songs (mostly on the topic of marriage or infidelity), she gave Hunter the history of a local cemetery and spoke at length about a local doctor who was "a very common sight riding around the streets of Springfield." She said that "he prepared his own medicines and carried them around with him." When Barclay came down with the flu, she recalled, the doctor called for two glasses of water and filled them halfway: "Then he poured a little bit of this from a little vial. . . . He tasted it a little more until he got it just the way he wanted it. . . . Whatever he put in that water was tasty! [And] . . . he got good results. . . . He weren't a regulation MD anyway."[12] This same doctor-on-horseback was fond of using coal oil and sugar to cure croup and employed castor oil in combination with turpentine as a laxative to rid children of worms.[13]

Occasionally the people Hunter met looked to him as a source rather than the other way around. When Hunter met with Mrs. Floy Huskey, she spent much of the interview leafing through the songbooks atop her pump organ. Some ways into the interview it was clear that Hunter wasn't getting what he wanted when he asked her, "Did your mother ever sing any songs about lords or ladies, like 'Lord Randall'?" to which Huskey replied, "She used to sing a lot of songs that I can't remember." In this instance, the potential contributor had responded to Hunter's ad in the hope that *he* would be able to supply her with the lyrics she could no longer recall.[14]

As time went on, Hunter increasingly turned to members of his own family for folkloric material. In September 1970 he interviewed his father-in-law, Myrl Mercer, a man of cheerful temperament who had vivid recollections of how singing played a part in his own childhood:

> I was a boy of about 8 years old and we moved from Sedalia about 12 miles north of Dixon. . . . We built the lines ourselves and put in the telephones. They were the kind that had the two dry cell batteries and you cranked them. . . . And there was 12 to 15 families that was on the line that time. . . . My Daddy—he always worked away from home—we had a hired man, and this hired man and my two sisters at night were entertainment for the people all up and down the line. They got on this telephone and they sing their songs. . . . "Once There was a Pollywog Sitting on a

Log," that was one of their favorites they sang, and any number of their old-timers. They had a book, but that book got lost. They carried on for hours at a time, for everybody up and down the line.[15]

Mercer told him, "When anybody between us and Dixon would ring . . . if anybody had hold of the line and it went through, then it would shock the tar out of 'em."

Mercer was yet another wealth of information about local cure-alls—something that continued to interest Hunter throughout his life. Mercer spoke of a widowed neighbor who had six or seven boys: "One of those boys was subject to a nosebleed and he always wore a little piece of lead around his neck on a string. . . . If he took his lead off and lay it to one side, his nose would go to bleed."[16] Hunter's father-in-law also made reference to the turpentine cure for worms, this time on Mercer's own daughter, Virginia: "And lo and behold, it worked."[17]

In the early seventies, fewer and fewer of Hunter's songsters sang without accompaniment. Such was the case with Floyd Holland and Kermit Moody (then in their eighties) of Mountain View, Arkansas, both of whom fell under the influence of the Carter Family repertoire and accompanied themselves on banjo while singing songs like "Curtain of Stars" and "Little Darling Pal of Mine." During their interview with Hunter in October 1971, Holland, who lived in Stone County his entire life, spoke of how he played a gourd banjo as a kid and made strings "out of sewing thread."[18] The first song he remembers learning was "Go Tell Aunt Rhody." "I was singing before I could talk," he said.

The visit with Moody and Holland was most memorable for their stories about Jimmy Driftwood's father, Neal Morris. They said that Morris Senior was "snake-bit": "He wore leggings. . . . He wore them every day. . . . The only time he ever put them off is when he went to bed." Moody talked about what it was like when Morris came to town: "Every kid he met on the street he'd stop and sing a song. . . . You could see him coming and he'd be smiling. He's gonna stop and talk to you. . . . He'd started singing before you got there."[19] Moody said that Driftwood "got most of his musical knowledge from Neal and Neal's dad" and that Neal had the better voice.[20] Ollie Gilbert also once remarked of the elder Driftwood: "He was a good singer for an old man!" and his rendition of "One Morning in May" left an indelible impression on her.[21]

When Hunter returned home after his afternoon with Moody and Holland, he added a rare comment to the tape that gives us a window into both the setting and the relationships that Hunter enjoyed with his musical acquaintances: "Mr. Holland lives in a mobile home trailer. It was rather warm in the trailer. The windows were all open. And when I left, I was out to the car loading my recorders. . . . I could hear the two old gentlemen talking and I believe that I was paid one of the nicest compliments that I had ever heard; I heard one of them say that 'he had the appearance of a real fine fella.' . . . They couldn't say anything better."[22]

## Finding a Permanent Home

By the early seventies, Hunter's collection of Ozark ballads had caught the attention of local scholars, and he seemed to have settled into a comfortable conversation with the academic world. In fact, his closest associates were not traveling salespeople or businessmen, like himself, but college professors and folklorists who were deeply learned in their fields. That said, he was deliberate in his decision to stay outside of the ivory tower in much the same way that he always chose to stay local, even when given the opportunity to present at more distant or high-profile events.

But if Hunter wasn't traveling beyond the Ozarks, copies of his tapes continued to make it to Washington, D.C., albeit in fits and starts. Joe Hickerson, who now held the title of head of the Archive of American Folk Song, received updates on Hunter's work from their mutual friends, the Schroeders, and by the early 1980s he arranged for duplication of the more recent Hunter recordings for inclusion in the archive.[23]

As exciting as connecting with the Library of Congress had initially been, Hunter's active exchange with Washington, D.C., appears to have mostly petered out, and he was now concerned that the songs of his beloved Ozarkers would become inaccessible to the general public. "I checked around at a couple or three universities, and they wanted to put it in the archives where nobody could get to it, and that didn't make sense," he said.[24] By the time Hunter was seeking a permanent home for his collection, he had already given Parler permission to make copies of all of his tapes for the University of Arkansas Folklore Research Project,[25] where he would later claim that he couldn't gain access to his own song collection, let alone anyone else's. Commented Hunter, "I found out that in one university I'd put it in the archives all right, to the point that I couldn't even hear my own tape.[26] . . . I begin to wonder, if I can't hear my tape, how are you gonna hear it?"[27] Comparing his views on the subject with those of Vance Randolph, he said:

Vance didn't trust libraries. He thought that you should give things like this to universities. And my experience with universities is that . . . the public can't get to it. . . . Vance was interested more in preserving stuff. . . . He thought scholarly people should be the ones to make use of it. And I disagree with him there, because I think the layman, the average person, is cut out. . . . That's wrong. There's more laymen than there are scholars, anyway.[28]

In 1972, counter to the advice of Randolph and other friends who urged him to place his recordings in an academic institution, he bequeathed his many tapes and correspondences to the Springfield–Greene County Library, where most of his original materials can still be found.[29] A vibrant resource center for the town of Springfield, it is easy to see why Hunter chose this place as his repository. In terms of his own materials, while there are many important pieces of correspondence, one will find regrettably little photographic documentation, since this was not part of Hunter's lexicon as a collector, something he later regretted. The original recordings of the ballads have now been digitized, as noted elsewhere. The audiotapes of Hunter's talks and conversations with people like Cathy Barton and the Schroeders have all been copied and distributed across the state by the Missouri State Historical Society. Here's what Hunter had to say about his decision to donate to the local library: "You can take the tape home. You can copy the tape. If you sing songs, maybe there's a song on there that you can pick up and," he noted magnanimously, "maybe you'll get rich."[30]

The early seventies were a particularly busy time for Hunter, since, in addition to festival work and local presentations, he was now preparing the ballads for inclusion in bound volumes that would become part of this collection. The successful donation of Hunter's materials to the Springfield–Greene County Library would have been far more difficult without the help of his youngest daughter, Jenny Sweet. A high schooler at the time, most of Sweet's older siblings had already left home, so the brunt of committing lyrics to type fell to her. When her father offered her a salary to do this work, she readily accepted, given that she now had to pay for both a car and upcoming college tuition.

Looking back on this time, Sweet described how she and her father would listen over and over again to the recordings, trying to get things right, going so far as to hold paper towel tubes up to the tape machine in an effort to clarify otherwise unintelligible words:[31] "He [Hunter] was really picky in a lot of ways; if he came across something that he didn't feel was authentic, true Ozark before, he didn't want it."[32] When she first started assisting her father, Sweet punched out the lyrics with a mechanical typewriter, so it is hardly surprising that she recalled how excited she was the day they went to a new store in town to purchase an electric typewriter.[33]

While in the midst of donating his tapes to the Springfield–Greene Library, Hunter began one last big sweep through the Ozarks, likely because of an inevitable uneasiness about any songs or stories he may have missed. Sometimes this meant revisiting old contacts; other times it meant casting a wider net for new ones. In August 1972 Almeda Riddle came to stay with Max and Virginia Hunter because she was singing at Southwest Missouri State University's first folk festival. It was Saturday when Riddle and Hunter decided to pay May Kennedy McCord a visit at the local nursing home. McCord was now in her nineties and suffering from profound deafness as well as dementia. The scene Hunter's tape painted was a bleak one: "I had visited May several months before. . . . I could notice quite a bit of deterioration . . . mentally. . . . May couldn't remember our names or really who we were, [but] she could remember the tunes that she played on the piano."[34] At one point in the interview, McCord asked Hunter and Riddle if they were married to each other. Neither visitor succeeded in getting her to sing. "As we left the nursing home and walked out to the car," Hunter related, "neither one of us said anything 'til we got out to the car. And the first thing Almeda said was 'Old age gets to all of us sooner or later.'"[35]

A few days after visiting McCord, Hunter enjoyed a more uplifting recording session, which harkened back to his earlier days of spontaneously seeking out strangers. He recalled:

> The way I found Mr. Charlie Horton was I was driving out of Marshall, Arkansas, east on Highway 27 early one morning, and hadn't gone about about [sic] a quarter of a mile when I just happened to look . . . down at a little house that set down below the highway and I saw a man setting on the front porch and I thought he was playing a banjo. . . . I went on up the road, turned around and came back, and just decided I'd drive down and see if I could visit with Mr. Horton. I didn't know his name and had never heard of him before. . . . He was very nice and very friendly, invited me in and got a chair out of the house—he and his wife live in a very small house, rather old. We set on the front porch and he played the banjo.[36]

Hunter recorded several of Horton's tunes, which made it onto the *Visits from the Ozarks* tapes but did not make it into his song collection.

During September 1972 Hunter spent an evening speaking with Benson and Fleecy Fox of Leslie, Arkansas. The Foxes were well connected with many of Hunter's other Arkansas singers and had already contributed a large number of ballads to the John Quincy Wolf Jr. Collection a decade back, but they were happy to oblige the Missouri collector with their stories and reflections when he came calling. Among Hunter's many singers, the Foxes were unique in their habit not only of singing together but also of doing so an octave apart. In addition to sharing their version of "The Nightingale," in which the soldier in the song appears instead as a "cowboy who wore the long hair," they sang play party songs such as "Roll the Tater." Said Benson Fox, "An old man by the name of Roy Mack . . . had a group of people who did play party songs. They don't meet anymore." To which Fleecy Fox added, "You line up, and a couple goes up and down, when they begin to roll they go around each other." What they described was an early version of what we now call a "freeze dance," which Benson Fox described as "When you yell 'tater!' then everybody stops."[37]

In addition to the songs they shared, Fleecy Fox spoke of her grandfather's musical legacy: "[He] had 13 kids . . . a great big house full of children. . . . . Way back then we didn't have anything. . . . He had the least of anybody. We used to go over there at night. He'd put a big pine knot in the fireplace [and] we'd all sit around it, and he'd sing those old songs to us. I guess he knew a bushel. And I just loved listening to him. There's a few of them stuck with me. Wish I'd kept a lot of them, but I didn't."[38]

Although the Springfield-Greene decision had been made and Hunter and the library were pulling materials together for the songbooks, Hunter wasn't finished with working in the field. He continued gathering material for his *Visits from the Ozarks* audiotapes, including his one and only hospital recording made in 1973 while interviewing his father-in-law, Myrl Mercer, who was at Cox Medical Center recovering from a lung operation.[39] Another late interview included a lengthy discussion with Bertha Lamar,[40] whose mother, Gladys Everly, contributed almost a dozen songs to his collection, but given Everly's fondness for printed songbooks, it is unclear how many lyrics she recalled from memory.[41] By the time he had donated his collection to the library, Hunter's inventory included not only songs but 720 jokes, 1,040 proverbial expressions, and 122 fiddle tunes as well.[42] As Hunter liked to tell it, his own tapes "if glued together and stretched out would run about 18 miles."[43]

In May 1978, during an Ozark Heritage Series concert at the Springfield–Greene County Library that featured Gordon McCann and his musical

Hunter with his bound song volumes, circa 1976. (Courtesy of the Spring-field–Greene County Library)

partner, master fiddler Art Galbraith,[44] Hunter introduced the program by reiterating the importance of oral history: "Oral history is important and should be taught in schools," he proclaimed, and "it should be made available to anybody that wants it."[45] With the energy of a man who had found a new calling, he announced that later in the month he would be giving a talk on this very topic for the Baptist Historical Society in Jefferson City. He then entertained the audience with a by now well-embellished explanation of why he had donated his tapes to the library: "I quit giving part of my collection to some people because I found out that they were putting it down in a bomb-proof shelter, forty stories underground, and once it got in there, I couldn't even get in there to hear my own tape! One of these days somebody's gonna come along and say . . . 'Look what I found down in this hole in the ground.'"[46] Hunter's choice of placing his collection at the Springfield–Greene County Library was the furthest thing from a "hole in the ground."

# 9

# MAX HUNTER'S MAP
# OF THE OZARKS

## Geographic Ponderings

In addition to Hunter's rule about never being in a rush or pressuring his sources, there was also his conviction never to collect ballads from beyond the Ozarks. But exactly what constitutes "the Ozarks" has long been debated both inside and outside of university walls. Springfield scholar Milton Rafferty, an authority on Ozark geology and geography put it this way: "The boundaries of the Ozarks are vague to most people and subject to interpretation and disagreement by the experts."[1] Longtime Ozark Folk Center folklorist W. K. McNeil echoed Rafferty's observation: "Perhaps no mountain region in North America is so poorly defined as the Ozarks. It is likely that any two authorities on the area will provide a slightly different map."[2] Both scholars ultimately looked to the rivers for geographic boundaries. McNeil described it as follows: "On the north is the Missouri; in the southwest the Arkansas; to the southeast the Black; on the east is the Mississippi and on the west is the Neosho. Within these borders the Ozarks form an almost perfect arc on the map."[3] But the cultural delineation of the region has even more layers, ones that continue to be explored by scholars like Blevins.[4] Given that Rafferty was from Springfield, it is possible that Hunter had attended one of his talks, but most of the ballad collector's ideas (however roughly formed) echoed those of Randolph.

Indeed, time spent with academically minded friends was rubbing off on Hunter, and his sense of himself as an amateur collector had made a shift. He had now been invited to speak in front of university audiences, at museums,

and at other civic centers. But if he began to be known as an expert in the field
of ballad collecting, this expertise did not necessarily extend itself to other
areas. In February 1974 Hunter cobbled together his one and only "thesis"
paper, titled "Pioneer Ozarker—Complex Man," which he introduced as "a
layman's talk." In Hunter's introductory comments on the writing process,
he acknowledged that there were essentially two potential Max Hunters and
that he needed to make a choice: "I practiced on a piece of tape to see where I
wanted the volume control. . . . I heard two people talking. One was a fellow
trying to pronounce his words fairly distinctly and the other one sounded
like me. I think I like me the best, so that's the way I'll do this tape."[5]

Hunter's twenty-seven-page essay was a collection of presentations he'd
given, starting with the Ozark Folklore Society's annual meeting in July 1970,
and he originally wrote it at the suggestion of Betsy Olson,[6] who, as Hunter
expressed it, was eager to bridge the "communication gap between the scholarly folklorists and the layman folklorists."[7] A veritable catch basin of impos-
sibly broad topics, which included the mysteries of Ozark geography, customs,
religious beliefs, and some of his own collecting experiences, it nonetheless
marked Hunter's effort at becoming part of a broader conversation about
the Ozark culture in which he lived and worked. Many of his thoughts on
regional boundaries and identity came under the direct influence not only of
Randolph but of Rayburn as well:[8] "I prefer to use the cultural line—the way
of life, the lifestyle patterns, the commonplace way of life," Hunter wrote:[9]

> How did the guy build his barn? How did he build his house? Did he
> put it on a foundation, or did he put it on stilts? How did he plow?
> And the mother. What'd she do? How'd she take care of the children?
> . . . People down below Poplar Bluff did not farm like my grandfather
> farmed in Christian County and Taney County, because my grandfather
> had one leg shorter than the other. He had to. He was walking around
> in the hills.[10]

Hunter also poked fun at regional boundaries: "Most people living here
think of it as all lake country. I know of several towns as much as 100 miles
apart that claim to be 'The Heart of the Ozarks.'"[11] He also once wrote, "I
have no argument with any group or individual when it comes to trying to
establish how big the Ozarks country is or where one might draw a boundary
line. This I know, any line would have to have a lot of curves in it."[12] And after
a lengthy preamble on the bewildering maps put out by both the Arkansas
Geological Society and the National Geographic Society, Hunter humorously

concluded, "It looks like the whole middle section of the United States is going to be Ozark Country."[13] Indeed, Hunter's sense of the Ozarks was largely both experiential and anecdotal. His admiration for the native intelligence of Ozarkers was another thread running through this paper: "Most of the pioneers were not book-learning educated, but they were not dumb."[14] And when he made statements such as "The pioneer Ozarker watched his environment much closer than we do," he turned to anecdotal evidence for ballast:

> One man told me that when he was a young boy . . . they used a team of oxen to break ground on some of their land and horses or mules for the other. . . . They knew that a team of oxen could go around the stumps because there wasn't any single trees or double trees to get tangled up. . . . On other ground, they would use a team of mules or horses because they were faster. The same way with pulling heavy loads of timber. They knew that an oxen on some grounds could out pull a team of horses or mules.[15]

Hunter would again explore regionally distinct methods of agriculture during his stint as a columnist in 1977 when he wrote about a disgruntled farmer who had come from the flatlands of Illinois and was baffled by his Ozark neighbor's farming techniques, which included planting "crops in the light and dark side of the moon" and turning breeding livestock toward or away from the sun to predetermine the sex of their offspring.[16]

## Of Hillbillies and Preachers

Hunter also took it upon himself to explore regional identity: "Perhaps the best way to tell if you are a native to the Ozarks is . . . when you are asked, you will tell people you are an Ozarker. But if you're not, you would probably tell them that you are an Ozarkian."[17] Hunter continued to explore this topic in a talk he gave for Adolf Schroeder's Festival of Missouri Folk Music in 1977. Introduced as "A Gentleman of the Ozarks,"[18] Hunter questioned the "gentleman" part while at the same time expanding upon the geographic part of the title. Tending toward the pedantic, Hunter then devoted the entire first part of his talk to differentiating these labels: "I am an Ozarker," he said, "because I was born in the Ozarks. I've lived in the Ozarks all my life, my great-great-grandparents came to the Ozarks in eighteen and forty, they lived and they died in the Ozarks on both sides of my family." He then went on to poke fun at those who use the other label: "An Ozarkian . . . this is my personal opinion—moves into the Ozarks, likes it . . . and then in a couple of, maybe, three years writes back home wherever they came from and says 'I'm a Hillbilly.'"[19]

If Hunter's relationship with the term "hillbilly" was both long-winded and equivocal, it simply reflected a cultural debate that had been fermenting on Springfield soil as far back as 1934. That is the year when the city was gearing up for its first folk festival and the chamber of commerce voiced opposition to "the 'hillbilly' stuff" that would (somewhat ironically) make this early event such a success.[20] While on the one hand Hunter seemed to take great pleasure in declaring his own hillbillyism to a university audience,[21] according to Bangs, he typically forbade the use of this term in his own household and instead followed the lead of Otto Rayburn and referred to his beloved singers as the "Hill People," believing this alternatively questionable appellation would garner them more respect.[22]

Hunter in a Western hat. (Photographer Bob Linder, *USA Today* Network, March 7, 1998)

The genuine "hillbilly," as Hunter liked to think of him, was fast disappearing and was being replaced by a damaging caricature. "The slapstick comedy of the hillbilly is ridiculous. . . . It is the professional hillbilly that appears in our commercial attractions," he complained.[23] This comment came directly out of his frustration with a folk festival culture that often piggybacked on tourism to promote such cultural stereotypes.

## Religion and Folklore

If Hunter, who grew up in the suburban sprawl of Springfield, harbored romantic ideas about his rural neighbors, he was less nostalgic toward the religious beliefs and practices of his ancestors: "Most of our older people had a strong, personal feeling toward religion. They were church-going people, almost to the point of radicalism."[24] His paper—rife with overgeneralizations—turned once again to anecdotal "evidence" in which he described the "strange religious scruples" he had witnessed at a brush arbor revival:[25]

> When I was 11 or 12 years old, I went to a revival service one night with one of my neighbors. . . . I saw a woman start shouting right in the middle of the preaching. She started hollering and waving her arms and she also passed out in front of the pulpit. About a couple of hours later, she came to and was so weak she couldn't walk. One of the strangest things I remember about this happening [was that] it was rumored that the woman was having a love affair with the preacher.[26]

A soft-spoken man, Hunter occasionally made observations about the extreme behaviors that religion (inside and outside of church walls) could inspire. He talked about the supposed evils of everything from dancing ("For a man and a woman to allow their bodies to touch, that is in public, was an extreme shame") to playing cards ("I have personally saw cards threw in a fire regardless of who they belonged to"). He also knew several people who "would not allow [a] fiddle in their home because they thought it was an instrument of the devil."[27] Hunter concluded, "Well, about the only thing left was whittling and then you had better be careful where you got the wood."[28]

Associations with religious extremism aside, both Max and Virginia Hunter regularly attended the Campbell Street Methodist Church in Springfield, and this ecclesiastical setting occasionally became part of the "field" in which he recorded stories, ballads, and other materials. In September 1971 Hunter spent much of a church supper at the back entrance of the church, recording the gruesome pastimes that Springfield native Otto Clayton had enjoyed in his youth.[29] In contrast to the ecclesiastical setting where the interview took place, Clayton also spoke of a number of cure-alls involving horse urine as well as love charms, including the following: "If a young girl would place a ruby under her tongue and look in the mirror, it would increase her love powers," and "A bag of dried cherry seeds, hidden and carried in a girl's clothing, will make her more attractive."[30] Hunter's field had indeed widened as he began to think about the culture that surrounded his beloved ballads, and he sometimes pushed societal boundaries in his eagerness to get interesting material.

Hunter's Ozark landscape also included several paranormal beliefs with which he had grown up. He recalled hearing his father describe how, when Hunter's grandmother died, "My grandfather had the boys cover the mirrors with bed sheets. When the casket with the body in it was brought to the home before the funeral, a candle was placed on a table at each end of the casket and was kept burning until the casket lid was closed." Hunter then attempted to find the rationale behind these rituals: "Whoever looks upon a dead person and then into the mirror will be the next to die. The lighted candle is to keep the evil spirits from stealing the soul out of the casket."[31] But Hunter's attempts at interpretation were random rather than systematic.

Regardless of where Ozark Country lay both psychologically and geographically, Hunter, like folklorists who had gone before, was deeply concerned about Ozark culture disappearing altogether: "I have stories of silver mines, gold mines, cabins, trails and so forth which are all covered over with water now."[32] The hill country appeared more imperiled to him than the flatlands: "The vacation resort centers have brought many outsiders into the hill country but this has not happened in the flat prairies yet. I'm talking about the northern part of the Ozarks."[33] And this changing landscape had a direct effect on collective cultural memory. Hunter matter-of-factly opined, "The present generation knows very little about the folklore of their forefathers."[34] As time went on, and Hunter spent more and more time with trained folklorists and scholars, he began to understand how his song-collecting activities could ameliorate some of this loss.

# 10

# MAX HUNTER AND THE FESTIVAL CIRCUIT

Despite the loss of his musical partner, Hunter would return to Eureka Springs for the Ozark Folk Festival year after year, with the exception of 1975, when he decided not to go: "I was on the program—I don't know how many years—until it got to the point that it wasn't folk anymore. . . . Everybody had their own speakers and microphone, and so much stuff was on the stage there wasn't no place for the performer, there wasn't anything folk about it, it was strictly a variety show."[1] In addition to Hunter's state of disenchantment with the Ozark Folk Festival, he had just taken on a consultancy position that same year with a newly created music festival in the Silver Dollar City theme park near Branson, Missouri. He embarked upon this new project with unbridled optimism: "There's a good possibility that it can become an annual event, . . . becoming even the biggest music festival of its type in America."[2] These were the words of a man in his prime who was enjoying his recognition and the influence that came with it.

The fanfare surrounding the Silver Dollar City festival included the making of a video titled *Music of the Mountains* that documented the evolution of this event and the music of several of its participants. As described in the authoritative voice of KDOE-TV narrator Bob Phillips, "The task of auditioning and selecting 125 musicians from widely divergent points in the Ozarks was a formidable one. Much of the work fell on Max Hunter of Springfield, Missouri; a widely known authority on mountain music."[3] Hunter himself described putting ads in newspapers and radio stations all over the Ozarks, and there was no lack of would-be performers; in fact, several had to be turned away because they either didn't meet his musical standards or simply showed up in "weird costumes." Hunter recalled, "For instance, one fellow showed up dressed as a pink cowboy. . . . His guitar was painted in pink, his boots were pink, his suit was pink, his hat was pink. I'm not so sure but what his beard was pink."[4]

Springfield natives Julia O'Reilly and Krisanne Parker, both of whom attended Missouri State University and came of age during the folk music revival, met Hunter through auditions for Silver Dollar City. Observed Parker, "There was a tremendous interest in traditional music. . . . There were people like me . . . [who] didn't necessarily grow up with the music, but simply fell in love with it."[5] Their ears were filled with the sounds of Peter, Paul, and Mary; Joni Mitchell; the Weavers; the Kingston Trio; and politico singer/songwriter Phil Ochs, yet they knew little or nothing of traditional Ozarks music.

Before auditioning, O'Reilly armed herself with two Joan Baez ballads. "We were so nervous," she recalls.[6] After she and Parker made it through the auditions, Hunter handed them cassette tapes with approximately twelve songs to learn in two weeks' time. And like many of the songs in his collection, the source recordings did not necessarily make for easy listening. But "Max was a salesman. . . . He could get anything out of anybody. He insisted that we could learn these tunes that we could hardly hear or read." Hunter was now ideally positioned to introduce a new generation to the songs that their parents and grandparents had failed to pass along. O'Reilly also recalls having attended a song swap with Jimmy Driftwood and Jean Ritchie in the Student Union at Missouri State. She said, "Max was a great networker. . . . He could sell water to a fish." Forty years later, O'Reilly, who now plays music for contra dances, among other folk music activities, says that these early festival days took her down an unexpected path.[7]

Parker related her experience with Hunter as well: "At the time, I had been playing and performing folk music (primarily for myself) I had learned off records. Despite my lack of oral tradition and musical background, he [Hunter] hired me." In keeping with the performance standards of Silver Dollar City, "The performers were sent a list of 'do's' and 'don'ts' prior to beginning. Nothing modern or urban: watches, make-up, jewelry, open-toed shoes, etc. And the music needed to be from the 1800s and traditional ballads, fiddle tunes with absolutely no bluegrass, country, recently composed songs."[8] Painted nails were *verboten*. Regarding these requirements, O'Reilly recalls, "Being young, we rolled our eyes a lot."[9]

Parker also performed for Hunter at the Ozark Folk Festival. "We sang harmonies on many of the songs, some of which were ballads," but Hunter voiced his disapproval about their doing so. "He was gentle, but . . . I've never forgotten this either. I can't listen to a traditional ballad that's being sung with harmonies and/or heavy instrumentation without thinking that the performer has lost the original spirit of the music," recalled O'Reilly.[10] Her comments illustrate that as times moved on and performing styles evolved, Hunter continued to draw deep lines in the sand regarding what constituted "traditional" performance, and working with him meant observing his rules.

But for Hunter, singing also created an expanded network for young vocalists who were being swept up in Missouri's and Arkansas's iteration of the folk music revival. The crystal-clear soprano vocals of both Parker and O'Reilly feature prominently in the *Music of the Mountains* video, in which narrator Bob Phillips describes the dramatic convergence of native talent. Most of the musicians started off as strangers to one another, but "on the evening before the festival began, the musicians were given a short briefing and assigned locations throughout Silver Dollar City. Then, with the business concluded, the performers gathered in the city square," where they took part in a "spontaneous, unrehearsed hoedown while the sun went down over the Ozarks."[11]

Despite the strictures kept on their performances, participation in the Mountain Folks Music Festival, as well as other events organized by Hunter, changed both women's musical lives forever. Parker described her pleasant experience with the festival:

> The Silver Dollar experience was really great; it was the first time I had heard players and singers who had grown up with the music. . . . There are not many names I remember from then, but I do remember Donnie Koontz, a fine musician, and his wife, Pearl, who played a washtub bass. Kim and Greg Becker performed on a regular basis—Kim on hammered dulcimer (the first time I had heard that instrument). . . . I was lucky to be introduced by Max to Almeda Riddle. Most of the performers were given rotating location assignments, but Almeda could be found on the porch of her cabin at any time.[12] I headed over on many of my breaks to spend time with her.[13]

Samuel Osterloh (who would later become a minister) was part of the band that Hunter put together for the Mountain Folks Music Festival in Branson.[14] In addition to Silver Dollar City, Osterloh frequently performed for Hunter at Missouri State University concerts along with musicians O'Reilly, Parker, Toby Nix, and Mike Howell. Osterloh, who graduated in 1977, recorded about twenty-five songs with this group and looks back on this moment in his life with the deepest nostalgia.[15] His greatest wish (forty and more years later)

A publicity shot of Krisanne Parker. (Photographer unknown, courtesy of Krisanne Parker)

was to be reunited with them (Nix had since passed away and the surviving members of the band are now geographically distant from one another).[16]

Many of the young performers whom Hunter summoned for Silver Dollar City would follow him to Eureka Springs. It was in 1976, shortly after his (likely) strategic boycott of the Ozark Folk Festival the previous year, that Hunter received an invitation from executive director Phil Bullock to become program director. As told by Hunter:[17]

> He called me up here one night and wanted to know if I'd be interested in talking to them about the program. . . . I drove down with my list of things that I wanted. . . . I said that he had not had a folk program in years. Well . . . they was . . . financially bankrupt—I don't know how many thousands of dollars they was in the red. They either had to quit or do something. I met with them—I wanted 100 percent control of the program, I wouldn't use anybody that they had had on there in the past. . . . And I knew I was gonna get some static because they had some singers who had been there every year and didn't need me.

Despite this bold statement, it seems likely that Hunter was overruled by Bullock with regard to the wholesale replacement of existing talent. Hunter ended up retaining several key people who had been with the festival from day one, chief among them the "Queen of the Hillbillies," May Kennedy

Silver Dollar City performance with fiddler Toby Nix, (unidentified guitar player), Krisanne Parker, and Samuel Osterloh, circa 1976. (Courtesy of Samuel Osterloh)

McCord (alternately known as "First Lady of the Ozarks"),[18] who had been the institutional face of the festival since 1948. But the way Hunter would later tell it, after stating his demands to Bullock, he hunkered down:

> I said I'm gonna go down to the bar and I'm gonna drink me a beer and if somebody don't come and get me by the time I have had a drink, I am going home. . . . I hadn't no more than hardly got the top off it 'til here come Mr. Bullock and said "Come on back, we decided to take it on your terms." So I started that—they were in the black—they paid off their mortgage on the museum, they put a new roof on it, they now have deeded it over to the city, they are financially solid right now.[19]

Hunter would go on to act as producer and director of the festival from 1976 to 1988.[20]

The original festival featured the Hilltoppers string band, whose fiddle player, Paralee Weddington, would be a mainstay at the festival for decades to come. Arkansawyer Fred High and his sister Mary Briscoe (both of whom sang without accompaniment) also appeared at the early festival, as did Jimmy Driftwood. But by the 1960s and 1970s, there were indeed cracks in the festival pavement as depicted in the flowery prose of festival historian Carroll Thompson: "Beside the genuine folklorists vanishing from the stage, each year more vacant seats appeared in the City Auditorium."[21] It was Hunter's job to get the ailing festival back on its financial feet while simultaneously bringing it back to its so-called roots.[22] Top on the list he alluded to was his rule about disallowing any songs written after 1900: "I've got a list I give to the performers and also post them on stage of songs that I don't want to hear."[23] Hunter also had strict rules about apparel and appearance: ladies had to wear dresses with long sleeves and skirts and (as in Branson) to avoid open-toed shoes, and men had to hide their long hair beneath their collars or under their hats.[24]

Hunter was far from the first organizer to issue rules around everything from festival attire to song repertoire. Back in 1944 Sarah Gertrude Knott and business partner M. J. Pickering had collaborated with the National Folk Festival Committee (of which they were a part) to publish a highly comprehensive and culturally inclusive folk festival handbook that discussed virtually every aspect of festival organizing and went so far as to include a "material guide" on specific cultures, dances, songs and instruments.[25] Although it is unlikely that Hunter consulted this guide, many of the actions he took at the Ozark Folk Festival mirrored suggestions that had been made thirty years prior, one of which could be found on page 12: "Little scenery is necessary. . . . It is not customary to mount folk festivals with elaborate stage sets or to present each folk group with a special effect." Thompson rhapsodized:

> The few bales of straw remaining on the stage for the performers to sit on until their names were called, were left. The addition of every empty park bench in Eureka Springs lined the sides and back of the stage area of the City Auditorium. Electrified amplifiers and electrified instruments were removed . . . and would not be replaced as long as Max Hunter served the Festival as its Program Director. . . . Therefore, the 29th Annual Ozark Folk Festival became a reunion of the preservation of Folk and the talent to present it in traditional accuracy.[26]

But Hunter's mission wasn't as simple as Thompson would have us believe; in fact, he would spend the next decade trying to transform a tourist event into a musical event with a deeper cultural impact. But in doing so, he would have to contend with a changing arts culture that was increasingly dominated by television broadcasts and imagery, as well as with the economic demands of Eureka Springs itself, which was and remains a draw for tourists. These external challenges aside, Hunter had the unique opportunity to showcase traditional songs as well as their singers, thus shining a light on two decades of ballad collecting.

His directorship also created a somewhat new dynamic between himself and Randolph, who occasionally asked for personal favors:

> Mr. and Mrs. Mike Flynn of Tulsa would like to perform at the Eureka Springs Festival. I have heard their songs in person and on tape. They sing old ballads and broadside songs, and I think they are damn good. If you can give them any special consideration it will be a favor to me personally. They are old friends of mine, and friends of many important people in Oklahoma, including our mutual friend Betsy Olson of Vinita. . . . Come and see us when you can. It has been a long time.[27]

But there is no evidence suggesting that Hunter acted on this recommendation, which is hardly surprising, given his rule about staying strictly in the Ozarks.

In addition to the presence of McCord, there were also a number of old-time fiddlers who participated in the festival, and most of them were top contestants from the fiddle contest held in Hunter's hometown only a few days ahead of the 1976 Ozark Folk Festival. This almost nonexistent lead time made for a great deal of excitement among the musicians, not to mention logistical challenges for the organizers. Immediately after learning that they would be performing at the Ozark Music Festival, musicians were handed the list of do's and don'ts. Consistent with his mission, Hunter insisted that instruments be acoustic and without amplification.

Despite Hunter's earlier conviction to wipe the performer slate clean, audiences benefited from the retention of Weddington, with whom Hunter enjoyed a particularly good rapport. She was in her late sixties when he first met her—a heavyset woman with a cane and a full-length prairie dress, who cut a large and voluble presence on stage. If her out-of-tune guitar accompaniment and vocals fell musically short, she made up for this with the solid fiddling she had learned from her father.[28] The matriarch of a family of musical daughters and the wife of a former moonshiner,[29] she had plenty of good stories to tell in addition to a well-timed sense of absurdity. Weddington, who, like McCord, in many ways embodied the Ozark Folk Festival, contributed as many as twenty-three songs to the Hunter Collection.

Other program favorites included the Humpy Holler Folk, a family band from Coal Hill, Arkansas. Ralph and Minnie Spencer had a wide and engaging repertoire of tunes and were unlike the majority of Hunter's contacts in that they sang most of their songs with harmonies and neatly arranged instrumental accompaniments reminiscent of the Carter Family. But if the Spencer family's music was less than traditional, they made up for this through their winsome way with audiences, whom they addressed at length on the history behind their homemade instruments.[30] Their son Stephen played a banjolin fashioned from a pressure cooker,[31] and other family members played a gourd banjo and a cigar box fiddle.[32] They also liked to discuss the importance of music to their family history. As Minnie explained, "The way Ralph and I met was in the cotton patch. We'd both had jobs hoeing weeds out of the cotton. . . . We did most all of our courting playing music because Ralph didn't have money to take me anyplace." (Hunter and his wife went on a recording expedition to the Spencers' home about a month after the festival in 1976.)

The Spencers, who developed their collective stage persona under Hunter's wing, represented the majority of Hunter's recruits insofar as they had spent their lives playing for one another in a domestic or town setting rather than for wider audiences. In 1978 they explained to a University of Missouri audience that they were "non-professional" musicians who had never "played in front of anybody" before they auditioned for the Ozark Folk Festival.[33] In addition to the older generation of performers, Hunter also brought in young interpreters of the old "gems"—people like Booneville, Missouri, musicians Cathy Barton and Dave Para. And several of the university students he had selected for Silver Dollar City followed him to Eureka Springs, chief among them O'Reilly and Parker.

According to Para and Barton—who went on to found the Big Muddy Folk Festival and became international emissaries of traditional Missouri music—much of Hunter's success at the Ozark Folk Festival was due to the fact that "he had contacts that no one else had."[34] The two women had fond memories of hanging out with Hunter in the lobby of the Basin Park Hotel: "Max would pick a table and just wait for people to come in. He was in his element," recalled Barton.[35] Like the Randolphs before her, Barton—a graduate student in folklore at the University of Bowling Green in Bowling Green, Kentucky—met Hunter at the Ozark Folk Festival, and her research activities provided many of the essential details about his life as a collector.

The year 1976 was one of opportunity for Hunter, who suddenly found himself at the center of activity in the Ozark folk world. Not only was this his first year as master of ceremonies at the Ozark Folk Festival (where he would continue to work in an official capacity for over a decade), but he was also invited to Washington, D.C., to participate in the Smithsonian Institution's

Hunter at the Weddington house in Busch, Arkansas, October 1972. (Courtesy of the Springfield–Greene County Library)

Festival of American Folklife. Word of Hunter's collecting work also made it to California, where a Los Angeles branch of the national Country Dance and Song Society invited him on an "all-expense-paid tour" including the cities of Austin, Tucson, San Diego, and even five of California's seven Claremont colleges.[36] But Hunter was too immersed in regional activities to take up either of these invitations.

Hunter's sudden busyness was reflected in a letter to the folklife festival's program director, Shirley Cherkasky, in which he turned down the Smithsonian's offer with a lengthy list of his current involvements. Chief among those activities was his upcoming directorship of the Ozark Folk Festival, his consultancy position at Silver Dollar City, and his production responsibilities for the folk festival at Southwest Missouri State University in Springfield.[37] After acknowledging that the Smithsonian invitation was indeed "an honor," Hunter asked for a "rain-check." Given that 1976 was America's bicentennial year, the latter was an impossibility, as the Smithsonian Festival of American Folklife would be extended over a never-duplicated twelve-week period and was scheduled to include a vast array of programming that would not be repeated. Hunter's written response to Cherkasky was anything but humble. Speaking of his ballad collection, he wrote, "It is perhaps one of the largest private regional collections in America."[38] And throughout the letter, Hunter made ample mention of his importance to the Ozark folk community: "I have a list of over 300 musicians and singers and over 200 craftsmen. These are some of the reasons I have been contacted by the various groups."[39]

All of this resume building culminated in the following pitch from the Missouri collector: "I read in the material that I received that 'talent scouts' have been searching the country for talent. This sounds like something I might be interested in so I would like to 'open the door.'" Then Hunter threw in a familiar calling card: "If it is worth anything I would like to refer you to a very personal friend as to my qualifications, Mr. Vance Randolph, Sunrise Manor, Fayetteville, Arkansas. This is just an idea."[40] Although it is impossible to know how this letter was received, viewing it from decades later, the manner in which Hunter put forth his agenda appears amateurish, and his rejection of the Smithsonian invitation seems narrow-minded. Indeed, there are no "rain checks" on such opportunities. But, similar to Ollie Gilbert (who at least ventured to D.C.), he remained focused on home and, by extension, the Ozarks region.

Although interviews with Hunter scarcely ever touched on matters of employment, it is worth noting that all of these musical activities took place around the edges of Hunter's life as a breadwinner. At the same time that he became involved with both the Ozark Folk Festival and Silver Dollar City, he was an employee of Southern Materials Company, a business he stayed with from 1965 to 1979, before becoming the owner of yet another refrigeration company. And although his life as a collector became the centerpiece of his public persona, he remained a businessman (albeit a semi-retired one) up until about six years before his death.

While Hunter was embarking on his activities at Eureka Springs and continuing to make a living as a salesman, he also took on a second season as "technical consultant" to the nine-day festival in Branson.[41] Hunter's position with Silver Dollar City—though occupying much of his mind at the time—was destined to be short-lived, likely because of what some labeled as his "rigid" ideas about how such events should be run. In addition, Hunter was now coming face-to-face with the evolution of the national folk revival, and it often ran against his apolitical and purist grain, as expressed in the introduction to his own collection:

Recently we've had a great crop of folk songs that were composed in the last three, four, five, six years. . . . I think most of these recently composed folknick songs could be filed under protest songs. There's a difference between going to some neighbor or friend's home for a song swap party and going into some night club and singing songs against something . . . to let people know you've been mistreated.[42]

Protest songs were not, in his estimation, real folksongs.

Although his second season at Branson had not been entirely agreeable, Hunter immediately started angling for a more permanent position, as indicated in a letter he wrote to the organizer, Jean Nichols: "I am in no way trying to put any pressure on you but if you have plans to continue to employ me I thought you might like to have some of my thinking. . . . If you have plans for a Mountain Folks Music at the new SDC [Silver Dollar City] location, I already have several personal friends in that area who 'pick and sing.'"[43]

As in his letter to the Smithsonian, Hunter's real agenda lay in the final paragraph, in which he again floated the idea of becoming a "talent scout" for Silver Dollar City: "I would be working with 'singers and pickers' all year."[44] Hunter offered to find craftspeople as well and gave examples of two people he already had in mind—one a candle maker and one a seamstress. Most telling of all, he invoked his skills as a salesman: "My thinking is that if Mountain Folks Music continues and grows, like I'm sure you want it to, a person like me is going to be needed more, not less. . . . Businesses have to have traveling salesmen. They have to have the 'personal contact.'"[45] Hunter was at his most ambitious. "A hobby has turned into an avocation and may very well turn into a vocation," he mused. The letter was virtually bursting with his ideas—too many at once for Nichols, the recipient, to take seriously. Hunter was ready to join the festival scene full-time and leave his refrigeration business behind, should the opportunity arise. In retrospect, if he'd been more measured in setting forth his ideas, Hunter just might have succeeded in fulfilling this dream.

But fresh on the heels of the 1976 festival at Silver Dollar City, he sent yet another letter to Jean Nichols; it was a seven-page "personal evaluation" of all the things that went wrong at the event. In this document, which speaks volubly of a wounded ego, Hunter made ample mention of his "stature" in the folk world, including his collaborations with such persons as Vance Randolph, the Schroeders at the University of Missouri–Columbia, and even ballad scholar Bertrand Harris Bronson. The letter expressed Hunter's strong opinions on how traditional music events should be run and the role of festival administrators. His analysis of Silver Dollar City was relentless and unforgiving: "Persons who fool around with events, like me and you, Jean . . . have to set in three seats," he wrote, putting himself on the same playing field as Nichols. "We have to set in the seat of the producer, we have to set in the seat of the performer and then we have to set in the seat of the audience. . . . When we lose sight of the last two, we are in trouble."[46] In short, he was telling her how to do her job.

This was Hunter at his most pedantic and most miffed; apparently his rule about excluding any songs after 1900 had been dismissed. He reported hearing everything from "Rocky Top" to "This Land Is Your Land": "If you remember, I came to your office and told you as far as I was concerned, I might as well go home. I was ashamed of what I heard." To which he added, in a scalding moment of sarcasm, "I will have to admit, the 1976 Mountain Folks Music Festival was one of the best 'bluegrass festivals' that I ever attended."[47] The rant then continued. Above all, Hunter objected to how the performers had been treated: "I think an apology is due every musician and singer. . . . I have never heard of a festival, as such, that did not pay the performers, in full, on the last day of their performance."[48] Affixed to this lengthy complaint was a five-page list of the rogue songs: "The following songs were heard being sung or played during the 1975 and 1976 Mountain Folks Music Festival and should not be used because they were composed or copyrighted after the year 1900."[49]

Hunter's evaluation letter was followed by yet another missive, which appears to have been unsent but reflects his wounded state of mind. In this draft he vacillated between assignment of blame and personal apology for his own misunderstandings, concluding, "From the feedback I got during the Mountain Folks Music Festival I felt that some of the musicians and singers thought I had more to do with the planning. . . . I had very little to do with it and some of the suggestions I made were ignored. I assure you it would have been quite different had I been consulted, that being the reason I was hired."[50] Unsurprisingly, Hunter's contract with Silver Dollar City was not renewed.

In the end, Hunter's falling out with Silver Dollar City boiled down to mostly one factor: his vision of folk festivals as the ideal vessel with which to promote traditional music was too narrow for the other organizers. There is little doubt that in this context Hunter might be viewed by performers and organizers alike as a curmudgeon—or, in today's lingo, a micromanager—who was not in sync with the times. To quote unabashed admirer Thompson back in Eureka Springs: "Some would say Max Hunter is almost fanatical where folk music and how it is presented are concerned."[51] Hunter, who was entering his fifth decade, elicits a familiar pattern among aging festival organizers, when youthful qualities of conviction and determination become perceived as rigidity.[52]

As previously alluded to, the disagreements that arose between Hunter and Silver Dollar City mirrored the difficulties that Jimmy Driftwood was experiencing around this same time as a result of his personal involvement with the economically and ideologically troubled Ozark Folk Center in Stone County, Arkansas. Both men were devoted to the promotion and continuity of traditional music, a devotion that often put them at odds with festival and concert organizers, who were focused first and foremost on the economic necessity of attracting an audience, one made up largely of tourists. The same insightful words with which biographer Michael Ann Williams described this stage in life for organizers John Lair and Sarah Gertrude Knott could just as easily be applied to Driftwood and Hunter a decade later, since these men "would both be challenged to keep their shows from becoming anachronisms."[53]

The cultural dissonances at Mountain View, Arkansas, and in Branson, Missouri, were microcosms of national trends. Folk music scholar Norm Cohen provided this perspective: "Gradually, the appreciation for traditional performances grew to the point where there were two audiences for the folk revival: those who preferred the smoother, more polished presentations of the urban revivalists, and those [like Hunter] who insisted on their music unadulterated."[54] Add to this the dying off of an older generation of traditional musicians, many of whom did not pass their craft on to younger generations.[55] Although Hunter didn't have a sophisticated knowledge of the strife in Stone County, his friendship with Ollie Gilbert (in particular) would certainly have made him aware of the controversies swirling around Driftwood and the folk center.

And while Mountain View may be unique in the degree to which cultural rifts took place there, it is not unique in its struggle to maintain an audience for traditional music. Hunter's experiences, particularly in Branson, taught him that "you can't do a straight folk program without a captive audience,"[56] words that were followed by a collective sigh on the part of his friends in Columbia. The story of the folk center mirrored that of other folk institutions, especially festivals that were in a constant struggle for survival. Even if Hunter's involvement with Silver Dollar City had continued, the Ozark Folk Festival would always be at the center of his musical universe.

The Branson chapter now at a close, Hunter would spend the next decade focused not only on the festival at Eureka Springs but also on running events closer to home. In August 1976, fresh on the heels of his falling out with Silver

Dollar City, Hunter threw his creative energy into a monthly folk music series at the Springfield Art Museum. The concerts would receive support through a matching grant from the Missouri Arts Council, and Hunter, having never before applied for a grant, was likely steered through the process by Becky Schroeder, who was simultaneously applying for folk music funding for University of Missouri programs.

In preparation for the museum series, the local paper published Hunter's call for auditions, which included his now-familiar stipulation that "electrified or amplified instruments, folk-rock or rock music will not be considered." Clearly in control mode after the Silver Dollar experience, Hunter requested that anyone who wanted to perform should write to him directly.[57] According to the Missouri Arts Council minutes from May 1977, the first year of concerts was a resounding success; concertgoers did not need to pay admission and there were "overflow audiences."[58]

On the heels of this positive trend, Hunter and the museum received another grant for the following season, and in February 1977 there was again a call for talent. This time the local paper emphasized that Hunter was "insisting on historical authenticity" for festival performers, and it blacklisted precisely 151 songs to be avoided at all costs. The journalist who put out the article also dutifully noted that the Springfield Museum folk series had now made it onto the Library of Congress's festival list as well as that of the National Folk Festival Association. In this same interview, Hunter boasted of having "85 different acts, over 200 fiddlers and about 300 individuals" at his programming fingertips.[59] All of this braggadocious energy seemed to emanate directly from his thwarted ambitions at Silver Dollar City. Although the reasons are unclear, there is no record of Hunter having put in a grant request for year three, but it seems likely that he had bitten off more than he could chew, given his ongoing directorship of the Ozark Folk Festival and his full-time refrigeration sales work.

The Branson episode now behind him, by the late 1970s Hunter was well integrated into the Ozarks folk music world, and his easy manner on stage won him master of ceremonies gigs for other local and regional events. He sporadically gave folksong presentations at the University of Missouri–Columbia under the auspices of his friends the Schroeders. In addition, he organized and often hosted several folk music events at Missouri State University in Springfield, perhaps the most significant of which was the fifth annual Ozark Folk Festival in April 1977. It is there that Art Galbraith and Gordon McCann made one of their first appearances together under the name Art's Country Pickers, a performance that would lead to many others in the ensuing years.[60]

## Working with McCann

During the early 1980s, continued musical collaborations with Gordon Mc-
Cann led to yet another musical endeavor: the organizing of fiddle contests both in Springfield and in Eureka Springs. It was hardly surprising that
Hunter would take an interest in this type of activity; Missouri fiddling (in
all its regional variation) has gained just as much attention in the Ozarks as
folksong collecting and performance, and Hunter himself was an erstwhile
collector of tunes.[61] In the spring of 1983, Hunter hired McCann as emcee
and Art Galbraith as one of the contest judges for a Springfield contest. These
competitions were initially designed to scout out talent for the Ozark Folk
Festival, and they often took place just days before the festival.

But while both of these Springfield businessmen shared a love of traditional
music, they did not always see eye to eye. According to the younger McCann,
Hunter—suddenly outside his area of expertise—had some unrealistic notions about how to run a fiddle contest, and this made for an uneasy working
relationship. Notes from McCann's field journals regarding the first contest
Hunter himself organized in April 1983 described some misconceptions on
the part of his Springfield neighbor. In his enthusiasm for Ozarks music,
Hunter initially chose to spread the fiddle competitions over three or four
days when there were barely enough contestants for two. Given the dictates
of their work schedules, the best fiddlers were rarely available to compete
until Saturday morning, but nothing McCann or Galbraith could say would
change Hunter's mind.[62] Not surprisingly, this first contest was a desultory
affair that attracted too few contestants and not enough talent.[63] The last fiddle
contest Hunter organized was in April 1987, and although it was shortened
by a day, the results were much the same. But despite the frustrations that
arose around this unsuccessful venture, McCann ultimately emerged as a
supporter of Hunter's song preservation work actively advocating for the
digitization of the ballad collection.[64]

McCann and Galbraith were hardly the first individuals to encounter
Hunter's stubborn streak. While Hunter's purist standards served him ad-
mirably as a ballad collector, they often got in the way of his success with
event organizing, which clearly required more flexible thinking. Meanwhile,
things were beginning to go less than smoothly with the Ozark Folk Festival;
Hunter had begun to express his frustration with the Ozark Folk Festival
while in the company of Dolf and Becky Schroeder, whom he could rely
upon to listen without casting judgment. "This is the first time in over the 10
years that I've had the program that I've run into any trouble at all," he told
them. But Hunter was increasingly locking horns with the other organizers,

likely because he had a finger in every pot.⁶⁵ If festival tasks were delegated, he was not happy with the outcome; he spoke of an overuse of spotlighting on the dancers and of the request to have taped rather than live music as their accompaniment, something he strongly opposed. Most of all, Hunter complained about the loss of spontaneity: "You can't choreograph a folk program, period. And if you try, and you rehearse it, you'll ruin it."⁶⁶

While Hunter was convinced that unstaged, unpolished musical interactions represented the true spirit of Ozarks music, there were other forces at play that would see folk music as a highly marketable commodity. Gradually, his relationship with Eureka Springs would begin to unravel as well. Hunter now embarked upon the last decade of his life, much of which would be spent looking back at his collecting work and the friendships he had made along the ballad trail. Regardless of the musical ground shift that was inevitably taking place under his feet, if not for the existence of the Ozark Folk Festival, Hunter would never have experienced a lifetime of conversation with both community and academic scholars, all of whom gave him a heightened perspective on the significance of his chosen avocation.

# 11

# ONE EYE ON THE PAST AND ONE ON THE FUTURE

## Local Recognition

Although his collecting days were now over, Hunter was far from idle. In fact, he had become something of a local celebrity, a phenomenon he liked to poke fun at. It is around this time that he received a letter from Eldorado, Arkansas, addressed to "Max Hunter/Folk Singer/Springfield, MO." "It got delivered to me like that," remarked Hunter. "Springfield is not a small town. It's over 100,000 population. I thought it was very nice that the post office department knew who I was, where I lived and could deliver that to me."[1] Then there was the woman who sent him a bunch of Bible scriptures about the world coming to an end and wanted Hunter to broadcast them everywhere he went. But perhaps the most unusual communication he received was from a local Springfield woman who wanted to collaborate on an opera: "She had been in the theatrical business for years and had a stage name. . . . She thought we could put together a folk opera and make 100 Jillion Dollars. Also, she said that her mother had composed the 'Kitty Wells' [song],[2] and she give me . . . all sorts of copy right dates that she supposedly had received."[3]

But aside from attracting the occasional eccentric, being in the community's public eye meant more opportunities to draw attention to the songs he had collected. One of these opportunities came in the form of an event in which Hunter was invited to speak to about one thousand high school students in their gym. One unidentified woman who attended this program said that it was quite memorable: "He [Hunter] was gonna sing two songs. There wasn't a sound in that whole building. They [the students] kept watching him and he sang for thirty minutes. The bell rang—the principal, the teachers, nobody moved. He said he wasn't a singer, but *boy* he captured those kids!"[4]

In addition to the preservation efforts already made on Hunter's behalf by the Library of Congress, interest in his ballad work had also reached Massachusetts professor Frederick Danker, who would spend innumerable hours sifting through Hunter materials at the Springfield–Greene County Library while researching the life and music of Ollie Gilbert and other Hunter sources.

An active schedule of public presentations filled the time Hunter had previously spent out in the field, and he could now enjoy the accolades and local recognition that came after twenty years of ballad hunting. During an interview with Cathy Barton in 1981, a year after Vance Randolph's passing, Hunter proclaimed, "For all purposes, I am through collecting and I'm satisfied with what I did and I think Vance Randolph probably paid the best compliment. . . . He said that he thought that between [what] Belden had collected and what I collected that he didn't think there needed to be any more. . . . There is enough work for a lifetime."[5]

The remarkably prolific and topically wide-ranging work of writer and photojournalist Ernie Deane—who in terms of productivity and approachability was a sort of Studs Terkel of the Ozarks—ran an "Ozarks Country" column for years in a variety of local papers. This column was instrumental to keeping his friend's accomplishments in the public eye. In 1980 Deane, who enjoyed keeping company with a number of prominent folklorists and musicians, wrote a clear-eyed overview of Hunter's achievement, saying, "Max started his collecting efforts just in time, considering that the Ozarks region began to undergo major changes after World War II. . . . Most of what he collected cannot be obtained today first-hand, because so many of his sources are dead."[6] Spearheaded by Dolf Schroeder, documentation of Hunter's work (as well as that of Loman Cansler) continued into the 1980s as part of the Missouri Origins Project and included a number of in-depth interviews with Hunter both at home and at historic sites such as Arrow Rock and Wilson Creek National Battlefield.[7]

On December 4, 1981, both Hunter and Cansler appeared on the same program at the Springfield–Greene County Library, something that would happen with increasing frequency given their mutual connection to the Schroeders.[8] In 1983 Hunter and Cansler received indirect accolades when the Schroeders sent Alan Jabbour, now director of the American Folklife Center, copies of the Missouri Origins interviews. In reply, Jabbour wrote, "It was a pleasure for me to see the two videotapes you have created, sensitively documenting the contributions and personal reflections of two distinguished Missouri folklorists. . . . Such collectors, arising not from the academy but from the grassroots, are an important part of the folklore and folklife movement."[9]

Out of sheer happenstance, Hunter began his work at a critical moment in musical history and surrounded himself with people whose academic work would bring much-needed attention to a fast-disappearing element of Ozark culture. Author Ted Anthony aptly described the energy at work during the late 1950s and early 1960s, when people like Mary Celestia Parler were "sending batches of students out from the sprawling university campus in Fayetteville to interview aging Ozarkers and preserve their stories for a modern age. This moment . . . was pivotal in developing connections between young university students and the older parts of the culture around them, and courses like Parler's were Petri dishes for the creativity fueling the rising folk revival."[10] The same could be said of Joan O'Bryant, who instilled a similar passion for fieldwork in her students. Emanating from John Lomax's nationwide documentation work in the early twentieth century onward,[11] there was a constant exchange of ideas between song collectors and folk music revivalists.[12]

Thanks to Dolf and Becky Schroeder's keen interest in ballad scholarship, in combination with the publication of several Missouri Folklore Society papers devoted to this topic, the collecting work of both Hunter and Cansler received increasing statewide attention. In 1986 both men were the recipients of the Missouri Folklore Society Award for Distinguished Achievement, and their friends the Schroeders—who held both men's ballad collections in equally high esteem—were instrumental in these nominations. Had Cansler lived seven more years, it seems likely that he and Hunter would have shared yet another late-life award. [13]

## Lost Landscapes

No longer in the field, it was now Hunter's turn to ring the death knell on the harvesting of traditional material, and by this time one look at the changing Ozark landscape would give his words more weight:

> When I first started collecting there wasn't any Tablerock Dam, wasn't any Beaver Dam, wasn't any Truman Dam, wasn't any Stockton Dam, wasn't any of these things and by the nature of building a dam you have to cover up the most beautiful part of the country and that's where

people lived and many of the people I collected from in the beginning had to move because the water has taken their home site. And when they move they don't live like they did. . . . I think you would have a hard time if you start out today . . . collecting a song that hasn't already been collected. . . . I don't think you would find any Fred Highs and Ollie Gilberts and Allie Parkers and Donnie Hammontrees—I don't think they exist anymore.[14]

Indeed, singers such as Goldie Schott and Allie Long Parker, among several others, had to relocate when engineers created Beaver Lake.[15]

Despite how he made his living, Hunter readily admitted that the prevalence of air-conditioning in particular was bad news for the perpetuation of oral tradition: "Nowadays people come in and the house is all closed up. . . . Your neighbor can die and you don't know it until you read it in the paper, where they buried him yesterday. . . . There were a few, very few music parties still being held."[16]

In saying these words, Hunter consciously echoed the thoughts of his mentor: "I am of the same opinion as Randolph[,] who once stated, 'the bulldozer is after us, and I'll be damned if I don't think he's overtaking us.'"[17] The bulldozer was not an abstract notion for Hunter, as he noted on one of his *Visits With* tapes: "There's a machine right in the back of the house . . . cutting new roads through a new development, and there's nothing I can do about it."[18] Another time when he was traveling between the houses of two banjo-playing brothers, Charlie and Barry Horton of Marshall, Arkansas, Hunter also made mention of road graders that were in the midst of permanently altering the landscape.[19]

## Surrounded by Scholars

It would be inaccurate to characterize Hunter as a Luddite given that he took an active interest in the development and improvement of recording technologies. However, as time went on, he became increasingly pessimistic about societal changes. In addition to environmental changes, mass media also factored into the wearing away of oral traditions, and Hunter blamed much of this cultural forgetfulness on the influence of television: "So, I'd say between TVs and water, this Ozark has changed a lot."[20] During interviews Hunter often made light of his accomplishments as a collector: "I had more fun and made more friends than I guess anybody ever will."[21] But there can be little doubt that as his musical pastime extended over decades, his sense of being on a cultural mission deepened.

Once quoted as saying "I think you can be too educated,"[22] Hunter would continue to express himself in rambling, run-on sentences and mixed tenses throughout his adult life, while at the same time garnering the greatest admiration from the academicians who would eventually surround him. Once when asked for advice on collecting, he responded, "Well, don't read any books, to start with."[23] And despite his affection for some of his more bookish friends, Hunter's attitude toward higher education and his own unfinished schooling would remain ambivalent throughout his life. As an endnote to materials donated to the Springfield–Greene County Library, Hunter criticized academics for making overgeneralizations about the Ozark population. "It seems, to me, they [academics] have not been able to experience the 'day by day' life style of our natives. They seem to study one or two persons and use that to fit us all," wrote Hunter,[24] who was capable of making the same sweeping judgments.

While on the surface Hunter seemed to take considerable pride in keeping *outside* the ivory tower, one of his proudest moments was hearing from a graduate student named Fern Denise Gregory. Enrolled at Central Missouri State University, Gregory was writing a thesis titled "Selected Child Ballad Tunes in the Max Hunter Collection of Ozark Folksongs."[25] She wanted to interview Hunter and was requesting his formal permission to use materials from the Springfield–Greene County Library. As described in Gregory's abstract, "The purpose of this thesis is to transcribe in musical notation selected Child Ballad tunes from the taped collection. Thirty-eight songs in ninety-one versions are contained herein."[26] And further on in her preface, summoning the music-first approach of Bertrand H. Bronson: "The importance of the ballad tune cannot be overestimated. . . . In a ballad the tune and the text are inseparable, for to really understand one it is necessary to include the other."[27]

But Gregory, like Bronson and many others before her, would find herself considerably challenged. "Many of the tunes are modal, monophonic, and are in a 'gapped' or pentatonic scale," she observed, and she followed in Hunter's purist footsteps when it came to musical transcription: "In the interests of preserving authenticity no attempt has been made to 'correct' any notes."[28] Gregory was in complete agreement with Bronson when she said that "music notation is 'desperately clumsy.'"[29] While listening to Hunter's recordings, this classically trained musician was both intrigued and bewildered by the music she encountered: "Rhythm does not often follow a strict pattern of regular beats and words are musically accented in manners that may sound strange to the schooled musician. . . . The freedom and fluidity of rhythmic meter, though difficult to capture in notation, are part of the charm of these folksongs."[30] Indeed, Gregory found rich academic fodder in the Hunter Collection.[31]

## What Really Mattered

By 1986, copies of many of the materials from the Max Hunter Collection were archived alongside those of Loman Cansler as part of the Schroeder Collection at the State Historical Society of Missouri in Columbia. So while Hunter's original reel-to-reel tapes, audiocassettes, and related documents remained at the Springfield-Greene, copies of these materials also continued to be disseminated elsewhere, including the dubbed tapes previously made by Mary Celestia Parler for the University of Arkansas.

All of this attention by local institutions reached its apex when, in December 1997, Hunter received a letter from Flora Maria Garcia of the Missouri Arts Council announcing that he was one of five recipients selected for the state's highest honor: the Missouri Arts Award.[32] The award ceremony was held on February 4 in Jefferson City, where Hunter and his family found themselves in the company of Governor Mel Carnahan, among other local dignitaries. "He [Hunter] was sick then and on oxygen, but he made the trip and accepted the award," recalled his daughter Linda.[33]

Now in failing health due to a lifetime of heavy smoking, it's unclear how much any of this fanfare mattered to the collector. As Springfield journalist Sara J. Bennett wrote on the heels of the ceremony, "The biggest reward for Hunter is hearing from people like the woman in Florida who discovered her grandmother [Olive Coberley] singing on one of his tapes, then played it for her own children." Hunter told Bennett, "You couldn't give me any amount of money for the things that these people have told me."[34] While he continued to take pleasure in recounting days gone by, Hunter had seemingly made peace with the end of the Ozark ballad trail: "I quit because there is nothing else out there anymore."[35] It was that simple.

That same year, in a follow-up to the arts award, Missouri State University music professors Michael and Kathleen Murray began the gargantuan process of digitizing the Max Hunter Folk Song Collection with an eye toward preserving its contents and making them universally accessible on the internet. This was not for the faint of heart; the Murrays began with no less than forty reel-to-reel tapes, and each tape was accompanied by the typewritten lyrics provided by Hunter and his daughter Jenny Sweet. First off, they needed to convert the original sound recordings to digital audiotape, after which the

DAT files would be transferred to compact discs. Murray and his team then created a searchable web page for each and every song, complete with the song title, the name of the singer, and the date and place it was recorded.[36]

Following in the footsteps of Gregory's Child ballad excursion, Kathleen Murray would have the most time-consuming task of all; since Hunter did not write down the tunes of the songs, it was Murray's job to create musical notation. As described by her husband, Mike, early on in the project, "Our transcriber takes an average of about an hour per song. We're being very meticulous and true to what's actually on the tapes." Murray herself used measured words to describe her grueling process: "It can be made much more interesting by the fact that lots of these songs have many verses and the verses aren't always sung the exact same way, so I get to put lots of footnotes on the finished product, so that we stay as true as possible to the original."[37] In the end, the Murrays would complete musical notation for 400 out of the 1,592 ballads in the collection before this part of the project was abandoned. Mike Murray later reasoned that there is no need for the written transcriptions, since the university used streaming audio to make the music readily accessible.

In the process of digitizing Hunter's collection, the Missouri State music department also struggled with how to handle the potentially offensive lyrics found in the Hunter Collection and finally came up with the following disclaimer: "Some of the songs date back several hundred years. Consequently, the lyrics of the songs represent the language, ideas, and prejudices of earlier eras and in some cases are blatantly offensive. Missouri State University does not endorse or condone the offensive language contained in these songs and provides this website only as a platform for the preservation and study of historical artifact."[38]

## The Next Generation

Assisting the Murrays with the Hunter tapes was a talented young grad student named Mark Bilyeu, who came from a long line of Christian and Taney County fiddle and banjo players. Working with the Max Hunter Folk Song Collection was a motivating experience for Bilyeu, who would later record his own interpretations of several of these Ozark ballads along with his wife, Cindy Woolf. Assisting with the collection gave Bilyeu a new sense of purpose. "I began to realize that I had this rich heritage behind me," Bilyeu commented during a videotaped profile of his family.[39] "I didn't realize how fortunate I was, and I wanted to know more about it. Collecting and preserving [traditional music] became a passion of mine."[40] Digitization was a critical step toward bringing Hunter's collection to the attention of the outside world.

Although a decade back, Springfield native Julie Henigan had opined that "relatively few people in the Ozarks—or the United States as a whole— still sing narrative songs,"[41] it would be more accurate to say that the digital transmission of previously discovered materials has caused a shift in the demographics of those who perform these materials. Ballad singers, while no longer firsthand sources, are frequently the urban or suburban offspring and, more often, the grand-offspring of folk revivalists, and unlike the majority of Hunter's torchbearers, these sons and daughters deliberately go about educating themselves through means other than oral transmission. There is also the unspoken expectation that musical performers of old songs and tunes should be scholars in the traditions they present.

Perhaps no one is as loyal a fan of Hunter's collecting efforts as vocalist and arts educator Judy Domeny Bowen of Rogersville, Missouri. Born in 1961, Bowen was always the first person to borrow the tapes from the Springfield–Greene County Library. Whenever a new one arrived, she would bring it home "and record from one cassette recorder to another" so as to have her own personal copies.[42] The songs Hunter had collected made a deep and lasting impression on her: "I would write down the words or take the tape player out to the garden while doing weeding. I could spend all day pulling weeds and singing songs. They helped me pass the time."[43]

Bowen's eager trips to the library and the formative hours she spent appreciating and learning his recordings is precisely what Hunter had in mind when he decided not to leave his collection to a university. In a 1979 interview with Cathy Barton, whose early discussions with Hunter provided the groundwork for much of this book, Hunter declared, "There's two things I'm proud of: I've never been run off by anyone, anywhere. I've made lots of friends. Another thing is that all this stuff is going in the library. . . . It ought to be out where people can get hold of it."[44]

Bowen first sang for Hunter in the mid-seventies, during an audition for his Springfield Art Museum series. "I did 'The Old Armchair' and 'The Blind Child,' and I got fifteen dollars!" she recalled with great pleasure. Although she worked with him only a few times, she got much of the inspiration for her two albums, *Yesterday's News* and *Calling Me Back: Folk Songs of the Ozarks*, from his collection. While sharing the stage with Hunter in 1983, Bowen gave a performance of one of her favorites, "The Lightning Express," first telling the audience that she had learned it from a lady who had learned it from her own mother. According to Bowen, as a young girl the singer of this ballad would conceal her face under a "bonnet and stand facing out the window, so her mother couldn't see the tears rolling down her cheeks."[45] In 1998 Bowen wrote a paper in which she made mention of several ballads from the Hunter Collection and examined her penchant for tragic storylines:

> The songs I liked best were the sad ones such as "Mary of the Wild Moor," "Babes in the Woods," "Barbry Allen," "The Brown Girl," "Little Blind Child," and "The Lightning Express." As a result, my repertoire today is heavy with sad songs. I liked them for their plaintive melodies. I liked them because they tugged at my heartstrings while the funnier songs once sung had no lingering meaning. Ballads have substance.
>
> Sometimes people ask me how I can sing so many sad songs and not make myself depressed. The songs have never depressed me, just interested me.[46]

Hunter understood that the next generation might take little or no interest in the songs that had been passed down from their elders: "When Fred High died his sons could[n't] care less about what he did."[47] And then there was the disappearance of Emma Dusenbury as experienced by Hunter: "We went down there—Joanie, Mary and I—trying to find her grave. We couldn't even find anybody that had ever heard of her; never knew she was around there. We asked, oh, I don't know how many places—the store, the post office, a filling station. . . . They thought that was a bunch of foolishness, singing those old songs like that."[48] The Dusenbury story was important to Hunter (as well as other folklorists) not only because his friend Vance Randolph had collected from her,[49] but also because it epitomized, in the most poignant way imaginable, the ephemeral nature of song transmission and the many ways in which song bearers were brushed aside rather than valued. As written so effectively in Robert Cochran's meditation "All the Songs in the World," "The scholars came in 1936 with their recording machines, and went away again, while Emma Dusenbury lived on in the same bonegrinding poverty until she died forgotten five years later and was buried by the county."[50]

It is practically indisputable that the old ways of oral transmission have died off, along with the people who sang for Hunter. But nowadays it would be a mistake to say that interest in Anglo-American balladry is dead. In fact, in recent years this interest has culminated in a weeklong event called Trad-Mad, in which ballad singers from the United States as well as "across the pond" gather in Plymouth, Massachusetts, to celebrate their love of the old gems, as well as a popular traditional song weekend in Becket, Massachusetts, specifically designed for young folksingers. Similar gatherings now take place across the country.

While today's singers often learn their material from digital sources rather than immediate family or community members, the digital age has created a veritable explosion of interest in balladry, so it is perhaps best to look at the shift in the conveyors of tradition rather than to mourn its complete disappearance. *Missouri Folklore Society Journal* editor Lyn Wolz, of the University of Kansas, who compiled the invaluable "Anglo-American Folk Music in Missouri: An Annotated Bibliography," once described Listservs "that function as online communities of scholars,"[51] and there are now several digital resources, too numerous to mention, for apprentice musicians in search of inspiration and instruction.

Writing lyrically on the life of ballads, Bertrand Bronson observed, "Vitality of tradition is to be measured by the amount of re-creative energy flowing into tradition at a particular time or place. Tradition is not a constant, nor should it be thought of as something strong at the outset and becoming always weaker, like the diminishing reverberations of a bell. . . . Like everything subject to growth and decay, it runs an uneven course."[52] As I write these words, many a bleary-eyed fiddler and ballad singer (a number of whom are the grandchildren of folk revivalists) is returning home from starry-night summer sessions at camps and traditional music gatherings all across the country.

In addition to changes in how songs are acquired and in the lifestyles of those who acquire them, current performers of both ballads and tunes are now expected to be authorities in the traditions they present. This is certainly true of the Shortleaf Band, a duo that tours under the auspices of the Missouri Arts Council and whose repertoire is centered on the Scots/Irish influence in the Ozarks region.[53] Both Michael Fraser (an apprentice of the late fiddler Bob Holt[54]) and Tenley Hansen do far more than sing and play; they provide the provenance of their selections while simultaneously educating audiences about the difference between old-time and bluegrass music.

Shortleaf, and bands of a similar ilk, often appear at the Old Time Music, Ozark Heritage Festival in West Plains, Missouri, a two-day event that got its start in 1995 and focuses on performers who are connected through cross-generational mentorships, such as those of the late Bob Holt and apprentice fiddlers David Scrivner and Ashley Hull Forrest, both of whom enjoy musical friendships with Gordon McCann. Although Hunter never had the chance to attend, several of his friends have, including the late Cathy Barton, Dave Para, and Judy Domeny Bowen, who still functions as emcee. Most significantly, several of the festival's singers, from Cindy Woolf and Mark Bilyeu to Kim Lansford, often invoke the Max Hunter Folk Song Collection when naming their sources.[55] In short, traditional music and song still have a significant presence in Missouri.

A survey of young folk artists in the Ozarks reveals a trend toward those who position themselves under the "roots" or "Americana" umbrella, thus avoiding the "folk" label altogether and allowing for unusual instrumentation and the occasional composition of ballads "in the spirit" of traditional material. The One More Dollar band, near West Plains, Missouri,[56] plays self-proclaimed "Ozarkana" music and sings ballads rooted in the 1920s and 1930s string band esthetic—music that would please their grandparents—while the collective expertise of the Ozark Highballers, out of Fayetteville, Arkansas,[57] encompasses nothing less than "classic" banjo techniques, pre–World War II harmonica styles, and the crafting of parlor guitars. Everyone is an expert in something, and most of these performers also describe themselves as "storytellers" or "folklorists." While it is useless to speculate how Hunter would have felt about the appearance of cellos and violas in folk trios and Gillian Welch wannabes, this expanded folk genre is a vibrant way forward for the old songs and tunes.

As for Hunter himself, his observations about musical acquaintances and their activities rarely made it onto paper, one exception being his short-lived folklore column for a Springfield publication. "Not too long ago," Hunter wrote, "one of the fellows that has something to do with the publishing of this magazine, called and wanted to know if I would be interested in writing an article about . . . interesting people and places, in the Ozarks."[58] In so doing, Hunter would briefly join the ranks of the many folklorists and cultural observers/promoters (Deane, Randolph, Rayburn, and McCord among them) who used their literary abilities to draw attention to their fieldwork and the Ozark region.[59] But Hunter was hardly a man of letters: "I told him, 'I ain't no writer.' He said, if I'd write the article, he'd take out all of the mistakes. That sounded like a fair enough offer, so if you find any mistakes, blame them on *him*."[60] Despite streaks of obstinacy and hubris, Hunter understood where he stood in the larger community of ballad chasers. With obvious admiration, Anthony wrote the following about him:

> Hunter's field work contained an elegant symmetry. The traveling salesman is an American archetype. . . . [Yet] Hunter was the opposite of the anonymous suit who entered a town and built only the relationships he needed to sell his wares. He wanted to know the people in these communities, to understand their lives and the way they told their stories. He was sowing enthusiasm—not merely for refrigerators but for folks' own culture, too.[61]

Hunter's attachment to the ineffable qualities behind the song is what drove him, and it's what led me to the writing of this book. In Hunter's words, "I don't think you can compose a folk song . . . because to me a folk song has to go through something. I don't know what it is. It's got to go through part of an oral tradition to get to be a folk song."[62]

## A Quiet Funeral

After all the excitement of the Missouri awards ceremony in 1998, Hunter began to grow increasingly ill from emphysema. Gordon McCann, having worked alongside Hunter during many local events, described the song collector's last public appearance at the Ozarks Celebration Festival held at Southwest Missouri State University. "What all had expected to be a brief appearance because of his failing health, became a full forty-five minute program in true Hunter style," McCann wrote shortly after this event, which took place August 29, 1998.[63] Hunter died on November 8, 1999, at the age of seventy-eight, just short of his sixtieth wedding anniversary and two months short of the year 2000, which, according to daughter Jenny, he so much wanted to see.[64] He died in the same town where he spent his entire life, with the exception of the one year he spent in California as a refrigeration machinist for the U.S. Navy,[65] a year that he rarely mentioned but that earned him military honors at his burial.

Oddly, there is no mention of any music having been played or songs having been sung at Hunter's memorial service. Linda Bangs did share one discomfiting moment from the time of her father's passing: two weeks after her father's death, Congressman Roy Blunt and representatives from the Library of Congress summoned her family to the newly constructed branch of the Springfield–Greene County Library, which had just opened: "They sprung it on us. . . . All of a sudden, here on this huge screen was Daddy."[66] The video Bangs was referring to was that of Hunter at Arrow Rock and was part of the Missouri Origins Project. After the viewing, Bangs told Congressman Blunt that although she and her mother appreciated what the Library of Congress was doing, the timing of the video was unfortunate.[67] It upset the entire family, whose least concern at that moment was to celebrate the life of their father as a public figure. Later, Bangs was further distressed to find out that her father's materials—some of which had been duplicated and some not—had been "spread out between everywhere. I wish they'd just picked one place. If I'd had my druthers, I would have liked it to stay here [in Springfield]."[68]

It is perhaps best to leave this biography of Hunter a decade earlier, in the year 1987, while he was hosting the fortieth year of the Ozark Folk Festival. A homemade videotape displayed a combination of stand-up comedian and historian with a folksy manner, who was at the apex of his life as a collector and promoter of old songs.[69] A sparsely haired, slight man of energetic manner, meticulously dressed in a plaid shirt, string tie, and perfectly pressed khaki trousers, Hunter made his way on and off the stage at strategic moments—surrounded by his beloved hay bales, Ozark cloggers in flouncy dresses, fiddlers, hammered dulcimers, and ballad singers of his own choosing.

Hunter continued to entertain audiences with his stories and to educate them about Ozark songs until his final days, and the journalists who listened for notes of regret found few or none. In the Arrow Rock interview that was aired during the celebration of his life at the Springfield-Greene, Hunter said,

Sketch of Hunter by artist Laura Cansler. (Courtesy of the Springfield–Greene County Library)

"You gotta stop somewhere. You can't keep collecting your whole life. . . . I don't find any remorse about it. I did what I wanted to do."[70] But in all the words written about Max Hunter before and after his passing, the statement read by then-governor Mel Carnahan during the Missouri Arts Council Awards ceremony remains the most meaningful to his family: "When Max came calling, people sang, and a dying culture lived again."[71] In a memoir addressed to her own children, Linda Bangs agreed, writing, "I think it says everything there is to say."[72] Well, perhaps not *everything*.

# NOTES

## Abbreviations

| | |
|---|---|
| AAFS/AFC | Archive of American Folk Song (Archive of Folk Culture) |
| Cansler Collection | Loman D. and Laura M. Cansler Collection |
| CALS | Central Arkansas Library Systems |
| Danker Tapes | Frederick Danker Tapes |
| MHC | Max Hunter Collection |
| MHFS | Max Hunter Folk Song Collection |
| McCann Collection | Gordon McCann Collection |
| MFS | Missouri Folklore Society |
| MFSR | Missouri Folklore Society Records |
| MOP | Missouri Origins Project |
| MSU-Springfield | Missouri State University Special Collections and Archives, Springfield |
| O'Bryant Collection | Joan O'Bryant Kansas Folklore Collection |
| OFC | Ozark Folksong Collection |
| ROH | Rackensack Oral Histories |
| Schroeder Collection | Adolf E. and Rebecca Schroeder Collection |
| SHSM | State Historical Society of Missouri |
| *Visits With* | *Visits from the Ozarks* CD collection |
| WFC | John Quincy Wolf Folklore Collection |

## Foreword

1. A detailed account of the complicated Ledbetter/Lomax arrangements is Charles Wolfe and Kip Lornell, *The Life and Legend of Leadbelly* (New York: HarperCollins, 1992). See especially chapters 15–19 (and the opening pages of chapter 21 for Richard Wright's blistering critique). For Thomas's presentation of Day in the context of the wider folk festival movement, see Michael Ann Williams, *Staging Tradition* (Urbana: University of Illinois Press, 2006). The collector/impresario told her own story in *The Traipsin' Woman* (New York: E. P. Dutton, 1933).

2. Abrahams's *A Singer and Her Songs: Almeda Riddle's Book of Ballads* was published in 1970 by Louisiana State University Press. Glassie's 1960s fieldwork with Ola Belle Reed, *Ola Belle Reed and Southern Mountain Music on the Mason-Dixon Line*, was issued (with remastered audio and more recent research by Clifford Murphy and Douglas Dowling Peach) by Dust-To-Digital in 2015. Ives's *Larry Gorman: The Man Who Made the Songs* was published in 1964 by Indiana University Press; his *Joe Scott: The Woodsman-Songmaker* appeared in 1978 from the University of Illinois Press. An excellent early study of a family tradition is Carl Fleischauer and Alan Jabbour, eds., *The Hammons Family: A Study of a West Virginia Family's Traditions* (booklet and two-LP discs, AFS L65-L66) (Washington, DC: Archive of Folk Culture, American Folklife Center, Library of Congress, 1973). An updated version of the booklet was published online in 2018. For an Ozark family tradition, see Robert Cochran, *Singing in Zion: Music and Song in the Life of An Arkansas Family* (Fayetteville: University of Arkansas Press, 1999).

3. W. K. McNeil, Introduction to Vance Randolph, *Ozark Folksongs* (Columbia: University of Missouri Press, 1980). The discussion of Hunter is on pages 20–21. Randolph's reputation has too long overshadowed the achievement of Mary Parler. McNeil himself, despite the overall excellence of his survey, grossly underrates Parler by noting that she "gathered numerous folksongs, as well as other types of folklore, from her students at the University of Arkansas." Parler was not Belden; she was (like Hunter, whose tapes she sometimes dubbed) an active field collector in her own right. Her collection has been made available online by the Special Collections Division at the University of Arkansas Library (https://digitalcollections.uark.edu/digital/collection/OzarkFolkSong). For background on Parler, see Rachel Reynolds, "Mary Celestia Parler (1904–1981): Folklorist and Teacher," in Cherisse Jones-Branch and Gary T. Edwards, eds., *Arkansas Women: Their Lives and Times* (Athens: University of Georgia Press, 2018).

4. John A. Lomax, *Adventures of a Ballad Hunter* (New York: Macmillan, 1947).

5. Stephen Petrus and Ronald D. Cohen, *New York and the American Folk Music Revival* (Oxford, UK: Oxford University Press, 2015); Chris Strachwitz and Alex Machado, *Hear Me Howling! Blues, Ballads & Beyond, As Recorded by the San Francisco Bay by Chris Strachwitz in the 1960s* (El Cerrito, CA: Arhoolie Productions, 2010). Arhoolie Records was acquired by Smithsonian Folkways Recordings in 2016.

James P. Leary, ed., *Folksongs of Another America: Field Recordings from the Upper Midwest, 1937–1946* (Madison: University of Wisconsin Press, 2015).

6. Nicholas Dawidoff, *In the Country of Country: A Journey to the Roots of American Music* (New York: Random House, 1998).

7. Booth Campbell and Frank Campbell, interviewed by Merlin Mitchell on March 16, 1950. Ozark Folksong Collection (reel 41, item 4), Division of Special Collections, University of Arkansas Library, https://digitalcollections.uark.edu/digital/collection/ OzarkFolkSong/id/3451/. Parler is listed as the transcriber, but in fact no transcript is provided.

8. Abrahams's apt description of Randolph appeared in his blurb for the reissue of Randolph's *The Ozarks: An American Survival of Primitive Society* by the University of Arkansas Press in 2017 (originally published by Vanguard Press in 1931).

## Preface

1. Joshua Heston, *State of the Ozarks* online newsletter, http://stateoftheozarks.net/ showcase/. Heston is based in Hollister, Missouri.

2. Caroline Paton (1932–2019) was a much-loved singer of traditional and contemporary songs who, along with her husband, Sandy, cofounded Folk-Legacy Records (now part of Smithsonian Folkways Recordings). She met me with me at the Old Songs Festival in 2016 and handed me an LP of Hunter's folksongs along with the liner notes.

3. Crankies are enjoying a comeback among today's folk artists. Often backlit, they are hand-cranked "moving panoramas" made out of paper as well as other materials. Crankies come in all sizes and were popular storytelling devices in nineteenth-century Europe. For more on crankies, see Panoramacouncil.org or www.Crankiefactory. com.

## Introduction

1. For a Harvard perspective on Child's life and work, see John Burgess, "Brief Life of a Victorian Enthusiast: 1825–1896," *Harvard Magazine*, June 2006, https:// harvardmagazine.com/2006/05/francis-james-child.html.

2. Stephen D. Winick, "Francis James Child and *The English and Scottish Popular Ballads*" (Library of Congress, n.d.), https://www.loc.gov/item/ihas.200196779/.

3. Francis James Child, ed., *The English and Scottish Popular Ballads*, 5 vols., from the collection of Francis James Child by Helen Child Sargent and George Lyman Kittredge (Boston: Houghton Mifflin, 1904), https://archive.org/details/englishscottish p1904chil/page/n19/mode/2up?ref=ol&view=theater.

4. "Broadsides are songs originally printed on one side of a sheet of paper and sold for a small fee. Many of these ballads found in Anglo-American tradition are classified in G. Malcolm Laws Jr., *American Balladry from British Broadsides* (Philadelphia: American Folklore Society, 1957). Stylistically, these ballads are frequently compared to

tabloids, for, like them, the broadsides generally deal with sensational subjects—robberies, murders and the like being the most common themes." W. K. McNeil, liner notes to *Not Far from Here: Traditional Tales and Songs Recorded in the Arkansas Ozarks*, Arkansas Traditions NR 12559, 1981, 3–4. These songs are often of a less compelling literary quality than the Child ballads. See also G. Malcolm Laws Jr., *Native American Balladry*, revised (Philadelphia: American Folklore Society, 1964), 5.

5. For a detailed discussion of the ages and origins of the Child ballads, see chapter 4 of M.J.C. Hodgart's *The Ballads* (New York: W. W. Norton, 1962).

6. Child, *English and Scottish Popular Ballads*, xi.

7. Gordon H. Gerould, *The Ballad of Tradition*, reprint (Oxford, UK: Oxford University Press, 1957), 3. For more regarding the narrative characteristics of the Child ballads, also see Laws, *Native American Balladry*, 3–4.

8. For more on the stylistic differences between the Child ballads and ballads that were composed and circulating in the United States from the late eighteenth through the early twentieth centuries, see Laws, *Native American Balladry*, 5.

9. Even though North American field recordings of songs in foreign languages had already been made, these artifacts mostly gathered dust in the archives of the Library of Congress until they were brought into the light of day more than half a century later. James P. Leary, *Folksongs of Another America: Field Recordings from the Upper Midwest (1937–1946)* (Madison: University of Wisconsin Press, 2015).

10. Cecil Sharp (1859–1924) was a musician and folk dance promoter who established the English Folk Dance Society, which later evolved into the Country Dance and Song Society on American soil.

11. Adolf Schroeder (1916–2013), known as "Dolf" to his friends and associates, was the son of German immigrants. Described as a "cultural gem" by musician Cathy Barton, he occasionally conducted his own fieldwork in German and French communities in Missouri.

12. Adolf E. Schroeder, "Missouri Folk Song," conference paper (Jefferson City, Missouri, April 11,1980). Audiocassette, vol. AC 137, transcription box 7, C3826; Folk Song and Folklore Collection, Adolf E. and Rebecca Schroeder Collection, State Historical Society of Missouri, Columbia, Missouri (hereafter "Schroeder Collection").

13. Ibid.

14. Rebecca B. Schroeder, "Henry Marvin Belden (1865–1954)," in *Dictionary of Missouri Biography*, ed. Lawrence O. Christensen et al. (Columbia: University of Missouri Press, 1999).

15. Susan L. Pentlin and Rebecca B. Schroeder, "H. M. Belden, the English Club, and the Missouri Folk-Lore Society," *Missouri Folklore Society Journal* 8–9 (1986–1987): 1–44. https://missourifolkloresociety.truman.edu/home/missouri-folklore-studies/belden/.

16. Susan L. Pentlin, "Maude Williams Martin: Early Ballad Collector in Missouri," *Missouri Folklore Society Journal* 6–7 (1986–1987): 54, https://babel.hathitrust.org/cgi/pt?id=inu.30000108643879&view=image&seq=61&q1=rosa 1986/. Belden's hand-

written dedication to his early student's copy of the collection read: "To Mrs. Frank Martin who as Maude Williams started this whole thing more years ago than we are likely to contemplate."

17. Pentlin and Schroeder, "H. M. Belden."

18. Henry Marvin Belden, *Ballads and Songs Collected by the Missouri Folk-Lore Society*, 3rd ed. (Columbia: University of Missouri, 1940).

19. Vance Randolph and Ruth Ann Musick, "Folksong Hunters in Missouri," *Midwest Folklore* 1, no. 1 (1951): 24.

20. Greg Olsen, "Mary Alicia Owen," State Historical Society of Missouri, Columbia, Missouri (hereafter "SHSM"), Historic Missourians, n.d., https://historicmissourians.shsmo.org/historicmissourians/name/o/owen/.

21. Robert B. Cochran, *Louise Pound: Scholar, Athlete, Feminist Pioneer* (Lincoln: University of Nebraska Press, 2009).

22. Pentlin and Schroeder, "H. M. Belden."

23. Rebecca B. Schroeder (1921–2018), known as "Becky" to her friends and associates, served as general editor of the University of Missouri Press's "Missouri Heritage Readers" for two decades. Along with her husband, "Dolf" Schroeder, she was a folk music patron and organizer.

24. Belden, *Ballads and Songs*, vol. 15, no. 1, xi.

25. R. Schroeder, "Henry Marvin Belden," 52–53.

26. Norm Cohen, "Ballad Collectors in the Ozarks," in *The Ballad Collectors of North America: How Gathering Folksongs Transformed Academic Thought and American Identity*, edited by Scott B. Spencer (Lanham, MD: Scarecrow Press, 2012), 39.

27. The term "ballet" has occasionally been used in place of the word "ballad." As described by song scholar Louise Pound, "*Ballad* is derived from *ballare*, to dance, and historically means dancing song; it is associated etymologically with *ballet*, a form of dance." For her in-depth discussion on this topic, see Pound's "Poetic Origins and the Ballad." Certain of Hunter's sources kept "ballet" books, including Almeda Riddle and Allie Long Parker. As described by the editors of the "Songs and Ballads" Special Issue of the *Missouri Folklore Journal*, "Hand-written 'ballet' books . . . were cherished by individuals and families up through the 20th century." For a brief discussion of Riddle's use of the term, see linguist Ruth Finnegan's *Oral Poetry: Its Nature, Significance and Social Context*, 2nd ed. (Bloomington: Indiana University Press, 1992), as well as Riddle's, *A Singer and Her Songs: Almeda Riddle's Book of Ballads* (Baton Rouge: Louisiana State University Press, 1970). Also of note, Mary Celestia Parler compiled written ballad lyrics in a project she labeled as "An Arkansas Ballet Book" (1965), box 3, Ozark Folksong Collection, University Libraries Digital Collections and Special Collections Department, University of Arkansas, Fayetteville (hereafter "OFC").

28. Lyn A. Wolz, "Anglo-American Music in Missouri: An Annotated Bibliography," *Missouri Folklore Society Journal* 4 (1982): 59.

29. Vance Randolph (1892–1980). For a brief description of Randolph's life as a writer, collector, and Ozark observer, see Kimberly Harper, "Vance Randolph," His-

toric Missourians, SHSM, https://historicmissourians.shsmo.org/historicmissourians/name/r/randolph/. For the most authoritative exploration, see Robert Cochran, *Vance Randolph: An Ozark Life* (Chicago: University of Illinois Press, 1985).

30. Early on, Randolph published several ballads in a newspaper column nostalgically titled "The Songs Grandfather Sang." See *Ozark Folksong Transcripts: Lyric and Melodic Transcriptions of Ozark Folksongs*, OFC. These entries stimulated interest in the ballads and helped him find more materials.

31. Cochran, *Vance Randolph*, 76–77.

32. Ibid., 91.

33. Vance Randolph, *Ozark Folksongs*, revised, 4 vols. (Columbia: University of Missouri Press, 1980). For discussion of how this work was received, see Cochran, *Vance Randolph*, 181–82.

34. Ruth Ann Musick (1899–1974). Judy Prozzillo Byers, "Ruth Ann Musick—The Show-Me Mountaineer: A Missourian Adopts West Virginia," *Missouri Folklore Society Journal* 8–9 (1986–1987): 89–114.

35. Randolph and Musick, "Folksong Hunters in Missouri." Musick was also a collector, having recorded as many as 354 song texts and 117 tunes from her native Missouri before relocating to West Virginia.

36. Ibid., 24.

37. Ethel C. Simpson, "Otto Ernest Rayburn (1891–1960)," in Central Arkansas Library System (hereafter "CALS"), *Encyclopedia of Arkansas*, July 31, 2018, https://encyclopediaofarkansas.net/entries/otto-ernest-rayburn-3003/. See also "Otto Ernest Rayburn Research Materials," University Libraries Special Collections, University of Arkansas, Fayetteville, n.d., https://libraries.uark.edu/specialcollections/research/guides/folklore/Rayburn.asp/.

38. Cochran, *Vance Randolph*, 88.

39. May Kennedy McCord (1880–1979). Locally famous in Springfield as the "Queen of the Hillbillies," McCord wore a variety of hats: prolific journalist, musical performer, and radio host, to name a few.

40. For more on this Springfield journalist, see Lucile Morris Upton Papers, State Historical Society of Missouri–Columbia. https://shsmo.org/collections/women-media/biographies/upton-lucile/.

41. Randolph and Musick, "Folksong Hunters in Missouri," 27.

42. Ibid., 28.

43. Ibid., 31.

44. Ibid., 26.

45. Charles Van Ravenswaay Papers, 1841–1990, SHSM, n.d., https://collections.shsmo.org/manuscripts/columbia/c3873/.

46. N. Cohen, "Ballad Collectors in the Ozarks," 38.

47. Louise Pound, *American Ballads and Songs* (New York: Charles Scribner's Sons, 1922).

48. During his relatively brief but profoundly productive career as a folklorist, Gordon found himself caught between the institutional demands of the Library of Congress and his own attraction to field investigation as well as the mechanical challenges that came along with it. For more on Gordon's life, see Debora Kodish, *Good Friends and Bad Enemies* (Urbana: University of Illinois Press, 1986).

49. Library of Congress, "The Ethnographic Experience: Sidney Robertson Cowell in Northern California," American Folklife Center, n.d., https://www.loc.gov/collections/sidney-robertson-cowell-northern-california-folk-music/articles-and-essays/the-ethnographic-experience-sidney-robertson-cowell-in-northern-california/. See also Peter Stone, "Sidney and Henry Cowell," Association for Cultural Equity, http://www.culturalequity.org/alan-lomax/friends/cowell/.

50. Mark A. Davidson, "Recording the Nation: Folk Music and the Government in Roosevelt's New Deal, 1936–1941" (PhD. diss., University of California Santa Cruz, 2015), https://escholarship.org/content/qt7960b6qq/qt7960b6qq.pdf. From Davidson's abstract: "The network of individuals involved in these projects reads like a who's who of folklore and folk music scholarship of the era."

51. Randolph, *Ozarks: An American Survival*, 21.

52. Brooks Blevins, "Collectors of the Ozarks: Folklore and Regional Image," unpublished paper presented at the grand opening of the Ozark Folksong Collection, University of Arkansas, Fayetteville, 2015, 15.

53. Brooks Blevins, *Hill Folks: A History of Arkansas Ozarkers and Their Image* (Chapel Hill: University of North Carolina Press, 2002), 4.

54. Blevins, "Collectors of the Ozarks," 17. At the start of the twenty-first century, John Lomax, an English professor at the University of Texas, addressed what he saw as the demoralization of folklore studies as a result of new ways of thinking: "Folklore's malaise seems particularly intense in its subfield of Anglo/American folksong" (Renwick 3). He called for a revitalization of this area of study through more wideranging comparative studies, specifically through the utilization of contemporary song databases (4). His ultimate aim: "I try to hear the folksong materials' own 'voice' rather than using them as a convenient mouthpiece" (xv). See Roger deVeer Renwick, *Recentering Anglo-American Folksong: Sea Crabs and Wicked Youths* (Jackson: University Press of Mississippi, 2001).

55. Harold Bell Wright, *Shepherd of the Hills* (New York: A. L. Burt, 1907), 16.

56. Ibid.

57. Lynn Morrow and Linda Myers-Phinney, *Shepherd of the Hills Country: Tourism Transforms the Ozarks, 1880s–1930s* (Fayetteville: University of Arkansas Press, 1999), 7.

58. Blevins, "Collectors of the Ozarks."

59. The Ozark Folksong Collection was officially opened on August 28, 2015. OFC, https://digitalcollections.uark.edu/digital/collection/OzarkFolkSong. Physical materials are housed in the University of Arkansas's Special Collections Department.

60. Blevins, "Collectors of the Ozarks."

61. Max Hunter, *Pioneer Ozarker: Complex Man*, audiocassette transcript, vol. AC 16–17, C3826: Folk Song and Folklore Collection, Schroeder Collection, SHSM, 1974, 16.

62. Randolph, *Ozarks: An American Survival*, 4. As encapsulated by American studies and folklore scholar Simon Bronner, Randolph's many writings regularly offered up images of "tradition-toting residents of the storied Ozarks as America's primitive ancestors drawn from British stock," something that readers could not get enough of. Simon Bronner, *Following Tradition* (Logan: Utah State University Press, 1998), 227.

63. Gordon McCann, "Documenting Ozarks Tradition and Culture, The Gordon McCann Collection," video recording, January 22, 2010, Missouri State University Special Collections and Archives (hereafter "MSU-Springfield"), *OzarksWatch Video Magazine*.

64. Ibid.

65. Ibid.

66. Robert Cantwell, *When We Were Good* (Cambridge, MA: Harvard University Press, 1996), 38.

67. W. K. McNeil and Williams M. Clements, eds., *An Arkansas Folklore Sourcebook* (Fayetteville: University of Arkansas Press, 1992), 25.

68. Cantwell, *When We Were Good*, 36.

69. According to Bronner, the concept of "the folk" has much to do with social classifications put forth by the Grimm brothers. See Bronner, *Following Tradition*, 223.

70. Ronald Cohen, *Rainbow Quest: The Folk Revival and American Society, 1940–1970* (Amherst: University of Massachusetts Press, 2002), 113.

71. "When I arrived in St. Louis in 1967, the folk music scene could best be described as moribund," commented writer and musician Paul Stamler. For a snapshot of the folk scene in St. Louis, see Paul J. Stamler, "Freaks and Fiddle Tunes: The Early 1970s Folk Revival in St. Louis," *Missouri Folklore Society Journal* 27–28 (2015): 18–30.

72. R. Cohen, *Rainbow Quest*, 144.

73. That said, late in his collecting days Hunter claimed to have no objection to professional performers making commercial use of his songs: "There might be three or four songs that these . . . artists, have got out of my collection. . . . And they changed them a little bit, and I have no argument with them because if you are going to put a song on a strictly commercial album . . . you may have to polish it." Max Hunter, "Home Interview with Donald Lance, A. E. Schroeder, Becky Schroeder, Virginia Hunter," audiocassette transcript, vol. AC 21, C3826: Folk Song and Folklore Collection, Schroeder Collection, 1981, 3.

74. For more on variation in lyrics, see Bertrand H. Bronson, *The Ballad as Song* (Berkeley: University of California Press, 1969): "Variation in folk-song is fascinating from many points of view—psychological, sociological, and aesthetic. It raises

abundant questions of great interest, but full of teasing perplexities" (101). For the democratic and uncurated process of variant development, see also Pound, *American Ballads and Songs*, xx–xxi.

75. Laws, *Native American Balladry*. The question of what defines the *American* ballad was also explored by John A. Lomax: "I contend that American ballads that have caught the spirit of the old ballads, however they may be lacking in impersonality, in form and in finish, do exist and are being made today." John A. Lomax, "Some Types of American Folk-Song," *Journal of American Folk-Lore* 28 (1915): 1.

76. Blevins, "Collectors of the Ozarks," 12.

77. Renamed Rhodes College in 1985.

78. McNeil and Clements, *Arkansas Folklore Sourcebook*, 53.

79. Born James Morris.

80. The Southern Folk Heritage Series, consisting of seven LPs, includes an astonishing variety of field recordings made during a two-month tour of the American South in the summer of 1959. Lomax was assisted by English folk singer Shirley Collins, who later wrote a book about this experience: *America Over the Water: A Musical Journey with Alan Lomax* (London: SAF Publishers, 2004). For more on these sessions, see Alan Lomax Collection, Manuscripts, Southern Folk Heritage Series, 1978, Manuscript/Mixed Material, American Folklife Center, Library of Congress, Washington, D.C. (hereafter, "Alan Lomax Collection"), https://www.loc.gov/item/afc2004004.ms160423/.

81. Almeda Riddle, *A Singer and Her Songs: Almeda Riddle's Book of Ballads*, ed. Roger D. Abrahams and George Foss (Baton Rouge: Louisiana State University Press, 1970).

82. Alan Lomax Collection, https://www.loc.gov/collections/alan-lomax-manuscripts/?q=southern+journey/. See also Tom Piazza, *The Southern Journey of Alan Lomax* (New York: W. W. Norton, 2013).

83. Louise Pound used the term "armchair researchers" to differentiate Hunter's immediate mentor from folklorists who did not do their own collecting. As (partially) quoted from Cochran's *Vance Randolph*, "'Mr. Randolph is not just another armchair researcher or one who sits in a library. . . . He takes to the open, goes from person to person among his scattered hillfolk'" (180–81). See Louise Pound, "Absorbing Folklore through the Rind," *New York Herald Tribune, Weekly Book Review*, August 1, 1948, 4. See also Scott B. Spencer, ed., *The Ballad Collectors of North America: How Gathering Folksongs Transformed Academic Thought and American Identity* (Lanham, MD: Scarecrow Press, 2012), 38.

84. Loyal Jones, *Minstrel of the Appalachians: The Story of Bascom Lamar Lunsford* (Boone, NC: Appalachian Consortium Press, 1984), 1.

85. Hunter, "Home Interview with Donald Lance et al.," Schroeder Collection.

86. Max Hunter, "Interviewed by Cathy Barton," audiocassette transcript, vol. AC 18–19, C3826: Folk Song and Folklore Collection, Schroeder Collection, 1981, https://catalog.hathitrust.org/Record/006932738/.

87. Fiona Ritchie and Doug Orr, *Wayfaring Strangers: The Musical Voyage from Scotland and Ulster to Appalachia* (Chapel Hill: University of North Carolina Press, 2014), 185.

88. Lucy Quigley, audio recording transcript, June 3, 1958, OFC, http://digital collections.uark.edu/cdm/singleitem/collection/OzarkFolkSong/id/3411/rec/3/.

89. N. Cohen, "Ballad Collectors in the Ozarks," 43.

90. Ibid., 45.

91. For a fascinating exploration of the effects of note taking on both researcher and field subjects, see Michelle Kisliuk's chapter "Undoing Fieldwork" as well as other essays in Gregory F. Barz and Timothy J. Cooley, *Shadows in the Field: New Perspectives for Fieldwork in Ethnomusicology* (New York: Oxford University Press, 1997).

92. Max Hunter, "Introduction to His Collection," audiocassette transcript, vol. AC 44, C3826: Folk Song and Folklore Collection, Schroeder Collection, 1982.

93. Floy Huskey, "Interview by Max Hunter," audio CD, vol. 8–10, *Visits from the Ozarks,* Springfield–Greene County Library, Springfield, Missouri (hereafter "*Visits With*"), 1971.

94. Max Hunter, "Introduction to the Ozark Song Collection," in *Songs of the Ozarks,* Schroeder Collection, 1969. On February 19, 1969, Hunter recorded a lengthy tape that he called "Introduction to the Max Hunter Collection." An amalgam of several recordings, this displayed Hunter at his most ponderous and pedantic.

95. Ibid.

96. Jenny Fillmer, "1906 Lynchings Grew from Tensions, Racism: Thriving Black Community Died," *Springfield [MO] News-Leader*, April 14, 2006. One of the most vivid depictions of Jim Crow laws at work in the city of Springfield can be found in the Roper Report published by the Springfield Chamber of Commerce on September 27, 1958: "We feel that it is shameful that all human beings, regardless of color, who have the price of a meal, the price of a night's lodging, or the price of a theatre ticket can't go into anyplace of their choosing and receive the same services and treatment accorded all persons." Phillip Roper, "Roper Report," Springfield Chamber of Commerce, September 27, 1958, Missouri State University Digital Collections, Katherine Lederer Ozarks African American History Collection.

97. Harold McPherson, "Black Legends of Springfield Music," *Ozarks Watch* 2, no. 6 (2017): 59–66. See also Harold McPherson interview, audio transcript, *Ozarks Watch Video Magazine*, February 23, 2015, Missouri State University, Digital Collections. Transcript can be accessed at http://purl.missouristate.edu/library/archives/Route66/ HAROLDMCPHERSONXT.

98. For more on non-"mountain" musical traditions in Arkansas, see McNeil and Clements, *Arkansas Folklore Sourcebook*, 71–79.

99. Julie Henigan, "Ozark Ballads as Story and Song," *Missouri Folklore Society Journal* 27 (2005): 165.

100. Francis B. Gummere, *The Popular Ballad* (Boston: Houghton Mifflin, 1907). As a student of Francis Child, Professor Gummere has been criticized for his neglect of native American balladry in favor of British balladry. Belden, *Ballads and Songs,* xii.

101. Max Hunter, "Interview with Joe Walker," audio CD, vol. 11–15, *Visits With,* 1960).

102. Belden, *Ballads and Songs* (1955), xii.

103. Kaitlyn McConnell, "Julie Henigan, Authority on Ozarks and Irish Tradition," *OzarksAlive!* (blog), May 26, 2021, https://ozarksalive.com/julie-henigan-authority-on-ozarks-and-irish-tradition/.

104. Henigan, "Ozark Ballads," 159.

105. William Eden, January 11, 1960, OFC, https://digitalcollections.uark.edu/digital/collection/OzarkFolkSong/id/999/rec/1.

106. Lucile Morris Upton, "Ballad Collector Says Folklore, History Are Hard to Separate," *Springfield [MO] Daily News,* October 14, 1974, D2.

107. Sarah Jane Nelson, "The Crooked Road Meets the Conservatory," *Fiddler Magazine* (Fall 2012): 19–21.

108. Jimmy Driftwood, liner notes to *Music of the Ozarks,* National Geographic Society 703, 1972.

109. Dorothy Scarborough Papers, 1886–1938, Baylor University, Waco, Texas, March 27, 2015, http://www.baylor.edu/lib/texas/.

110. Herbert Halpert Collection (AFC 2004/008), Archive of Folk Culture, American Folklife Center, Library of Congress, Washington, D.C. (hereafter "AAFS/AFC"). See also Herbert Halpert Collection, Memorial University of Newfoundland, Queen Elizabeth II Library, Archives and Special Collections, https://www.library.mun.ca/asc/specialcollections/collections/halpert.

111. Sarah Jane Nelson, "A Salesman amidst Scholars: Ozarks Song Collector Max Hunter," *CDSS News,* 2016, 14–15.

## Chapter 1. Singing on the Way to Church

1. Max Hunter, "Festival of Missouri Folk Music and Dance," audiocassette transcript, vol. AC 8, C3826: Folk Song and Folklore Collection, Schroeder Collection, 1977.

2. Ted Anthony, *Chasing the Rising Sun: The Journey of an American Song* (New York: Simon and Schuster, 2007), 107.

3. Norm Cohen, *Folk Music: A Regional Exploration (Greenwood Guides to American Roots Music)* (Westport, CT: Greenwood Press, 2005), 110.

4. Max Hunter, "A Word about Fakelore," *Just for the Record,* September 1977, 17. According to Findagrave.com, Penelope Redfearn (Taylor) was born in 1790 in North Carolina and died in Springfield, Missouri, in 1858. https://www.findagrave.com/memorial/24618232/penelope-redfearn/.

5. Hunter, "Pioneer Ozarker," AC 16–17:17, Schroeder Collection, 1974.

6. Jonathan Fairbanks and Clyde Edwin Tuck, "Past and Present of Greene County, Missouri, ca. 1914," Springfield–Greene County Library, https://thelibrary.org/lochist/history/paspres/.

7. Ibid. This soporific tendency purportedly helped James escape the notice of his aggressors.

8. Max Hunter, "Max Hunter on His Ancestors," audio CD, vol. 1–3, *Visits With*, 1960.

9. Linda Bangs, telephone interview by author, December 26, 2015.

10. Max Hunter, "Visit to Columbia," November 13, 1986, Schroeder House, vol. AC 37, C3826: Folk Song and Folklore Collection, Schroeder Collection, 1986.

11. Hunter, "Home Interview with Donald Lance, et al.," Schroeder Collection.

12. Missouri Friends of the Folk Arts, "I'm Old but I'm Awfully Tough," booklet accompanying LP *I'm Old but I'm Awfully Tough: Traditional Music from the Ozark Region*, MFFA 1001 (1977), 6.

13. The mill was likely torn down in November 1948. For more on its history, see Lucile Morris Upton, "Ancient Eisenmayer Mill Building, Springfield Landmark, to Be Razed," *Springfield [MO] Leader and Press*, November 14, 1948, 32-D2. See also Eisenmayer Family Papers (SP0032), State Historical Society of Missouri Research Center–Springfield.

14. Hunter, "Interviewed by Cathy Barton," AC 18–19:2, Schroeder Collection.

15. Ibid.

16. Ibid.

17. Max Hunter, "Interview in Arrow Rock, MO," interview by Cathy Barton, November 17, 1982, audiocassette, vol. AC 26, C3826; copy of videocassette available in C3852 Missouri Origins (v.c. 1, 5–7, 85), transcript, box 7, Schroeder Collection.

18. Gordon McCann, "Documenting Ozarks Tradition and Culture," Gordon McCann Collection, Missouri State University Special Collections and Archives, Springfield, Missouri (hereafter "McCann Collection").

19. This was the last in a series of warm-up festivals held ahead of the first National Folk Festival in St. Louis that same year.

20. "Gleaners Class Entertained," *Springfield [MO] Leader and Press*, June 12, 1927.

21. Max Hunter, "An Evening with Max Hunter," vol. AC 3 (A), C3826: Folk Song and Folklore Collection, Schroeder Collection, 1976.

22. Rebecca B. Schroeder, "Springfield Public Library Acquires Valuable Collection of Ozark Folksong," *Show-Me Libraries*, Missouri State Library, Jefferson City, MO, 1972.

23. Hunter, "Interview in Arrow Rock, MO," Schroeder Collection. Hunter referred to the harmonica as a "French harp."

24. Lucile Morris Upton, "Max Hunter Diligently Searching Ozarks for Authentic Old Songs," *Sunday Springfield [MO] News and Leader*, July 15, 1962.

25. Hunter, "Pioneer Ozarker," 1974, AC 16–17:16, Schroeder Collection.

26. Ibid. For more on folk remedies, also see McNeil and Clements, *Arkansas Folklore Sourcebook*, 5.

27. Vance Randolph, *Ozark Magic and Folklore* (New York: Dover Publications, 1964), 92–93.

28. Hunter, "Pioneer Ozarker," 1974, AC 16–17:16, Schroeder Collection.

29. Hunter, "Interviewed by Cathy Barton," AC 18–19:1, Schroeder Collection.

30. Lamar, "Interview with Max Hunter Regarding Her Mother," *Visits With*.

31. Ibid.

32. Randolph, *The Ozarks*, 109.

33. Lamar, "Interview with Max Hunter Regarding Her Mother," *Visits With*.

34. Ibid.

35. We know from Belden's *Ballads and Songs* that schoolteacher Goldy Hamilton contributed a good number of ballads from what was then called Kirksville Normal School and later became Truman State University (preface ix).

36. Lamar, "Interview with Max Hunter Regarding Her Mother," *Visits With*.

37. Krisanne Parker, email interview by author, January 12, 2017. Years later, when he hosted a variety of folk festivals, Hunter strongly discouraged harmonization in "traditional" ballad performance.

## Chapter 2. A Traveling Salesman in Eureka

1. Hunter, "Visit to Columbia," November 13, 1986, Schroeder House," Schroeder Collection.

2. Hunter, "Interviewed by Cathy Barton," AC 18–19:6, Schroeder Collection.

3. Anthony, *Chasing the Rising Sun*, 113.

4. Hunter, "Interviewed by Cathy Barton," AC 18–19:2, Schroeder Collection. During his years as a traveling salesman, Hunter worked with industrial suppliers such as Kraft Cheese, Goodyear Rubber, Allen-Bradley Motor Controls, and B. F. Goodrich. Further information on his work life was provided by a letter to Alan Jabbour at the Library of Congress dated October 7, 1977.

5. Max Hunter, "Introduction to His Collection," audiocassette transcript, vol. AC 44, 3826: Folk Song and Folklore Collection, Schroeder Collection, May 20, 1982. Adolf Schroeder made a recording of Hunter's original introduction first recorded on February 19, 1969.

6. David Morton, "Armour Research Foundation and the Wire Recorder: How Academic Entrepreneurs Fail," *Technology and Culture* 39 (1998): 213–44. The American incarnation of the Telegraphone was invented on a whim by electrical engineer Marvin Camras as a favor to a cousin who was an opera buff and "would sing in his bathroom while taking a bath. He thought he sounded every bit as good as the opera singers and wanted to record himself." Described as "short-lived but clever," it was able to "capture sound in the form of magnetic impulses on a very fine steel wire."

7. Ibid., 213.

8. Ibid., 220.

9. Hunter, "Interviewed by Cathy Barton," Schroeder Collection.

10. Hunter, "Home Interview with Donald Lance et al.," audiocassette, vol. AC 21, C3826, October 4, 1981, audiocassette transcript, folders 4–5 Schroeder Collection.

11. Ibid., AC 21:4.

12. Linda Bangs, interview by author, Springfield, MO, June 21, 2016.

13. Cathy Barton, "Kentwood Arms Motel," audio recording transcript, folder 5, (Springfield, MO: Academic Support Center, University of Missouri–Columbia, May 17, 1982), 9–10; audiocassette recording, vol. AC 25, C3826, copy of videocassette recording (VC 18–21), Missouri Origins Project (hereafter "MOP") C3852, Schroeder Collection. Getting better equipment like the Webcor reel-to-reel recorder meant returning to his earliest sources to get better and more complete recordings.

14. Lucile Morris Upton, "Max Hunter Diligently Searching Ozarks for Authentic Old Songs," *Sunday News and Leader*, July 15, 1962, D2.

15. Anthony, *Chasing the Rising Sun*, 107.

16. Michael Ann Williams, *Staging Tradition: John Lair and Sarah Gertrude Knott* (Urbana: University of Illinois Press, 2006), 13. The festival handbook that Knott and her associates developed gave this advice: "Keep the door wide open to everybody." Evening Bulletin Folk Festival Association, *The Folk Festival Handbook: A Practical Guide for Local Communities* (Philadelphia, 1944), 16.

17. See David Whisnant, "White Top Festival: What We Have [Not] Learned," Southwest Virginia Higher Education Center, Abingdon, Virginia, August 6, 1998, http://faculty.buffalostate.edu/fishlm/articles/whitetop.htm.

18. Cochran, *Vance Randolph*, 134. The next Ozark warm-up to the national event took place in Springfield in mid-April. Despite this initial success, the festival was moved to Rolla the succeeding year and quickly lost much of its Ozarkian character.

19. Hunter, "Home Interview with Donald Lance et al.," AC 21:4, Schroeder Collection.

20. Ralph Spencer, "Festival of the Folk Arts, November 17, 1978," audiocassette transcript, vol. AC 12–13, C3826: Folk Song and Folklore Collection, Schroeder Collection, 1978, 4.

21. Richard D. Starnes et al., *Southern Journeys: Tourism, History, and Culture in the Modern South*, ed. Richard D. Starnes (Tuscaloosa: University of Alabama Press, 2003), 60.

22. Rayburn served as producer and director of the Ozark Folk Festival from 1952 to 1959.

23. Brooks Blevins, "Hillbillies and the Holy Land: The Development of Tourism in the Arkansas Ozarks," in Starnes et al., *Southern Journeys*, 60. Writing of Rayburn's first publishing venture, a magazine titled *Ozark Life: The Mirror of the Ozarks*, Ethel Simpson commented, "The sixteen-page paper struck the tone that continued in virtually every periodical Rayburn ever undertook from then on, a tone that the late twentieth century calls boosterism or hype." See Ethel C. Simpson, "Otto Ernest Rayburn (1891–1960)," in CALS, *Encyclopedia of Arkansas*, n.d., https://encyclopedia ofarkansas.net/entries/otto-ernest-rayburn-3003/.

24. Blevins, "Hillbillies," 60. For a fascinating look at the etymology and evolution of the word "hillbilly," see Archie Green, "Hillbilly Music: Source & Symbol," *Journal of American Folk-Lore* 78, no. 309 (1965): 204–228.

25. Hunter, "Home Interview with Donald Lance et al.," AC 21:4, Schroeder Collection.

26. Mary Celestia Parler and Vance Randolph, liner notes to *Ozark Folksongs and Ballads Sung by Max Hunter*, Folk-Legacy Records FSA 11, 1963. Also see Jim Baker, *Preserving Folklore and Traditional Music, and Keeping It Accessible, Ozarks Watch Video Magazine*, Ozarks Public Television, 1999, https://watch.opb.org/video/ozark swatch-video-magazine-preserving-folklore-and-traditional-music-and-making-it/.

27. Carroll S. Thompson, *The First 39 Years of the Ozark Folk Festival* (Eureka Springs, AR: Self-published, 1987). The author makes brief reference to Bob Duncan: "Bob Duncan, ballad collector and singer from Oklahoma, and author of the book, *The Dickey Bird Was Singing*, and his wife felt California calling and moved there to both become movie script writers."

28. Hunter, "Home Interview with Donald Lance et al.," Schroeder Collection.

29. Hunter, "Home Interview with Donald Lance et al.," AC 21:1, Schroeder Collection.

30. Hunter, "Interviewed by Cathy Barton," AC 18–19:4, Schroeder Collection.

31. Randolph, *The Ozarks*, 167.

32. Vance Randolph cited this method at least twice, both in *The Ozarks* (169) and in *Ozark Mountain Folks* (192–93).

33. Randolph, *The Ozarks*, 167.

34. Parler and Randolph, liner notes to Hunter, *Ozark Folksongs and Ballads*.

35. Hunter, "Pioneer Ozarker," February 12, 1974, audio recording transcript of audiocassette, vol. 16–17, C3826, folder 2, box 7, Schroeder Collection.

36. Charles J. Finger, *Frontier Ballads. Songs from Lawless Lands. Heard and Gathered by Charles J. Finger* (London: William Heinemann, 1927).

37. Loman Cansler, audio recording transcript, March 15, 1982, Schroeder Collection.

38. Wes Cook, "Old Songs Reflect Emotions of Today," *Casa Grande (AZ) Dispatch*, 1970, 16.

39. Hunter, "Pioneer Ozarker, 1974," AC 16–17:21, Schroeder Collection.

40. Donald M. Lance, "Chroniclers of an Era: Loman Cansler and Max Hunter, Missouri Collectors of Traditional Music, Songs, and Lore," *Missouri Folklore Society Journal* 20 (1998): 70. Decades before, Vance Randolph described how he would occasionally handle unwilling singers: "Very often he refers me to some other old singer, and volunteers minute directions as the best route to the other singer's cabin. I always make a careful note of this information but do not make any motion to leave." See Randolph, *The Ozarks*, 168–69.

41. Loman Cansler, interviewed by Cathy Barton and Lois Gandt, audio recording partial transcript, vols. 95–96, folder 1, C3826 of video cassette recording, C3852, at Schroeder Home, Schroeder Collection, October 17, 1981, 14.

42. Lance, "Chroniclers of an Era," 70. See "Cansler, Loman."

43. Max Hunter, "Interview with Max Hunter at His Home," vol. AC 38 (A), C3826: Folk Song and Folklore Collection, Schroeder Collection, 1987.

44. Max Hunter, "Presentation on Ozarks Music" for Festival of Missouri Folk Music and Dance, audiocassette, vol. AC 9, C3826, audio recording transcript, folder 2, Schroeder Collection, July 29, 1977.

45. Hunter, "Introduction to the Ozark Song Collection," 2, Schroeder Collection.

46. Max Hunter, "Letter to Loman Cansler," November 27, 1958, Schroeder Collection.

47. Sara J. Bennett, "Keeping Ozarks Culture Alive," *Springfield [MO] News-Leader*, March 7, 1998, 6B.

48. Donald M. Lance, "Max Hunter Remembers Vance and Mary," *Missouri Folklore Society Journal* 4 (1982): 7.

49. Bennett, "Keeping Ozarks Culture Alive," 6B.

50. Hunter, "Home Interview with Donald Lance et al.," Schroeder Collection.

51. Ibid.

## Chapter 3. Rules of Collecting and How Hunter Got His Songs

1. Edgar A. Albin, "The Arts," *Springfield [MO] Leader and Press*, September 19, 1971, 38.

2. Blake Perkins, "Fred High (1978–1962)," in CALS, *Encyclopedia of Arkansas*, https://encyclopediaofarkansas.net/entries/fred-high-5370/. As cited on this page, the town was named after Fred High's family.

3. Hunter, "Interview in Arrow Rock, MO," November 17, 1982, 4, Schroeder Collection.

4. Linda Bangs, email interview by author, June 10, 2017.

5. Linda Bangs, interview by author, June 21, 2016.

6. Ibid.

7. Ibid.

8. William Eden, reel 324, item 3, OFC. Collected by Mary Celestia Parler and Max Hunter, Monte Ne, Arkansas, January 11, 1960.

9. For more on the social mores around dancing, see *The Search for Yokum Creek*, directed by Henwar Rodakiewicz, produced by University of Arkansas, CBS, 1954, https://www.youtube.com/watch?v=oJX5vQFDln4. "Better not call it dancing," Parler explained. "They call it playing games." Play parties allowed for singing accompaniment without instruments, and hand holding but no other physical contact.

10. William Eden, reel 324, item 3, OFC.

11. Albin, "The Arts," 38.

12. Hunter's visit took place a full twenty years before Stilley would become known as "The Preacher Man of Hogscald Hollow," famous for his divinely inspired musical craftsmanship. For more on Stilley's life and work, see Kelly Mulhollan, *True Faith,*

*True Light: The Devotional Art of Ed Stilley* (Fayetteville: University of Arkansas Press, 2015). According to the *Encyclopedia of Arkansas*, "Aunt" Fannie Pricket[t] was Anna Frances Prickett, an elderly resident of Hogscald Hollow who gave the young Stilley room and board in exchange for help with her farming chores. Hunter also recorded songs from her children, Lucy and David Prickett.

13. Adolf E. Schroeder and Rebecca Schroeder, "Introduction to Schroeder Collection," Schroeder Collection.

14. Lance, "Chroniclers of an Era," 78.

15. Nicole Beaudry, "The Challenges of Human Relations in Ethnographic Enquiry," in *Shadows in the Field: New Perspectives for Fieldwork in Ethnomusicology*, ed. Gregory Barz and Timothy J. Cooley (New York: Oxford University Press, 1997), 229.

16. The Dene are the indigenous people of Canada.

17. Beaudry, "Challenges of Human Relations," 230.

18. Barz and Cooley, *Shadows in the Field*. See also Robert A. Georges and Michael A. Jones, *People Studying People: The Human Element in Fieldwork* (Berkeley: University of California Press, 1980).

19. Jody Bilyeu, Jenny Sweet, et al., "Gordon McCann Ozarks Folk Music Collection," University Plaza Hotel, Springfield, Missouri, November 12, 2005, https://www.youtube.com/watch?v=Tzv8wnzpILE&feature=youtu.be.

20. Ibid.

21. Ibid.

22. Max Hunter, "Festival of Missouri Folk Music and Dance," 1977, Schroeder Collection.

23. Hunter, "Interviewed by Cathy Barton," AC 18–19:68, Schroeder Collection.

24. Max Hunter, "Folklore: The Universal Language," recorded from the audience by A. E. Schroeder at the University of Missouri–Columbia, November 6, 1980, AC 14–15, Schroeder Collection.

25. Hunter, "Interview in Arrow Rock, MO," November 17, 1982, 3, Schroeder Collection.

26. Hunter, "Interviewed by Cathy Barton," AC 18–19:10, Schroeder Collection.

27. Hunter, "Interview in Arrow Rock, MO," November 17, 1982, 4, Schroeder Collection.

28. Hunter, "Festival of Missouri Folk Music and Dance," 1977, Schroeder Collection.

29. Blevins, *Hill Folks*, 4.

30. Interestingly, McNeil used Ohrlin (a man of geographically wide-ranging experiences, to make this point: "His repertoire consists of material from many parts of the United States, but that fact doesn't make him atypical, because folksingers . . . have always performed songs from various other regions." McNeil and Clements, *Arkansas Folklore Sourcebook*, 43.

31. The "lady" referred to was Almeda Riddle.

32. Max Hunter, "Hunter on Riddle," audio recording, 1970, Frederick Danker Tapes, Waltham, Massachusetts (hereafter "Danker Tapes").

33. Max Hunter and Judy Domeny Bowen, "Marilyn Prosser interview," audio recording, 1983, MSU-Springfield.

34. Hunter, "Festival of Missouri Folk Music and Dance," 1977, Schroeder Collection.

35. Steve Koehler, "Man Leaves Legacy of Ozarks Song," *Springfield [MO] News-Leader*, November 9, 1999, 1A.

36. Max Hunter, "Talk given during 'Festival of the Folk Arts and Music,'" audio recording transcript, University of Missouri–Columbia, 1978.

37. Tom Womack, "Collecting Music of the Ozarks," *Columbia [MO] Daily Tribune*, July 30, 1977.

38. Hunter, "Festival of Missouri Folk Music and Dance," 1977, Schroeder Collection.

39. Henigan, "Ozark Ballads," 173.

40. Cathy Barton and Dave Para, phone interview by author, May 2015.

41. Hunter, "Introduction to the Ozark Song Collection," Schroeder Collection.

42. Ibid., 2.

43. For a discussion of lyric modification, see **Selected Notes on the Ballads and Songs (online)**.

44. Max Hunter, "Collecting Ozark Folksongs," audiocassette, vol. AC 9, C3826: Folk Song and Folklore Collection, Schroeder Collection, 1977, 9B.

45. Hunter, "Festival of Missouri Folk Music and Dance," 1977, Schroeder Collection.

46. Ibid.

47. Hunter and Domeny Bowen, "Marilyn Prosser interview," 1983, MSU-Springfield.

48. Max Hunter Collection, Missouri State University, Springfield, Missouri, https://maxhunter.missouristate.edu/.

49. Hunter, "Pioneer Ozarker," audiocassette transcript, vol. AC 9:9B, C3826: Folk Song and Folklore Collection, Schroeder Collection, 1977.

50. Henigan, "Ozark Ballads," 173. "[Only] three of the eleven singers interviewed by Ozark ballad scholar John Quincy Wolf on the subject claimed never to have made any alterations in the songs they learned."

51. See D. K. Wilgus, *Anglo-American Folksong Scholarship since 1898* (New Brunswick, NJ: Rutgers University Press, 1959), for a more in-depth discussion on the topic of "bowlderization" and editing of traditional lyrics.

52. Graves, *English and Scottish Ballads*, xxiv.

53. Bangs, interview with author, December 26, 2015.

54. Max Hunter, "Max Hunter: Ozark Song Collector," videocassette transcript, vol. VC 4, C3852 MOP Collection, 1980–1985, State Historical Society of Missouri–Columbia, 1986.

55. Ibid.

56. Bangs interview.

57. Albin, "The Arts," 38.

## Chapter 4. The Child Ballads and Other Bounty

1. Rachel Reynolds Luster, "Mary Celestia Parler (1904–1981)," CALS, *Encyclopedia of Arkansas*, n.d.

2. Parler and Randolph, liner notes to Hunter, *Ozark Folksongs and Ballads*, 9.

3. Hunter, "Home Interview with Donald Lance et al.," Schroeder Collection.

4. Parler and Randolph, liner notes to Hunter, *Ozark Folksongs and Ballads*, 9. "Some of the songs that he [Virgil Lance] recorded for Max Hunter in February, 1958, are older than the eighteenth century, but 'Sweet Lovely Jane' has not been traced back beyond 1855. It appears as 'A True Song' in *American Rhymes by a Southern Poet*, printed at Knoxville, Tennessee, by John B. J. Kinsloe, 1855."

5. Neil Byer and Carla Lance, "Where the Ole White River Flows," audio recording transcript, reel 199, item 3, OFC, 1954.

6. Virgil Lance, "Rose of Erin (Erin's Green Shore)," audio recording transcript, reel 147, item 8, OFC, 1953.

7. Parler and Randolph, liner notes to Hunter, *Ozark Folksongs and Ballads*, 2.

8. "The Nightman" (Child 003) is a greatly revered song about how a young man outwits the devil in disguise. Max Hunter, "An Evening with Max Hunter," vol. AC 3 (A), C3826: Folk Song and Folklore Collection, Schroeder Collection, October 9, 1976.

9. Hunter, "Festival of Missouri Folk Music and Dance," July 29, 1977, Schroeder Collection. "The boy in 'The Jew's Garden' [Child 155] was less fortunate because he ends up having his head cut off by the 'Jewess' next door." When Hunter performed this song at a festival in 1977, he gave it a longer than usual preamble, saying, among other things, "I know some people who sing this . . . change a word because they think there's some racial problem with it. I don't. It's a known fact that things like this [murder] did happen, and if you don't think so, look in 'The Prioress's Tale' in Chaucer, and see if you don't read the same story. . . . He was killed, and he still wouldn't stop singing [about Christianity]."

10. Allie Long Parker, "Allie Long Parker 'Talk,' Hogscald Hollow, Arkansas, 1958," OFC, https://digitalcollections.uark.edu/digital/collection/OzarkFolkSong/id/4140/rec/1/.

11. Katie McCluer, "Who You Are Depends on Who You Was," *Springfield [MO] Daily News*, July 9, 1974. Since writing paper was so expensive, this was common practice. McCluer writes, "Hunter has found handwritten examples of these in such unexpected spots as underneath wallpaper and on the backs of old calendars."

12. Paul Stubblefield, "He Hunts for Folk Songs in the Ozarks," *Kansas City Star*, December 17, 1972.

13. Lance, "Chroniclers of an Era," 37.

14. David and Lucy Prickett were the children of "Aunt" Fannie Pricket[t], from whom Hunter collected several songs when she was in her mid-eighties.

15. Commentary accompanying Hunter's recording of the song "The Baggage Coach Ahead" on September 7, 1958, in Osceola, Missouri, reel 255–56, item 22, OFC, http://digitalcollections.uark.edu/cdm/singleitem/collection/OzarkFolkSong/id/654/rec/5/.

16. T. R. Hammond, "The Baggage Coach Ahead," audio recording, Max Hunter Folk Song Collection, Osceola, Missouri (hereafter "MHFS," 1958, Cat. #0226 (MFH #34), https://maxhunter.missouristate.edu/songinformation.aspx?ID=226/.

17. Denny Elrod, "The Coleman House., *Exploring Izard County* (blog), April 15, 2009, https://exploreizard.blogspot.com/search?q=coleman+house/.

18. "Talk: Autobiographical [J. W. Breazeal]," Springfield, Missouri, April 27, 1958, OFC, https://digitalcollections.uark.edu/digital/collection/OzarkFolkSong/id/3383/rec/1/. This was what Guy Logsdon referred to as "the early frontier version of shape-note notation." See Guy Logsdon, "Shape-Note (Fa-Sol-La) Singing," in *The Encyclopedia of Oklahoma History and Culture* (Oklahoma City: Oklahoma Historical Society, n.d.), https://www.okhistory.org/publications/enc/entry.php?entry=SH007/.

19. While the roots of this system began in New England during the late 1700s, it flourished down South, especially amid religious congregations. See "Shape Note Singing," Collection: The Library of Congress Celebrates the Songs of America, Library of Congress, https://www.loc.gov/collections/songs-of-america/articles-and-essays/musical-styles/ritual-and-worship/shape-note-singing/.

20. Mary Celestia Parler, "Letter to Pearl Brewer," January 10, 1960, Mary Celestia Parler Papers, MC 1501, boxes 1–2, OFC. This letter, which includes personal annotations intended for Hunter, was instructional insofar as it outlined a brief history of the songs Brewer shared.

21. Parler and Randolph, liner notes to Hunter, *Ozark Folksongs and Ballads*, 13.

22. Sue Jackson, "Introduction (to accompany reel 432) Folk Songs from Mrs. Pearl Brewer," Fayetteville, Arkansas, Fall 1963, OFC, http://digitalcollections.uark.edu/cdm/singleitem/collection/OzarkFolkSong/id/4960/rec/17/.

23. Parler and Randolph, liner notes to Hunter, *Ozark Folksongs and Ballads*, 13.

24. Ibid., 16.

25. Belden, *Ballads and Songs*, 29. When a student of Belden's collected this song in 1916 from Josephine Casey of Kansas City, we learned that the boar hunting song (which included elements of the supernatural) was used as a lullaby in the singer's family: "'Miss Casey is a grandniece of General Zachary Taylor of Mexican War fame. . . . General Taylor and President James Madison were great-great-grandsons of James Tyler, who came from Carlisle, England, to Orange County, Virginia, in 1638, and both were hushed to sleep by their negro 'Mammies' with the strains of *Bangum and the Boar. . . .* The air itself is even older than the words. A Danish maid in the service of Miss Casey's sister burst into tears when she heard the song. When

asked the reason she said, 'It makes me homesick. In Denmark, we young people used to dance to that air, which is a very old one.'"

26. John Rogers, "Salesman Documented Way of Life in the Missouri Ozarks," *St. Louis Dispatch*, May 24, 1998.

27. Hunter, "Evening with Max Hunter," 1976, Schroeder Collection.

28. Hunter, "Interview with Max Hunter at His Home," 1987, Schroeder Collection.

29. Ibid.

30. Robert B. Cochran, *Singing in Zion: Music and Song in the Life of One Arkansas Family* (Fayetteville: University of Arkansas Press, 1999), 35.

31. Hunter, "Introduction to the Ozark Song Collection," Schroeder Collection. Read more on the lyrics and history of this Bald Knobber's song at https://ozarkshistory .blogspot.com/2013/09/the-ballad-of-bald-knobbers.html.

32. Randolph, *Ozark Folksongs*, rev. ed., 1–4: 11.

33. Randolph, *Ozark Folksongs*, rev. ed., 2: 114–17.

34. Robert B. Waltz and David G. Engle, "The Bald Knobber Song," *The Ballad Index*, Fresno State University, Fresnostate.edu/folklore/ballads/R154.html. For a broader look at their history, see Matthew James Hernando, "The Bald Knobbers of Southwest Missouri, 1885–1889: A Study of Vigilante Justice in the Ozarks" (PhD diss., Louisiana State University, 2011), https://digitalcommons.lsu.edu/gradschool _dissertations/3884.

35. "Talk: Biographical [William Eden]," Monte Ne, AR, January 11, 1960, OFC, http://digitalcollections.uark.edu/cdm/singleitem/collection/OzarkFolkSong/id/996/ rec/1/.

36. Listed as "Philbreck" in the Max Hunter Folk Song Collection.

37. Herbert Philbrick, "Interview by Max Hunter," audio CD, October 28, 1959, *Visits With*. In subsequent years Philbrick said this was likely "Fandango," which has no lyrics.

38. Hunter, "Introduction to the Ozark Song Collection," Schroeder Collection.

39. Ibid.

40. Ibid.

41. Hunter, "Home Interview with Donald Lance et al.," AC 21:18, Schroeder Collection.

42. Philbrick interview, *Visits With*.

43. Ibid. Parler dubbed the interview of Hunter and Philbrick for her own collection. This happened several times with other Hunter materials.

44. Philbrick interview, *Visits With*.

45. Ibid.

46. Ibid.

47. Ibid.

48. They consisted of "The Western Water Tank," a dying hobo song, a fragment of "How Can a Boy Be Forgetful of Mother," and "I've a Tender Recollection." Hunter was likely the guitarist providing the accompaniment.

49. Philbrick interview, *Visits With.*

50. Hunter, "Festival of Missouri Folk Music and Dance," July 29, 1977, AC 10, side 1, Schroeder Collection.

51. Bangs, interview with author, June 21, 2016.

52. Hunter was not alone in this shortcoming as observed by McNeil and Clements. With regard to Vance Randolph's *Ozark Folksongs*, "There is too little information about informants and specific recording sessions, about attitudes of singers towards the songs." This weakness was common among other song collections as well. McNeil and Clements, *Arkansas Folklore Sourcebook*, 45, 53.

53. Steve Koehler, "Man Leaves Legacy of Ozarks Song." *Springfield [MO] News-Leader*, November 9, 1999, 1.

54. Hunter, "Presentation on Ozarks Music," Schroeder Collection.

55. Hunter, "Interviewed by Cathy Barton," Schroeder Collection.

56. Bangs, interview with author, June 21, 2016.

57. Hunter, "Festival of Missouri Folk Music and Dance," July 29, 1977, Schroeder Collection.

58. Hunter, "Pioneer Ozarker," 1974, Schroeder Collection.

59. Ibid.

60. Hunter, "Introduction to the Ozark Song Collection," Schroeder Collection. After recording his introduction in February, he also created a handwritten draft in June 1969.

61. Hunter, "Interviewed by Cathy Barton," Schroeder Collection.

62. Hunter, "Visit to Columbia," AC 37:13, Schroeder Collection.

63. Paul Stubblefield, "He Hunts for Folk Songs in the Ozarks," *Kansas City Star*, December 17, 1972.

64. Max Hunter, "Hunter Collecting Experiences," audiocassette, vol. AC 44 (B), C3826: Folk Song and Folklore Collection, Schroeder Collection, 1982.

65. Barton, "Kentwood Arms Motel," Springfield, Missouri. Interview with Cathy Barton et al., May 17, 1982, C3852, audiocassette. vol. 25, audio recording transcript, box 7, folder 5, MOP.

66. Spencer, "Festival of the Folk Arts, November 17, 1978," Schroeder Collection.

67. Hunter, "Talk given during 'Festival of the Folk Arts and Music,'" Schroeder Collection.

68. Hunter was particularly proud of the bawdy version of "Strawberry Roan," which he collected from cowboy song collector Glenn Ohrlin of Mountain View, Arkansas, in May 1969; it featured foul language as well as graphic details of sexual encounters with pimps and prostitutes. The variant he collected from Ollie Gilbert three years later was considerably tamer. Ohrlin's "Bawdy Strawberry Roan" is also known as "The Castration of the Strawberry Roan" (on *Just Something My Uncle Told Me*, vol. LP0141, Rounder Records, 1981). See Guy Logsdon, *"The Whorehouse Bells Were Ringing" and Other Songs Cowboys Sing* (Urbana: University of Illinois Press, 1989), 86–96. See also Elijah Wald, "Castration of the Strawberry Roan," *Old*

*Friends: A Songobiography* (blog), March 3, 2018, https://www.elijahwald.com/song blog/castration-strawberry-roan/.

69. Leary, *Folksongs of Another America*, 137–39. According to Leary, the expression "shoot the cat" was a euphemism for male ejaculation or vomiting; it can be found on both sides of the Atlantic and first appeared in a nineteenth-century sailing magazine.

70. Fred High, interview, "History of Fred High's Life," audio recording, n.d., Lyon College, John Quincy Wolf Folklore Collection (hereafter "WFC"), https://web.lyon.edu/wolfcollection/songs/highhistory1245.html.

71. Hunter, "Introduction to the Ozark Song Collection," Schroeder Collection.

72. Spencer, *Ballad Collectors of North America*, 37.

73. Georges and Jones, *People Studying People*, 21.

74. Ibid., 66.

75. Hunter, "Max Hunter: Ozark Song Collector," Schroeder Collection.

76. Blake Perkins, "Fred High (1878–1962)," CALS, *Encyclopedia of Arkansas*, https://encyclopediaofarkansas.net/entries/fred-high-5370/.

77. Hunter, "Pioneer Ozarker," 1974, Schroeder Collection.

78. Ibid.

79. Ibid.

80. Hunter, "Max Hunter: Ozark Song Collector."

81. Hunter, "Interviewed by Cathy Barton," Schroeder Collection.

82. Hunter recalled this decades later when in discussion with the Schroeders. Max Hunter, "Visit to Columbia," November 13, 1986, C3826, vol. 37, AC 37:13, Schroeder Collection.

83. For more on the popularity of the stage Irish tradition in America, see Mick Moloney's essay "Irish Ethnic Recordings and the Irish-American Imagination," in American Folklife Center, *Ethnic Recordings in America: A Neglected Heritage* (Library of Congress, 1982), 85–102.

84. Hunter, "Visit to Columbia," AC 37:13, Schroeder Collection.

85. Hunter, "Interviewed by Cathy Barton," Schroeder Collection.

86. Hunter, "Interviewed by Cathy Barton," September 1977, Schroeder Collection; Max Hunter, Festival of Missouri Folk Music and Dance, in Columbia, July 29, 1977, transcript p. 7, C3826, audiocassette recording, vol. 9, audio recording transcript, folder 2, 7, Schroeder Collection.

87. American Folklife Center, *Ethnic Recordings in America*, 85–102.

88. Smith would have known McCord from Eureka Springs and from performing alongside her on Springfield, Missouri's KWTO radio program *Hoedown*.

89. Georgine Cawood, "Introduction (to accompany reels 397–398), Folk Ballads of Fred Smith Collected by Georgine Cawood," audiocassette transcript, reels 397–98, OFC, 1963, https://digitalcollections.uark.edu/digital/collection/OzarkFolkSong/id/3074/rec/4/.

90. This is another term for handheld Irish "bones," which are wooden sticks used for percussive accompaniment.

91. Cawood, "Introduction, Folk Ballads of Fred Smith," 5–6.

92. Ibid., 7.

93. Lance, "Chroniclers of an Era," 82–83.

94. Associated Press, "West Plains, MO Dance Hall Explosion, April 1928," *Syracuse Herald*, April 14, 1928. See also Lin Waterhouse, *The West Plains Dance Hall Explosion* (Charleston, SC: History Press, 2010).

95. For an in-depth discussion of negotiation in fieldwork, see Georges and Jones, "Clarification and Compromise," in *People Studying People*.

96. Hunter, "Interviewed by Cathy Barton," Schroeder Collection.

97. Max Hunter, "A Word about Fakelore," *Just for the Record* 1, no. 5 (August 1977).

98. Hunter, "Interviewed by Cathy Barton," Schroeder Collection.

99. Odis Bird, "Little Billy," audio recording, Marshall, Arkansas, August 6, 1958, Cat. #0160 (MFH #346), MHFS, https://maxhunter.missouristate.edu/songinformation.aspx?ID=160.

100. Hunter, "Interviewed by Cathy Barton," Schroeder Collection.

101. Hunter, "Evening with Max Hunter," 1976, Schroeder Collection.

102. Hunter, "Pioneer Ozarker," 1974, Schroeder Collection.

103. Parler and Randolph, liner notes to Hunter, *Ozark Folksongs and Ballads*, 7.

104. Olive Coberley interview, October 7, 1958. This is a duplicate recording that A. E. Schroeder made of Hunter's original recording, which can be heard on audio-cassette re-recording, C3826, vol. 42, December 5, 1981, MHFS/MSU-Springfield, Schroeder Collection. The following is the URL for the Ozark Folksong Collection (OFC) copy of the pre-song interview: https://digitalcollections.uark.edu/digital/collection/OzarkFolkSong/id/672/rec/1/.

105. Hunter, "Interviewed by Cathy Barton," Schroeder Collection.

106. Coberley, interview.

107. Hunter, "Interviewed by Cathy Barton," AC 18–19:12, Schroeder Collection.

108. Belden, *Ballads and Songs*, 68.

109. Hunter, "Interviewed by Cathy Barton," Schroeder Collection.

110. Ibid.

111. Raymond Sanders, interview, audio recording transcript, 1969, p. 41, Rackensack Oral History Collection, University of Central Arkansas (hereafter "ROH").

112. Vaughn Brewer and his wife, Kay, were fortunate to receive grants from the National Endowment for the Arts, which supported their folkloric efforts in Arkansas's Timbo/Mountain View Region. For scholars, the most valuable outcome of the folk revival in Mountain View was the oral history work that was done after the formation of the Rackensack Folklore Society at the University of Central Arkansas. The Rackensack interviews provide invaluable information on some of Hunter's most significant sources—first and foremost, Ollie Gilbert.

113. Sanders interview, audio recording transcript, 2, ROH.

114. Ibid.

115. Ibid., 25.

116. Ibid., 33.

117. Ibid., 34–35.

118. Ibid., 35–36.

119. Ibid.

120. Anthony, *Chasing the Rising Sun*, 116.

121. This song is a variant of "Omie Wise."

122. Anthony, *Chasing the Rising Sun*, 117.

123. Ibid., 126.

124. Ibid., 115.

125. Ibid., 127.

126. Ibid., 128.

127. Reba Dearmore, "Interview by Max Hunter," audio CD, *Visits With*, vol. 4–7, 1969.

128. Ibid.

129. Ibid.

130. It seems likely that Dearmore would have sent Hunter a cassette of her songs, given that there is no mention of any field trip to Maryland.

131. McNeil said this was important "not only to gain a better understanding of what each individual knew but also to achieve a greater comprehension of the material that most appealed to them." McNeil and Clements, *Arkansas Folklore Sourcebook*, 45.

132. Reba Dearmore, "Letter to Max and Virginia from Gaithersburg, MD," February 12, 1972, Max Hunter Collection, Springfield–Greene County Library, Springfield, Missouri (hereafter "MHC").

133. There is no record of Hunter having collected from this singer.

134. Dearmore, "Letter to Max and Virginia," February 12, 1972, MHC.

135. Ibid.

136. Hunter's version of "Our Goodman," titled "Five Nights Drunk," and Hickerson's rendition of the broadside ballad "Reynardine" were both included in volume 1 of Sandy and Caroline Paton's Folk-Legacy album *The Continuing Tradition*. For notes on these songs, see *Ballads: A Folk-Legacy Sampler*, liner notes, vol. 1, *The Continuing Tradition*, Folk-Legacy Records CD-75, 1981, https://folkways-media.si.edu/liner_notes/folk-legacy/FLG00075-LP.pdf.

## Chapter 5. Singing Grandmas and the Musical Tribes of Stone County

1. Ollie Gilbert, "Interview by Vaughn Brewer and Frederick Danker," audio recording transcript, 1969, 1, ROH.

2. Now Rhodes College.

3. Blevins, *Hill Folks*, 250.

4. Freda Cruse Hardison, "Ollie Eva Woody Gilbert (1892–1980)," in CALS, *Encyclopedia of Arkansas History and Culture*, http://www.encyclopediaofarkansas.net/encyclopedia/entry-detail.aspx?entryID=622.

5. Hunter, "Max Hunter: Ozark Song Collector," Schroeder Collection.

6. Hardison, "Ollie Eva Woody Gilbert," CALS.

7. Ollie Gilbert, "Interview by Max Hunter," audio CD, vol. 10–11 (track 1), *Visits With*, 1971.

8. Gilbert, "Interview by Vaughn Brewer and Frederick Danker," ROH, 90–91.

9. Willadean George Barnes, "Interview by Vaughn Brewer," audio recording transcript, 1981, 17–18, ROH.

10. Ibid., 11.

11. Gilbert, "Interview by Vaughn Brewer and Frederick Danker," 24, ROH.

12. Barnes, "Interview by Vaughn Brewer," 17–18, ROH.

13. Ollie Gilbert, "Interview by Max Hunter and Fred Danker," audio recording, vol. 15, Danker Tapes, n.d. Jimmy Driftwood was also present during this interview.

14. Marion A. Hughes, *Three Years in Arkansas* (Chicago: Donohue & Co., 1904).

15. Ollie Gilbert, Jimmy Driftwood, and Cleda Driftwood, "Interview by Vaughn Brewer and Kay Brewer," audio recording transcript, 1969, 6, ROH.

16. Ibid., 115–16.

17. Gilbert, "Interview by Max Hunter," audio CD, vol. 8–9 (track 2), *Visits With*, 1971; Gilbert, "Interview by Max Hunter," audio CD, vols. 8–9, *Visits With*, August 31, 1971.

18. Barnes, "Interview by Vaughn Brewer," 8–9, ROH.

19. Ibid.

20. Gilbert, "Interview by Max Hunter and Fred Danker," Danker Tapes, n.d.; Ollie Gilbert, "Interview by Max Hunter," Danker Tape #15. Jimmy Driftwood was also present.

21. Shirley Collins and Dolly Collins, *The Harvest Years*, sleeve notes, EMI 228 404-2, Mainly Norfolk, 2008.

22. Gilbert, "Interview by Max Hunter," *Visits With*, 1971.

23. Barnes, "Interview by Vaughn Brewer," 6, ROH.

24. Ibid., 10.

25. Ibid., 14.

26. Ibid., 13.

27. Ibid., 15.

28. Gilbert, Driftwood, and Driftwood, "Interview by Vaughn Brewer and Kay Brewer," 1969, 23–24, ROH.

29. Ibid., 142–43.

30. Ibid., 41.

31. Hunter, "Evening with Max Hunter," Schroeder Collection, 1976.

32. Jimmy Driftwood, liner notes to *Aunt Ollie Gilbert Sings Old Folk Songs to Her Friends*, Rimrock, Inc., RLP-495, Concord, Arkansas, 1975.

33. Susan Gilbert Kemp, "Interview by Vaughn Brewer and Frederick Danker," audio recording transcript, 1981, ROH [Hardison, "Ollie Eva Woody Gilbert (1892–1980)."]

34. Gilbert, "Interview by Max Hunter and Fred Danker," Danker Tapes, n.d.

35. Kemp, "Interview by Vaughn Brewer and Frederick Danker," 37, ROH.

36. Gilbert, "Interview by Vaughn Brewer and Frederick Danker," 90–91, ROH.

37. For an in-depth breakdown of Stone County's musical factions resulting from the long-standing tensions between traditionalists and musicians who welcomed the commercialization of folk performance, see Page H. Stephens, "The Case of Missing Folk Music: A Study of Aspects of Musical Life in Stone County, Arkansas, from 1890–1980," *Mid-America Folklore* 10, nos. 2–3 (1982): 58–69, https://babel.hathitrust.org/cgi/pt?id=inu.30000116555941&view=image&seq=120&q1=The%20Case%20of%20Missing%20Folk%20Music.

38. Gilbert, "Interview by Max Hunter and Fred Danker," Danker Tapes, n.d.

39. Ollie Gilbert, "Interview by Max Hunter," audio recording transcript, March 11, 1970, ROH.

40. Gilbert, "Interview by Max Hunter and Fred Danker," Danker Tapes, n.d.

41. Ollie Gilbert, "Interview by Max Hunter," audio recording transcript, June 25, 1969, 17, ROH.

42. Ibid., 99–100.

43. Lucile Morris Upton, "Ballad Collector Says Folklore, History Are Hard to Separate," *Springfield [MO] Daily News*, October 14, 1974, 16. Hunter always insisted that women told dirtier jokes than men.

44. Hunter, "Festival of Missouri Folk Music and Dance," 1977, Schroeder Collection.

45. Cathy Barton and Dave Para phone interview by author, May 2015.

46. Barnes, "Interview by Vaughn Brewer," 12, ROH.

47. Danker and Brewer's exhaustive interviews with Gilbert would become an essential part of the Rackensack Folklore Collection, which is housed at the University of Central Arkansas.

48. Gilbert, "Interview by Max Hunter and Fred Danker," Danker Tapes, n.d.

49. Gilbert, "Interview by Vaughn Brewer and Frederick Danker," 10–11, ROH.

50. Gilbert, Rackensack interview at the University of Central Arkansas, June 25, 1969, 5, ROH.

51. Hunter, "Evening with Max Hunter," 1976, Schroeder Collection.

52. Ibid.

53. "Daddy Sang Bass," composed by Carl Perkins and made famous by Johnny Cash; "Hound Dog," composed by Jerry Leiber and Mike Stoller and made famous by Elvis Presley; "Last Thing on My Mind," composed by Tom Paxton.

54. Gilbert, "Interview by Vaughn Brewer and Frederick Danker," 58, ROH. The original Carter Family consisted of Sara Carter; her husband, A. P. Carter; and Sara's sister-in-law and first cousin, Maybelle Carter.

55. See Kenneth S. Goldstein's foreword to Louise Pound, *American Ballads and Songs* (New York: Charles Scribner's Sons, 1972), ix. See also Pound's own words on the topic of "vitality" in tradition (xxxi–xxxii).

56. Cochran, *Singing in Zion*, 88.

57. Kemp, "Interview by Vaughn Brewer and Frederick Danker," 6, ROH.

58. Gilbert, Driftwood, and Driftwood interview, "Interview by Vaughn Brewer and Kay Brewer," 1969, 12, ROH.

59. Kemp, "Interview by Vaughn Brewer and Frederick Danker," 9, ROH.

60. Gilbert, "Interview by Max Hunter and Fred Danker," audio recording, vol. 11, Danker Tapes, 1971.

61. Gilbert, Driftwood, and Driftwood, "Interview by Vaughn Brewer and Kay Brewer," 1969, 24, ROH.

62. Gilbert, "Interview by Vaughn Brewer and Frederick Danker," June 25, 1969, 1, ROH.

63. Cathy Barton and Dave Para, phone interview by author, April 14, 2017.

64. Stephens, "Case of Missing Folk Music," 65–66.

65. Hunter, "Evening with Max Hunter," Schroeder Collection

66. Riddle, *Singer and Her Songs*, 137–38.

67. John Quincy Wolf Jr., "Folksingers and the RE-Creation of Folksong," *Western Folklore* 26, no. 2 (April 1967).

68. Riddle, *Singer and Her Songs*, 112.

69. Max Hunter, "Festival of Missouri Folk Music and Dance," Schroeder Collection, 1977.

70. Frederick Danker, audio recording, vol. 6 (203–204), Danker Tapes, 1970.

71. Hunter, "An Evening with Max Hunter," vol. AC 3 (B), C3826: Folk Song and Folklore Collection, Schroeder Collection, 1976.

72. More details about the background of this song can be found in Riddle, *Singer and Her Songs*.

73. The latter stricture was either ignored by Hunter, since this homespun ballad made it into his collection, or permission was granted after the recording was made. Danker Tapes, 1970.

74. Frederick Danker, audio recording, vol. 6 (203–204), Danker Tapes, 1970.

75. Danker Tapes, vol. 6, February 10, 1970.

76. Letter from Almeda Riddle to Max Hunter, May 22, 1974, MHC.

77. Ibid.

## Chapter 6. Circle of Friends

1. Lance, "Max Hunter Remembers Vance and Mary."

2. Hunter, "Interviewed by Cathy Barton," Schroeder Collection

3. Hunter, "Home Interview with Donald Lance et al.," AC 21:19, Schroeder Collection.

4. Ibid.

5. Ibid., AC 21:2, Schroeder Collection.

6. Hunter, "Home Interview with Donald Lance et al.," Schroeder Collection.

7. Carlisle (yet another musically inclined English major), earned her master's degree from the University of Arkansas through the writing of her thesis, "Fifty Ballads and Songs from Northwest Arkansas." Clements describes her as "a major informant for Vance Randolph when he was collecting material for his *Ozark Folkways*." McNeil and Clements, *Arkansas Folklore Sourcebook*, 47.

8. Hunter, "Home Interview with Donald Lance et al.," Schroeder Collection.

9. Ibid., AC 21:3, Schroeder Collection.

10. Ibid., AC 21:4, Schroeder Collection. Also corroborated in Cochran, *Vance Randolph*, 147.

11. Hunter, "Interview with Max Hunter at His Home," Schroeder Collection, 1987.

12. Cochran, *Vance Randolph*, 147–48. The "Keeley Cure" got its start in Dwight, Illinois, in 1879 and attracted a number of high-profile individuals during its early days. As described by Cochran, "The 'secret remedy' was hypodermically injected four times each day . . . while a spoonful of tonic with water was taken every two hours."

13. Hunter, "Home Interview with Donald Lance et al.," AC 21:2, Schroeder Collection; Lance, "Max Hunter Remembers Vance and Mary," 3.

14. Hunter, "Home Interview with Donald Lance et al.," AC 21:6, Schroeder Collection.

15. Lance, "Max Hunter Remembers Vance and Mary," 5.

16. Ibid.

17. Letter from Vance Randolph to Max Hunter, November 21, 1965, box 2, MHC; letter from Mary Celestia Parler to Max Hunter, November 21, 1965, box 2, MHC.

18. Cochran, *Vance Randolph*, 140.

19. Lance, "Max Hunter Remembers Vance and Mary," 6.

20. Randolph received a loan of wax cylinder recording equipment from Alan Lomax at the Archive of American Folksong in 1941. See Cochran, *Vance Randolph*, 175–77.

21. Vance Randolph, *Ozark Mountain Folks* (New York: Vanguard Press, 1932), 205–206. This passage was written ten years before Randolph received recording equipment from Alan Lomax.

22. Lance, "Max Hunter Remembers Vance and Mary," 9.

23. Vance Randolph, *Pissing in the Snow and Other Ozark Folktales* (Urbana: University of Illinois Press, 1976).

24. Lance, "Max Hunter Remembers Vance and Mary," 4.

25. Letter from Mary Celestia Parler to Max Hunter, December 5, 1958, box 2, MHC.

26. Mary Celestia Parler, "Further Interview with Mr. Herbert Philbrick," notes associated with audio recording, Crocker, Missouri, October 28, 1959, reel 347, item 7,

OFC, http://digitalcollections.uark.edu/cdm/singleitem/collection/OzarkFolkSong/id/700/rec/1.

27. Letter from Parler to Hunter, December 5, 1958. In fact, Frances Majors, a student of Parler, contributed fifteen ballads to the Hunter Collection in Fayetteville, Arkansas, and Wichita, Kansas.

28. Ibid. "Joanie" refers to Joan O'Bryant.

29. Ibid. Hunter had an open invitation to attend Parler's folklore classes.

30. Letter from Loman Cansler to Max Hunter, October 20, 1958, MHC.

31. Lance, "Max Hunter Remembers Vance and Mary," 16.

32. Highlights of Antone's visit included the butchered delivery of an Israeli folksong, "which I imagine is his show piece, and which I feel sure is lovely if sung straight, but he blasted [it] like our preacher in Mena"; the attempted tuning of the guitar ("he got it worse out of tune"); and several poorly executed "naughty number[s]". Letter from Parler to Hunter and Joan O'Bryant, December 5, 1958.

33. Ibid.

34. Rachel Vukas, "Joan O'Bryant," *Missouri Folklore Society Journal* 11–12 (1989–1990): 125.

35. Hunter, "Interview with Max Hunter at His Home," 1987, Schroeder Collection.

36. In addition to Anglo-American ballads, O'Bryant recorded Native American songs, Irish songs, Spanish songs, German songs, and songs from the Mennonite community. Gayle Davis and Rachel Shorthill, *The Unburnished Mirror: An Interpretive Study of Folklore and Content Description of the Joan O'Bryant Collection*, ed. Leonard Messineo Jr. (Wichita, KS: Wichita Public Library, ca. 1984), 25.

37. Vukas, "Joan O'Bryant," 125.

38. While harnessing student field power might have given O'Bryant an advantage in terms of amassing material, it also proved problematic in terms of accuracy, as several tapes are labeled "unidentified performer" and those that are identified often have names misspelled or list incorrect sources

39. Davis and Shorthill, *Unburnished Mirror*, 9.

40. Ibid.

41. Ibid., 10–14.

42. Hunter, "Interview with Max Hunter at His Home," 1987, Schroeder Collection.

43. Southern variant for "whips."

44. Letter from Parler to Hunter, December 5, 1958.

45. Cawood, "Introduction (to accompany reels 397–98), Folk Ballads of Fred Smith Collected by Georgine Cawood," OFC, https://digitalcollections.uark.edu/digital/collection/OzarkFolkSong/id/3074/rec/4.

46. Hunter, "Interview with Max Hunter at His Home," 1987, Schroeder Collection.

47. Many of the individuals O'Bryant spent time with shared her dynamic qualities, among them the much-celebrated folklorist and performer Barre Toelken, who mentored and inspired young students during his professorial years, first at the University of Oregon and later at the Utah State University; scholar William E. Koch,

who authored *Folklore from Kansas: Customs, Beliefs, and Superstitions*; and itinerant musical historians Keith and Rusty McNeil of California.

48. Max Hunter, "Audio Letter to Joan O'Bryant," audiocassette, vol. AC 34, C3826: Folk Song and Folklore Collection, Schroeder Collection, 1961.

49. Ibid.

50. Dwight Nichols was the owner of the Crescent Hotel.

51. Hunter, "Audio Letter to Joan O'Bryant," Schroeder Collection.

52. Joan O'Bryant, *Folksongs and Ballads of Kansas*, LP, Folkways Records FW02338, 1957. See also Joan O'Bryant, *American Ballads and Folksongs*, Folkways Records SA 2338, 1958.

53. Folklorist Herbert Halpert was a close friend of Vance Randolph.

54. Hunter, "Interview with Max Hunter at His Home," 1987, Schroeder Collection.

55. Ibid.

56. Ibid.

57. Bangs interview with author, June 21, 2016.

58. Max Hunter, Joan O'Bryant, and Mary Celestia Parler, *Songs of the Ozarks*, audiocassette, vol. AC 33, C3826: Folk Song and Folklore Collection, Schroeder Collection, 1962. They called themselves "The Three Dials." D. K. Wilgus also makes brief mention of this obscure recording in "Record Reviews," *Journal of American Folk-Lore* 77, no. 303 (March 1964): 94–96.

59. Albin, "The Arts," *Springfield [MO] Leader and Press*, September 19, 1971.

60. Letter from Vance Randolph to Max Hunter, July 18, 1974.

61. Lance, "Max Hunter Remembers Vance and Mary," 14.

62. Hunter, "Home Interview with Donald Lance et al.," Schroeder Collection.

63. Letter from Randolph to Hunter, July 18, 1974.

64. Cochran, *Vance Randolph*, 218.

65. Letter from Vance Randolph to Virginia Hunter, November 7, 1974.

66. Vance Randolph, *Blow the Candle Out: Unprintable Ozarks Folksongs and Folklore*, vol. 2 (Fayetteville: University of Arkansas Press, 1992), 677–78. This particular song, "No Balls at All," which went unrecorded by Hunter but was caught by other collectors, appears under many different titles, Roud Song Index, no. 10136, https://www.vwml.org/search?q=no%20balls%20at%20all&is=1/.

67. Letter from Vance Randolph to Max Hunter, December 13, 1978.

68. Letter from Max Hunter to D. K. Wilgus, November 2, 1976.

69. Lance, "Max Hunter Remembers Vance and Mary," 21.

70. Hunter, "Visit to Columbia," Schroeder Collection.

71. Ibid.

## Chapter 7. The Importance of Columbia

1. Letter from Rebecca B. Schroeder to Max Hunter, May 8, 1972, box 4, MHC.

2. Letter from Rebecca B. Schroeder to Max Hunter, May 18, 1973, box 4, MHC.

3. Letter from Adolf E. Schroeder to Max Hunter and Virginia Hunter, June 8, 1976, box 4, MHC.

4. Katie McCluer, "Who You Are Depends on Who You Was," *Springfield [MO] Daily News*, July 9, 1974.

5. Ibid.

6. Letter from Roy Blunt to Max Hunter, n.d.

7. Letter from Rebecca B. Schroeder to Max Hunter, June 9, 1977.

8. Letter from Rebecca B. Schroeder to author, May 12, 2015.

9. Max Hunter, "Interview with Max Hunter at His Home," vol. AC 38 (B), C3826: Folk Song and Folklore Collection, Schroeder Collection, 1987.

10. Ibid.

11. Ibid.

12. Ibid.

13. Davis and Shorthill, *Unburnished Mirror*.

14. Hunter, "Interview with Max Hunter at His Home," Schroeder Collection, 1987. The book contained multiple contributors.

15. Loman D. and Laura M. Cansler Collection (n.d.), SHSM, https://collections .shsmo.org/manuscripts/columbia/c4018.

16. Wolz, "Anglo-American Music in Missouri," 64.

17. Letter from Cansler to Hunter, October 20, 1958, MHC. Author of *The Dicky Bird Was Singing: Men, Women, & Black Gold*, Oklahoma folk singer Bob Duncan was emcee for the Ozark Folk Festival before moving to Hollywood, California, with his wife, Wanda, to become a script writer.

18. Davis and Shorthill, *Unburnished Mirror*, 9.

19. Letter from Cansler to Hunter, October 20, 1958, MHC.

20. Letter from Loman Cansler to Max Hunter, July 26, 1963.

21. This restriction was lifted by his widow, Laura Cansler, in 2004.

22. Dave Para and Cathy Barton, phone interview with author, April 14, 2017.

23. "Hillbillies' Memory Banks Loaded, Folklorist Claims," *Springfield [MO] Leader and Press*, July 9, 1974. Hunter's definition made sense only on the most superficial level. M.J.C. Hodgart wrote, "The only satisfactory definition of a 'folksong' is a song that has been transmitted orally: that is, learnt by word of mouth by one generation from preceding generations, without the assistance of the written word." But he added this important caveat: "That definition could be applied to the ballads in this country but for the fact that there has been no such thing as purely oral transmission here for the last four hundred and fifty years. . . . Purely oral transmission can exist only among an entirely illiterate community . . . and such a community has hardly existed in England or Scotland during the recorded history of the ballads." M.J.C. Hodgart, *The Ballads* (New York: W. W. Norton, 1962), 11.

24. Letter from Loman Cansler to Max Hunter, March 5, 1959, MHC.

25. Ibid.

## Chapter 8. More Than a Hobby

1. This archive would become part of the American Folklife Center in 1974.

2. Max Hunter, "Letter to Folklore Division at Library of Congress," March 14, 1970, box 1, MHC. Hunter actively collected ballads through 1976.

3. Bronson was an English professor at University of California, Berkeley, and the author of important works of scholarship, including *The Traditional Tunes of the Child Ballads*, vols. 1–4 (Princeton, NJ: Princeton University Press, 1959–1972).

4. Hunter, "Letter to Folklore Division at Library of Congress," MHC. A year later he would give Alan Jabbour permission to dub reel 2 for Professor D. K. Wilgus of UCLA, who was doing a study of "Cue Ball" variants. Alan Jabbour, "Letter to Max Hunter," January 21, 1971, 21, AAFS/AFC.

5. Hunter, "Letter to Folklore Division at Library of Congress," MHC.

6. Alan Jabbour, "Letter to Max Hunter," June 11, 1970, AAFS/AFC.

7. Alan Jabbour, "Letter to Max Hunter," May 1, 1970, AAFS/AFC.

8. Max Hunter, "Letter to Alan Jabbour," May 9, 1970, AAFS/AFC.

9. Hunter, "Pioneer Ozarker," 1974, AC 16–17:22, Schroeder Collection.

10. Hunter, "Introduction to the Ozark Song Collection," 1 (Addendum), Schroeder Collection.

11. Hunter, "Introduction to the Ozark Song Collection," Schroeder Collection.

12. Audrey Barclay, "Interview by Max Hunter," audio CD, vol. 1–3, *Visits With*, 1970.

13. Vance Randolph made mention of several of these same remedies. See Randolph, *Ozark Magic and Folklore*, 93.

14. Floy Huskey, "Interview by Max Hunter," CD 8–10, *Visits With*, October 11, 1971.

15. Myrl Mercer, "Interview with Max Hunter," audio CD, vol. 11–15, recording #483, *Visits With*, 1970. During this time period, people also entertained themselves with "telephone fiddling." See Howard Wight Marshall, *Play Me Something Quick and Devilish: Old-Time Fiddlers in Missouri* (Columbia: University of Missouri Press, 2012), 212.

16. Mercer, "Interview with Max Hunter," 1970.

17. Ibid.

18. Floyd Holland and Kermit Moody, "Interview by Max Hunter," audio CD, vol. 8–9, *Visits With*, 1971. Holland also claims that they used to make banjo heads from both dog and cat hides instead of sheepskin.

19. Ibid.

20. Ibid.

21. Gilbert, "Interview by Max Hunter," 1971.

22. Holland and Moody, "Interview by Max Hunter," *Visits With*, 1971.

23. Joseph Hickerson, "The Max Hunter Duplication Project," email to the author, June 22, 2015. The project, which consists of audio copies of the Max Hunter Col-

lection of ballads, is located in the American Folklife Center (AFC 1970/061). The project took place in 1970 and 1971 and was also overseen by Alan Jabbour, who preceded Hickerson as director of the Archive of American Folk Song.

24. Maryanne Thompson, "For Posterity's Sake," *Springfield [MO] News-Leader*, July 23, 1987.

25. Parler, "Further Interview with Mr. Herbert Philbrick," October 28, 1959, OFC. See Parler note attached to reel 347, item 7, "FolkProject347t7use."

26. Hunter was referring to the University of Arkansas.

27. Max Hunter, "Folklore: The Universal Language," recorded from the audience by A. E. Schroeder at the University of Missouri–Columbia, November 6, 1980, AC 14–15, Schroeder Collection.

28. Lance, "Max Hunter Remembers Vance and Mary," 7.

29. Equipped with its own coffee shop/bakery, the library is a welcoming and culturally stimulating oasis, particularly during the scorching summer months. Spending days there in research, we saw entire families coming in and out, conversations going on, and individuals (like ourselves) stationed at tables going through archival materials. The original reel-to-reel recordings of the ballads themselves have now been digitized, as noted elsewhere. The audiotapes and transcripts of Hunter's talks and conversations with people like Cathy Barton and the Schroeders have all been copied and distributed across the state by the Missouri State Historical Society.

30. Hunter, "Folklore: The Universal Language," Schroeder Collection.

31. Sweet et al., "Gordon McCann Ozarks Folk Music Collection." Courtesy of the McCann Collection.

32. Ibid.

33. Ibid.

34. Max Hunter, audio CD, vol. 18–20, *Visits With*, 1972.

35. Ibid.

36. Max Hunter, "Outside of Marshall, AR," audio CD, vol. 22–24, *Visits With*, 1972.

37. Benson Fox and Fleecy Fox, "Interview with Max Hunter," audio CD, vol. 10–11 (track 2), *Visits With*, 1972.

38. Fleecy Fox, "Interview with Max Hunter," audio CD, vol. 8–10, *Visits With*, 1972.

39. Myrl Mercer, "Interview with Max Hunter," audio CD, vol. 22–24, *Visits With*, 1973. Mercer died a month later.

40. Bertha Lamar, "Interview with Max Hunter Regarding Her Mother."

41. Ibid.

42. Lance, "Chroniclers of an Era," 58.

43. Lucile Morris Upton, "Ballad Collector Says Folklore, History Are Hard to Separate," *Springfield [MO] Daily News*, October 14, 1974, 16.

44. For a detailed profile of the musical life of Galbraith, see several entries in Howard Wight Marshall's *Play Me Something Quick and Devilish*.

45. *Ozark Heritage Series*, Ozark Heritage Series, McCann Collection, 1978, https://digitalcollections.missouristate.edu/digital/.

46. Ibid.

## Chapter 9. Max Hunter's Map of the Ozarks

1. Milton Rafferty, "The Ozarks as a Region: A Geographer's Description," *OzarksWatch* 1, no. 4 (1988): 1–5. Rafferty was a professor of geology at Missouri State University.

2. W. K. McNeil, liner notes to *Not Far from Here: Traditional Tales and Songs Recorded in the Arkansas Ozarks*, Arkansas Traditions NR12559, 1981, 3.

3. Ibid.

4. Brooks Blevins, *A History of the Ozarks*, vol. 1: *The Old Ozarks* (Urbana: University of Illinois Press, 2018). See also Steve Pokin, "Answer Man: Where Exactly Is the Ozarks?" *Springfield [MO] News-Leader*, February 17, 2018, https://www.news-leader.com/story/news/local/ozarks/2018/02/18/answer-man-when-people-say-ozarks/338906002/.

5. Hunter, "Pioneer Ozarker," 1974, AC 16–17:1, Schroeder Collection.

6. Olson sang some ballads with Hunter as part of the 1977 Ozark Folk Festival and was acquainted with his collecting work through the University of Missouri–Columbia's Academic Support Center. See Ernie Deane, "Folk Festival Full of Talent," *Springfield [MO] Daily News*, November 2, 1977, 60.

7. Hunter, "Pioneer Ozarker," 1974, AC 16–17:1, Schroeder Collection.

8. According to Thompson, the festival went into a steep decline until Hunter revived it in 1976.

9. Hunter, "Pioneer Ozarker," 1974, AC 16–17:9, Schroeder Collection.

10. Hunter, "Festival of Missouri Folk Music and Dance," 1977, Schroeder Collection.

11. Hunter, "Pioneer Ozarker," 1974, AC 16–17:2, Schroeder Collection.

12. Max Hunter, "Ozark Folklore Field Collector," *Just for the Record* 1, no. 6 (September 1977): 9.

13. Hunter, "Pioneer Ozarker," 1974, AC 16–17:1, Schroeder Collection.

14. See journalist Ernie Deane's brief essay on "The Noble 'Hillbilly'" in Ernie Deane, *Ozarks Country* (Branson, MO: Ozarks Mountaineer, 1975), 27–28. See also Hunter, "Pioneer Ozarker," 1974, AC 16–17:8, Schroeder Collection.

15. Hunter, "Pioneer Ozarker," 1974, AC 16–17:9, Schroeder Collection.

16. Hunter, "Word about Fakelore."

17. Hunter, "Pioneer Ozarker," 1974, AC 16–17:2, Schroeder Collection.

18. Hunter, "Festival of Missouri Folk Music and Dance," 1977, Schroeder Collection.

19. Ibid.

20. Cochran, *Vance Randolph*, 135–39.

21. Hunter, "Festival of Missouri Folk Music and Dance," 1977, Schroeder Collection.

22. Linda Bangs, phone interview by author, November 2, 2015.

23. Hunter, "Pioneer Ozarker," 1974, AC 16–17:26, Schroeder Collection. Speaking of cultural stereotypes, it seems likely that Hunter would have been familiar with the television program *Five Star Jubilee*. According to author and record collector Wayne Glenn, one of the many reasons this program came to an end was because residents of Springfield "thought that hillbilly was a dirty word . . . and that Springfield deserved better than to be trying to make money and trying to put out an image on national T.V. to 9 million people, that Springfield was the headquarters of hillbillies. They didn't want any part of that." See Wayne Glenn, Ozark Jubilee interview by Thomas A Peters, video recording, February 27, 2014, Ozarks Voices, Missouri State University Libraries, https://www.youtube.com/watch?v=_hmDEBB-Goc/.

24. Hunter, "Pioneer Ozarker," 1974, AC 16–17:12, Schroeder Collection.

25. Brush arbor revival gatherings, which had their beginnings in Tennessee and Kentucky in the late eighteenth century, were initiated by Presbyterian minister James McGready. These spontaneous meetings also became popular in the Ozarks, where people gathered under a makeshift shelter of trees and shrubs while listening to the preachings of a "circuit rider." See Donna Scott, "It's a Brush Arbor Meeting," *Bittersweet* 3, no. 1 (Fall 1975), https://thelibrary.org/lochist/periodicals/bittersweet/fa75d.htm.

26. Hunter, "Pioneer Ozarker," 1974, AC 16–17:12–13, Schroeder Collection.

27. Ibid., AC 16–17:13, Schroeder Collection.

28. Ibid., AC 16–17:14, Schroeder Collection.

29. Otto Clayton, audio CD, vol. 4–7, *Visits With*, 1971. One of the activities he described involved tying cats together by their tails and throwing them over the clothesline.

30. Hunter, "Pioneer Ozarker," 1974, AC 16–17:17, Schroeder Collection. Randolph had observed that "superstitions relating to love, courtship and marriage are legion in the Ozark country." See Randolph, *The Ozarks*, 88.

31. Hunter, "Pioneer Ozarker," 1974, AC 16–17:18, Schroeder Collection.

32. Ibid., AC 16–17:4, Schroeder Collection.

33. Ibid., AC 16–17:26, Schroeder Collection.

34. Ibid., Schroeder Collection.

## Chapter 10. Max Hunter and the Festival Circuit

1. Thompson, *First 39 Years*.

2. Bob Phillips, *Music of the Mountains*, audio copy of videotape, vol. AC 2 (side 1), C3826: Folk Song and Folklore Collection, Schroeder Collection, 1975.

3. Ibid.

4. Ralph Spencer, "Festival of the Folk Arts, November 17, 1978," AC 12–13:6, Schroeder Collection.

5. Krisanne Parker, email to author, January 12, 2017.

6. Julia O'Reilly, phone interview by author, January 18, 2017.

7. Ibid.

8. Parker, email to author.

9. Ibid.

10. O'Reilly, interview by author.

11. Phillips, *Music of the Mountains*.

12. The McHaffie Homestead cabin was built in 1843.

13. Parker, email to author.

14. At the time of this writing, Osterloh was executive director of the Ethnic Field Ministry in Orlando, Florida, and was also producing the evangelical Jesus Film Project.

15. Osterloh shared these tapes with the author and expressed his interest in donating them to a university archive.

16. Samuel Osterloh, email to author, March 9, 2017.

17. Thompson, *First 39 Years*.

18. Ibid.

19. Hunter, "Interviewed by Cathy Barton," AC 18–19:31–32, Schroeder Collection.

20. Lance, "Chroniclers of an Era," 111–12.

21. Thompson, *First 39 Years*.

22. Ibid.

23. Hunter, "Interviewed by Cathy Barton," AC 18–19:33, Schroeder Collection.

24. Ibid.

25. Evening Bulletin Folk Festival Association, *The Folk Festival Handbook: A Practical Guide for Local Communities* (Philadelphia, 1944). https://babel.hathitrust.org/cgi/pt?id=inu.39000005756999&view=page&seq=3&skin=2021/. See page 27 for specific mention of the Child ballads.

26. Thompson, *First 39 Years*.

27. Letter from Vance Randolph to Max Hunter, "Good Friday," April 8, 1977, box 2, MHC.

28. Betty Fussell, *The Story of Corn* (Albuquerque: University of New Mexico Press, 2004), 261.

29. Ibid.

30. R. Spencer, "Festival of the Folk Arts, November 17, 1978," AC 12–13:6–18, Schroeder Collection.

31. This four-string instrument typically has a banjo body and a mandolin neck and tuning mechanisms.

32. Ralph spoke at length about the difficulty of finding cigars in wooden boxes since by the mid to late seventies, they were all made of cardboard. See Minnie Spencer, "Festival of the Folk Arts, November 17, 1982," audiocassette transcript, vol. AC 12–13, C3826: Folk Song and Folklore Collection, Schroeder Collection, 1982, 16.

33. Ibid., AC 12–13:13, Schroeder Collection.

34. Barton and Para, interview, May 2015.
35. Barton and Para, interview, April 14, 2017.
36. "West Los Angeles Garland Society Letter," July 15, 1976, MHFS, box 2, MHC.
37. Max Hunter, "Letter to the Smithsonian," June 1, 1976, boxes 1–2, MHC.
38. Ibid.
39. Ibid.
40. Ibid.
41. Phillips, *Music of the Mountains*.
42. Hunter, "Introduction to the Ozark Song Collection," Schroeder Collection. Hunter made a tape that clearly reflected the company he was now keeping.
43. Letter from Max Hunter to Jean Nichols, "Evaluation: Mountain Folks Music Festival, Silver Dollar City, MO," June 24, 1976, box 3, MHC.
44. Ibid.
45. Ibid.
46. Ibid.
47. Ibid.
48. Ibid.
49. Ibid.
50. Max Hunter, "Draft Letter to Silver Dollar City," n.d., box 3, MHFS.
51. Thompson, *First 39 Years*.
52. Note the parallels with these predecessors in particular: "The stubbornness and tunnel vision that propelled John Lair and Sarah Gertrude Knott to center stage in their forties served them less well as they each entered their second half century." Williams, *Staging Tradition*, 94.
53. Ibid.
54. N. Cohen, *Folk Music*, 233.
55. Blevins, *Hill Folks*, 257.
56. Hunter, "Evening with Max Hunter," 1976, Schroeder Collection.
57. Max Hunter, "Audition Notice," *Springfield [MO] Leader and Press*, August 28, 1976.
58. "Missouri Arts Council Meeting Minutes," St. Louis, Missouri, May 6, 1977, Missouri Arts Council.
59. Don Underwood, "Folk Music Attracts Nonmuseum Goers: Ozarks Historian Insists on Authenticity," *Springfield [MO] News-Leader*, February 12, 1977.
60. Marshall, *Play Me Something Quick*, 96.
61. Marshall observes in his introduction, "I am often surprised by how many people know that Missouri is a big fiddling state. Perhaps this is because we have more fiddlers' contests than most states and is due to the celebrity of Missouri fiddlers, spanning styles and eras" (3). See also Howard Wight Marshall, *Fiddler's Dream: Old-Time Swing, and Bluegrass Fiddling in Twentieth-Century Missouri* (Columbia: University of Missouri Press, 2017).
62. Gordon McCann, "McCann Journal," April 21, 1983, 1109, McCann Collection.

63. Ibid.

64. Gordon McCann, letter to John Prescott, Professor of Music at Southwest Missouri State University, advocating for digitization of the Max Hunter Collection, n.d., MHFS.

65. He was likely referring most to LeAnne Lindstedt, although the reference is not entirely clear. See Thompson, *First 39 Years*.

66. Hunter, "Visit to Columbia," Schroeder Collection.

## Chapter 11. One Eye on the Past and One on the Future

1. Max Hunter on his collecting experiences and fan mail as recorded by Adolf E. Schroeder during a visit to Springfield, Missouri, May 20, 1982. Audiocassette, vol. AC 44 (B), C3826: Folk Song and Folklore Collection, Schroeder Collection.

2. "Kitty Wells," as sung by Frank Pool, Fayetteville, Arkansas, January 6, 1958, Cat. #0015 (MFH #338).

3. Max Hunter on his collecting experiences and fan mail as recorded by Adolf E. Schroeder during a visit to Springfield, Missouri, May 20, 1982. Audiocassette, vol. AC 44 (B), Schroeder Collection.

4. Jenny Sweet et al., "Gordon McCann Ozarks Folk Music Collection," University Plaza Hotel, Springfield, Missouri, November 12, 2005, https://www.youtube.com/watch?v=Tzv8wnzpILE&feature=youtu.be.

5. Hunter, "Interviewed by Cathy Barton," Schroeder Collection.

6. Ernie Deane, "Ozarks Country," *Cabot [AR] Star-Herald,* November 21, 1980.

7. Headed by Professor Adolf E. Schroeder, the part of the project concerning balladry resulted in three videos—*Down in Missouri with Loman Cansler; Max Hunter: Ozark Song Collector;* and *Ballads, Bones, and Fiddle Tunes*—and was funded by both the Missouri Arts Council and the University of Missouri–Columbia Development Fund. Begun in 1981, the resulting Missouri Origins Project materials became part of the Schroeder Collection in 1984.

8. This program, organized by the Missouri Cultural Heritage Center in Columbia, took place December 4, 1981, at the Springfield–Greene County Library in Springfield, Missouri.

9. Alan Jabbour, "Letter to the Schroeders," January 18, 1983, AAFS/AFC, Library of Congress. The videos Jabbour was referring to were based on interviews with Cathy Barton and were part of the Missouri Origins Project.

10. Anthony, *Chasing the Rising Sun*, 112.

11. N. Cohen, *Folk Music*, 329.

12. Spencer, *Ballad Collectors of North America*, 3.

13. Cansler died in 1992.

14. Hunter, "Talk given during 'Festival of the Folk Arts and Music.'" Hammontree sang several bawdy and comedic songs for Hunter, in addition to songs of local significance, such as "The Battle of Wilson Creek."

15. Hunter, "Home Interview with Donald Lance et al.," Schroeder Collection. See also Lance, "Max Hunter Remembers Vance and Mary," 22–23.

16. Hunter, "Home Interview with Donald Lance et al.," Schroeder Collection. See also Lance, "Max Hunter Remembers Vance and Mary," 22–23.

17. Hunter, "Pioneer Ozarker," 1974, Schroeder Collection.

18. Max Hunter, audio CD, vol. 1–3 *Visits With*, 1970.

19. Max Hunter, Charlie and Barry Horton, "Interview by Max Hunter," audio CD, vol. 20–22, *Visits With*, August 23, 1972.

20. Hunter, "Interviewed by Cathy Barton," Schroeder Collection.

21. Max Hunter, "Collecting Missouri Folksongs," audio recording of Annual Meeting of the Missouri Folklore Society (MFSR), audiocassette, vol. AC 53–54, C 2045, SHSM, November 14, 1986.

22. Hunter, "Interviewed by Cathy Barton," AC 18–19:3, Schroeder Collection.

23. Hunter, "Max Hunter: Ozark Song Collector," Schroeder Collection.

24. Max Hunter, "Afterword to Ozark Folksong Collection" (n.d.), MHFS.

25. This paper was submitted toward Fern Gregory's master's degree in music at the School of Arts and Sciences, Central Missouri State University, Warrensburg, Missouri. Only one year before, a student by the name of Alice Kinslow Kugler submitted a thesis titled "Transcriptions of Selected Songs from the Max Hunter Collection of Ozark Folksongs" toward her master's in music education at Holy Names College in Oakland, California, but to my knowledge, Hunter never made mention of Kugler. A copy of the Kugler thesis can be obtained through the duplication service at the Archive of American Folk Culture (https://www.loc.gov/duplicationservices/) or by contacting the Paul J. Kushing Library at Holy Names College, Oakland, California.

26. Fern Denise Gregory, "Selected Child Ballad Tunes in the Max Hunter Collection of Ozark Folksongs" (master's thesis, Springfield, Central Missouri State University, 1979), 1.

27. Ibid., 6.

28. Gregory, abstract, in ibid.

29. Gregory, "Selected Child Ballad Tunes," 10. For an in-depth discussion of these challenges, see Bertrand H. Bronson, *The Traditional Tunes of the Child Ballads: With Their Texts, According to the Extant Records of Great Britain and America*, vol. 1 (Princeton, NJ: Princeton University Press, 1959).

30. Gregory, "Selected Child Ballad Tunes," 11.

31. Early on, Gregory, now Dr. Alexandra D. F. Gregory, of Duquesne University, spent two weeks student teaching for Alice Kugler, a music educator whom she greatly admired. Gregory went on to enjoy a successful career in musical performance and scholarship. It is an odd coincidence that both Kugler and Gregory, unbeknownst to the other, worked with the Hunter Collection.

32. "Artlogue," Summer 1998, Missouri Arts Council. This annual award pays "tribute to individuals and organizations who have made significant contributions to the state's cultural life."

33. Linda Bangs, "My Dad Max Hunter" (unpublished, November 2015).

34. Bennett, "Keeping Ozarks Culture Alive," 6B.

35. Ibid.

36. The Max Hunter Folk Song Collection can be accessed and searched at https://maxhunter.missouristate.edu/.

37. Kathleen Murray, quoted in Jim Baker, *Preserving Folklore and Traditional Music, and Keeping It Accessible. OzarksWatch Video Magazine*, Ozarks Public Television, 1999.

38. "Disclaimer," MHFS, n.d., https://maxhunter.missouristate.edu/disclaimer.htm.

39. Tom Carter, host, *Family Singing: A Musical Portrait, OzarksWatch Video Magazine*, Ozarks Public Television, August 2005, https://video.optv.org/video/ozarks watch-video-magazine-family-singing-a-musical-portrait/.

40. Mark Bilyeu, phone interview by author, January 8, 2016.

41. Henigan, "Ozark Ballads," 176.

42. Sweet et al., "Gordon McCann Ozarks Folk Music Collection."

43. Judy Domeny, "Terrible Songs: Missouri Tragedies in Music," *Missouri Folklore Society Journal* 20 (1998): 121–22.

44. Hunter, "Introduction to the Ozark Song Collection," Schroeder Collection.

45. Max Hunter and Judy Domeny Bowen, "Interview with Marilyn Prosser," audio recording, August 15, 1983, MSU-Springfield.

46. Domeny, "Terrible Songs," 121.

47. Lance, "Max Hunter Remembers Vance and Mary," 22.

48. Robert B. Cochran, "'All the Songs in the World': The Story of Emma Dusenbury," *Arkansas Historical Quarterly* 44 (1985): 15.

49. Max Hunter said, "I think he became pretty well acquainted with her. Back then he'd go and stay two or three days at a time. And if he found out those people were hungry, he'd go and buy some food." See Hunter, "Visit to Columbia," Schroeder Collection.

50. Cochran, "'All the Songs in the World,'" 15.

51. Wolz, "Anglo-American Music in Missouri," 124.

52. Bronson, *Ballad as Song*, 105.

53. Shortleaf Band, https://www.shortleafband.com/shortleaf-videos.

54. See Marshall, *Play Me Something Quick and Devilish*.

55. See more about Cindy and Mark at "The Creek Rocks," n.d., http://www.thecreekrocks.com/about.

56. One More Dollar, http://onemoredollarband.com/.

57. The Ozark Highballers, https://www.theozarkhighballers.com/.

58. Max Hunter, "Ozark Folklore," ed. Stephen D. Ansley, *Just for the Record* 1, no. 3 (1977): 16.

59. N. Cohen, "Ballad Collectors in the Ozarks," 44.

60. Hunter, "Ozark Folklore."

61. Anthony, *Chasing the Rising Sun*, 114.

62. Hunter, "Talk given during 'Festival of the Folk Arts and Music,'" Schroeder Collection.

63. Gordon McCann, "Letter to SMSU," n.d., McCann Collection.

64. Sweet et al., "Gordon McCann Ozarks Folk Music Collection."

65. Hunter served in the navy from 1942 to 1943.

66. Bangs interview with author, June 21, 2016.

67. Ibid.

68. The original reel-to-reel tapes and several folders of correspondence and related materials can be found at the Springfield–Greene County District Library.

69. The videotape was created by his youngest daughter, Jenny.

70. Hunter, "Max Hunter: Ozark Song Collector," Schroeder Collection.

71. These words were read by Governor Mel Carnahan during the Missouri Arts Council Awards ceremony in 1998.

72. Bangs, "My Dad Max Hunter."

# SELECTED BIBLIOGRAPHY

## Archival Sources

Archive of American Folk Song (now known as Archive of Folk Culture) (AAFS/
AFC). Library of Congress, Washington, D.C.

Loman D. and Laura M. Cansler Collection (Cansler Collection). State Historical
Society of Southern Missouri. Columbia, Missouri.

Central Arkansas Library Systems (CALS). *Encyclopedia of Arkansas*. Little Rock,
Arkansas. https://encyclopediaofarkansas.net/.

Frederick Danker Tapes (Danker Tapes). 1970. Waltham, Massachusetts. Audiocassette recordings of interviews with traditional singers primarily in Stone County,
Arkansas.

Eisenmayer Family Papers (SP0032). State Historical Society of Missouri Research
Center–Springfield.

Herbert Halpert Collection (AFC 2004/008). Archive of Folk Culture. American
Folklife Center. Library of Congress, Washington, D.C.

Max Hunter Collection (MHC). Springfield–Greene County Library. Springfield,
Missouri.

Max Hunter Folk Song Collection (MHFS). Missouri State University. Springfield,
Missouri. https://maxhunter.missouristate.edu/.

Max Hunter. *Visits from the Ozarks* (*Visits With*). CDs, 1959–1972. Springfield–Greene
County Library, Springfield, Missouri.

Alan Lomax Collection. Manuscripts. Southern Folk Heritage Series, 1978, Manu-
script/Mixed Material. American Folklife Center. Library of Congress, Washington, D.C.

Gordon McCann Collection (McCann Collection). Missouri State University Special Collections and Archives. Springfield, Missouri. https://digitalcollections
.missouristate.edu/digital/.

Missouri Folklore Society (MFS). Columbia, Missouri, and Truman State University, Kirksville, Missouri. https://missourifolkloresociety.truman.edu/.

Missouri Folklore Society Records (MFSR). 1906–1931, 1971–2016. State Historical Society of Missouri. https://files.shsmo.org/manuscripts/columbia/C2045.pdf/.

Missouri Origins Project (MOP). University of Missouri Academic Support Center. Columbia, Missouri.

Missouri State University Digital Collections, Katherine Lederer Ozarks African American History Collection. https://cdm17307.contentdm.oclc.org/digital/collection/Lederer/.

Missouri State University Libraries. https://libraries.missouristate.edu/.

Missouri State University Special Collections and Archives (MSU-Springfield). Springfield, Missouri. https://libraries.missouristate.edu/archives.htm/.

Joan O'Bryant Kansas Folklore Collection (O'Bryant Collection). Special Collections and University Archives. Wichita State University, Kansas.

Ozark Folksong Collection (OFC). University Libraries Digital Collections and Special Collections Department. University of Arkansas. Fayetteville, Arkansas. https://digitalcollections.uark.edu/digital/collection/OzarkFolkSong/.

Rackensack Oral Histories (ROH). University of Central Arkansas Archives. Conway, Arkansas. https://uca.edu/archives/rackensack-history/.

Dorothy Scarborough Papers, 1986–1938. Baylor University, Waco, Texas.

Adolf E. and Rebecca Schroeder Collection (Schroeder Collection). State Historical Society of Missouri, Columbia, Missouri.

"Cecil Sharp's Appalachian Diaries: 1915–1918." Vaughan Williams Memorial Library. London, England. https://www.vwml.org/browse/browse-collections-sharp-diaries/.

State Historical Society of Missouri (SHSM). Columbia, Missouri. https://shsmo.org/.

John Quincy Wolf Folklore Collection (WFC). Regional Studies Center. Lyon College. Batesville, Arkansas.

Lucile Morris Upton Papers. State Historical Society of Missouri–Columbia. https://shsmo.org/collections/women-media/biographies/upton-lucile/.

## Other Sources

American Folklife Center. "The Ethnographic Experience: Sidney Robertson Cowell in Northern California." n.d. https://www.loc.gov/collections/sidney-robertson-cowell-northern-california-folk-music/articles-and-essays/the-ethnographic-experience-sidney-robertson-cowell-in-northern-california/

———. Ethnic Recordings in America: A Neglected Heritage. Washington, D.C.: Library of Congress, 1982.

Anthony, Ted. Chasing the Rising Sun: The Journey of an American Song. New York: Simon and Schuster, 2007.

"Artlogue." Summer 1998. Missouri Arts Council Archives. St. Louis, MO.

Baker, Jim. Preserving Folklore and Traditional Music, and Keeping It Accessible. Ozarks Watch Video Magazine. Ozarks Public Television, 1999.

Barz, Gregory F., and Timothy J. Cooley. *Shadows in the Field: New Perspectives for Fieldwork in Ethnomusicology.* New York: Oxford University Press, 1997.

Beaudry, Nicole. "The Challenges of Human Relations in Ethnographic Enquiry." In Barz and Cooley, *Shadows in the Field,* 224–45.

Belden, Henry Marvin. *Ballads and Songs Collected by the Missouri Folk-Lore Society.* 3rd ed. University of Missouri Studies. Vol. 15, no. 1. Columbia: University of Missouri Press, 1966. Originally published 1940.

Bilyeu, Jody, Jenny Sweet, et al., "Gordon McCann Ozarks Folk Music Collection." Presentation, University Plaza Hotel, Springfield, Missouri, November 12, 2005, https://www.youtube.com/watch?v=Tzv8wnzpILE/.

Blevins, Brooks. *Hill Folks: A History of Arkansas Ozarkers and Their Image.* Chapel Hill: University of North Carolina Press, 2002.

———. "Hillbillies and the Holy Land: The Development of Tourism in the Arkansas Ozarks." In *Southern Journeys: Tourism, History, and Culture in the Modern South,* edited by Richard D. Starnes et al., 42–65 (Tuscaloosa: University of Alabama Press, 2003).

———. *A History of the Ozarks.* Vol. 1: *The Old Ozarks.* Urbana: University of Illinois Press, 2018.

Bronner, Simon. *Following Tradition.* Logan: Utah State University Press, 1998.

Bronson, Bertrand H. *The Ballad as Song.* Berkeley: University of California Press, 1969.

———. *The Traditional Tunes of the Child Ballads: With Their Texts, According to the Extant Records of Great Britain and America.* Vols. 1–4. Princeton, NJ: Princeton University Press, 1959–1972.

Burgess, John. "Brief Life of a Victorian Enthusiast: 1825–1896." *Harvard Magazine,* June 2006.

Cantwell, Robert. *When We Were Good.* Cambridge, MA: Harvard University Press, 1996.

Child, Francis James, ed. *The English and Scottish Popular Ballads,* 5 vols. Boston: Houghton Mifflin, 1904. https://archive.org/details/englishscottishp1904chil/page/n19/mode/2up?ref=ol&view=theater/.

Cochran, Robert B. "'All the Songs in the World': The Story of Emma Dusenbury." *Arkansas Historical Quarterly* 44 (1985): 3–15.

———. *Louise Pound: Scholar, Athlete, Feminist Pioneer.* Lincoln: University of Nebraska Press, 2009.

———. *Singing in Zion: Music and Song in the Life of One Arkansas Family.* Fayetteville: University of Arkansas Press, 1999.

———. *Vance Randolph: An Ozark Life.* Chicago: University of Illinois Press, 1985.

Cohen, Norm. "Ballad Collectors in the Ozarks." In *The Ballad Collectors of North America: How Gathering Folksongs Transformed Academic Thought and American Identity,* edited by Scott B. Spencer. Lanham, MD: Scarecrow Press, 2012.

———. *Folk Music: A Regional Exploration.* Westport, CT: Greenwood Press, 2005.

Cohen, Ronald. *Rainbow Quest: The Folk Revival and American Society, 1940–1970.* Amherst: University of Massachusetts Press, 2002.

Collins, Shirley. *America Over the Water: A Musical Journey with Alan Lomax.* London: SAF Publishers, 2004.

———, and Dolly Collins. *The Harvest Years.* Sleeve notes. EMI 228 404-2. Mainly Norfolk, 2008.

Davidson, Mark A. "Recording the Nation: Folk Music and the Government in Roosevelt's New Deal, 1936–1941." PhD dissertation. University of California Santa Cruz, 2015.

Davis, Gayle, and Rachel Shorthill. *The Unburnished Mirror: An Interpretive Study of Folklore and Content Description of the Joan O'Bryant Collection.* Edited by Leonard Messineo Jr. Wichita, KS: Wichita Public Library, 1984.

Deane, Ernie. *Ozarks Country.* Branson, MO: Ozarks Mountaineer, 1975.

Domeny, Judy. "Terrible Songs: Missouri Tragedies in Music." *Missouri Folklore Society Journal* 20 (1998): 121—22.

Driftwood, Jimmy. Liner notes to *Music of the Ozarks.* National Geographic Society 703, 1972.

Duncan, Bob. *The Dicky Bird Was Singing: Men, Women, & Black Gold.* New York: Rinehart & Co., 1952.

Evening Bulletin Folk Festival Association. *The Folk Festival Handbook: A Practical Guide for Local Communities.* Philadelphia, 1944.

Finger, Charles J. *Frontier Ballads. Songs from Lawless Lands. Heard and Gathered by Charles J. Finger.* London: William Heinemann, 1927.

Finnegan, Ruth. *Oral Poetry: Its Nature, Significance and Social Context,* 2nd ed. Bloomington: Indiana University Press, 1992.

Fussell, Betty. *The Story of Corn.* New York: University of New Mexico Press, 2004.

Georges, Robert A., and Michael A. Jones. *People Studying People: The Human Element in Fieldwork.* Berkeley: University of California Press, 1980.

Gerould, Gordon H. *The Ballad of Tradition.* Reprint. Oxford, UK: Oxford University Press, 1957.

Graves, Robert. *English and Scottish Ballads.* London: William Heinemann, 1957.

Green, Archie. "Hillbilly Music: Source & Symbol." *Journal of American Folk-Lore* 78, no. 309 (1965): 204–228.

Gregory, Fern Denise. "Selected Child Ballad Tunes in the Max Hunter Collection of Ozark Folksongs." Master's thesis. Central Missouri State University, 1979.

Gummere, Francis B. *The Popular Ballad.* Boston: Houghton Mifflin, 1907.

Henigan, Julie. "Ozark Ballads as Story and Song." *Missouri Folklore Society Journal* 27 (2005): 157–86.

Hodgart, M.J.C. *The Ballads.* New York: W. W. Norton, 1962.

Hughes, Marion. *Three Years in Arkansaw.* Chicago: M. A. Donohue & Co., 1904.

Jones, Loyal. *Minstrel of the Appalachians: The Story of Bascom Lamar Lunsford.* Boone, NC: Appalachian Consortium Press, 1984.

Kodish, Debora. *Good Friends and Bad Enemies*. Urbana: University of Illinois Press, 1986.

Lance, Donald M. "Chroniclers of an Era: Loman Cansler and Max Hunter, Missouri Collectors of Traditional Music, Songs, and Lore." *Missouri Folklore Society Journal* 20 (1998).

———. "Max Hunter Remembers Vance and Mary." *Missouri Folklore Society Journal* 4 (1982): 7.

Laws, G. Malcolm, Jr. *American Balladry from British Broadsides*. Philadelphia: American Folklore Society, 1957.

———. *Native American Balladry: A Descriptive Study and a Bibliographical Syllabus*. Rev. ed. Philadelphia: American Folklore Society, 1964.

Leary, James P. *Folksongs of Another America: Field Recordings from the Upper Midwest, 1937–1946*. Madison: University of Wisconsin Press, 2015.

Lomax, John A. *Adventures of a Ballad Hunter*. New York: Macmillan, 1947.

———. "Some Types of American Folk-Song." *Journal of American Folk-Lore* 28 (1915).

Marshall, Howard Wight. *Fiddler's Dream: Old-Time Swing, and Bluegrass Fiddling in Twentieth-Century Missouri* (Columbia: University of Missouri Press, 2017.

———. *Play Me Something Quick and Devilish: Old-Time Fiddlers in Missouri*. Columbia: University of Missouri Press, 2012.

McNeil, W. K. Introduction to Vance Randolph, *Ozark Folksongs*. Columbia: University of Missouri Press, 1980.

———. Liner notes to *Not Far from Here: Traditional Tales and Songs Recorded in the Arkansas Ozarks*. Arkansas Traditions NR12559, 1981.

———, and Williams M. Clements, eds. *An Arkansas Folklore Sourcebook*. Fayetteville: University of Arkansas Press, 1992.

McPherson, Harold. "Black Legends of Springfield Music." *Ozarks Watch* 2, no. 6 (2017): 59–66.

Missouri Friends of the Folk Arts (MFFA). "I'm Old but I'm Awfully Tough." Booklet accompanying LP *I'm Old but I'm Awfully Tough: Traditional Music of the Ozark Region*. MFFA 1001, 1977.

Morrow, Lynn, and Linda Myers-Phinney. *Shepherd of the Hills Country: Tourism Transforms the Ozarks, 1880s-1930s*. Fayetteville: University of Arkansas Press, 1999.

Morton, David. "Armour Research Foundation and the Wire Recorder: How Academic Entrepreneurs Fail." *Technology and Culture* 39 (1998): 213–44.

Mulhollan, Kelly. *True Faith, True Light: The Devotional Art of Ed Stilley*. Fayetteville: University of Arkansas Press, 2015.

Nelson, Sarah Jane. "The Crooked Road Meets the Conservatory." *Fiddler Magazine* (Fall 2012): 19–21.

———. "A Salesman amidst Scholars: Ozarks Song Collector Max Hunter." *CDSS News*, 2016, 14–15. https://www.cdss.org/images/newsletter_archives/articles/CDSS_News_spring_2016_salesman.pdf/.

Parler, Mary Celestia, and Vance Randolph. Liner notes to Max Hunter, *Ozark Folksongs and Ballads Sung by Max Hunter*. Folk-Legacy Records FSA 11, 1963.

Pentlin, Susan L. "Maude Williams Martin: Early Ballad Collector in Missouri." *Missouri Folklore Society Journal* 8–9 (1986–1987): 45–70.

———, and Rebecca B. Schroeder. "H. M. Belden, the English Club, and the Missouri Folk-Lore Society." *Missouri Folklore Society Journal* 8–9 (1986–1987): 1–44.

Piazza, Tom. *The Southern Journey of Alan Lomax*. New York: W. W. Norton, 2013.

Pound, Louise. *American Ballads and Songs* (New York: Charles Scribner's Sons, 1922).

———. "Poetic Origins of the Ballad." (1921). Faculty Publications, Department of English. 43. https://digitalcommons.unl.edu/englishfacpubs/43/?utm_source=digital commons.unl.edu%2Fenglishfacpubs%2F43&utm_medium=PDF&utm _campaign=PDFCoverPages/.

Prozzillo Byers, Judy. "Ruth Ann Musick—The Show-Me Mountaineer: A Missourian Adopts West Virginia." *Missouri Folklore Society Journal* 8–9 (1986–1987): 89–114.

Rafferty, Milton. "The Ozarks as a Region: A Geographer's Description." *OzarksWatch* 1, no. 4 (1988): 1–5. https://cdm17307.contentdm.oclc.org/digital/collection/p17307coll1/ id/499/.

Randolph, Vance. *Blow the Candle Out: Unprintable Ozark Folksongs and Folklore*. Vol. 2. Fayetteville: University of Arkansas Press, 1992.

———. *Ozark Folksongs*. Revised. 4 vols. Columbia: University of Missouri Press, 1980.

———. *Ozark Magic and Folklore*. New York: Dover Publications, 1964.

———. *Ozark Mountain Folks*. New York: Vanguard Press, 1932.

———. *The Ozarks: An American Survival of Primitive Society*. New York: Vanguard Press, 1931.

———. *Pissing in the Snow and Other Ozark Folktales*. Urbana: University of Illinois Press, 1976.

———, and Ruth Ann Musick. "Folksong Hunters in Missouri." *Midwest Folklore* 1, no. 1 (1951): 23–31.

Renwick, Roger deVeer. *Recentering Anglo-American Folksong: Sea Crabs and Wicked Youths*. Jackson: University Press of Mississippi, 2001.

Riddle, Almeda. *A Singer and Her Songs: Almeda Riddle's Book of Ballads*. Edited by Roger D. Abrahams and George Foss. Baton Rouge: Louisiana State University Press, 1970.

Ritchie, Fiona, and Doug Orr. *Wayfaring Strangers: The Musical Voyage from Scotland and Ulster to Appalachia*. Chapel Hill: University of North Carolina Press, 2014.

Schroeder, Rebecca B. "Henry Marvin Belden (1865–1954)." In *Dictionary of Missouri Biography*, edited by Lawrence O. Christensen, William E. Foley, Gary R. Kremer, and Kenneth H. Winn. Columbia: University of Missouri Press, 1999.

Spencer, Scott B, ed. *The Ballad Collectors of North America: How Gathering Folksongs Transformed Academic Thought and American Identity*. Lanham, MD: Scarecrow Press, 2012.

Starnes, Richard D., Brooks Blevins, Harvey H. Jackson III, Ted Ownby, Daniel S. Pierce, Harvey Newman, Brenden C. Martin, et al. *Southern Journeys: Tourism, History, and Culture in the Modern South*. Edited by Richard D. Starnes. Tuscaloosa: University of Alabama Press, 2003.

Stephens, Page H. "The Case of Missing Folk Music: A Study of Aspects of Musical Life in Stone County, Arkansas, from 1890–1980." *Mid-America Folklore* 10, nos. 2–3 (1982): 58–69.

Stone, Peter. "Sidney and Henry Cowell." Association for Cultural Equity. http://www.culturalequity.org/alan-lomax/friends/cowell/.

Thomas, Jean. *The Traipsin' Woman*. New York: E. P. Dutton, 1933.

Thompson, Carroll S. *The First 39 Years of the Ozark Folk Festival*. Eureka Springs, AR: Self-published, 1987.

Vukas, Rachel. "Joan O'Bryant." *Missouri Folklore Society Journal* 11–12 (1989–1990): 123–28.

Various Artists. *The Continuing Tradition*. Vol. 1: *Ballads, A Folk-Legacy Sampler*. Liner notes. Folk-Legacy Records FS1–75, 1981. https://folkways-media.si.edu/liner_notes/folk-legacy/FLG00075-LP.pdf.

Waterhouse, Lin. *The West Plains Dance Hall Explosion*. Charleston, SC: History Press, 2010.

Whisnant, David. "White Top Festival: What We Have [Not] Learned." Southwest Virginia Higher Education Center, Abingdon, Virginia, August 6, 1998. http://faculty.buffalostate.edu/fishlm/articles/whitetop.htm/.

Wilgus, D. K. *Anglo-American Folksong Scholarship since 1898*. New Brunswick, NJ: Rutgers University Press, 1959.

———. "Record Reviews." *Journal of American Folk-Lore* 77, no. 303 (March 1964): 94—96.

Williams, Michael Ann. *Staging Tradition: John Lair and Sarah Gertrude Knott*. Urbana: University of Illinois Press, 2006.

Winick, Stephen D. "Francis James Child and *The English and Scottish Popular Ballads*." Library of Congress, n.d. https://www.loc.gov/item/ihas.200196779/.

Wolf, John Quincy, Jr. "Folksingers and the RE-Creation of Folksong." *Western Folklore* 26, no. 2 (1967): 101–111.

Wolfe, Charles, and Kip Lornell. *The Life and Legend of Leadbelly*. New York: HarperCollins, 1992.

Wolz, Lyn A. "Anglo-American Music in Missouri: An Annotated Bibliography." *Missouri Folklore Society Journal* 4 (1982): 51–104.

Wright, Harold Bell. *Shepherd of the Hills*. New York: A. L. Burt, 1907.

# INDEX

Abrahams, Roger, x, xvi, 12
African American/Black folk music, 4, 6, 14–15, 17
All-Ozarks Festival, 23
Amalgamated Folksong Collectors Union, 125
American Folklife Center (formerly Archive of American Folk Song), 7, 87–88, 126–27, 134, 162–63
Anthony, Ted, 33, 85–86, 163, 171
Appalachian ballads, 2–3, 7–9, 13, 17, 19
Arkansas Folk Festival, 95, 100

Bailey, Nathan, 59
Bain, Chloe, 49
Bald Knobbers, 63
ballad studies and collecting: "ballad," defined, 2; ballad emendation and, 53; "ballet books/song ballets" in, 4–5, 15, 39, 57, 179n27; basis in Anglo-American songs, 2–3, 8, 15; of Belden (*see* Belden, Henry Marvin); broadside ballads/"stall ballads" in, 2, 11, 56, 58–59, 62–63, 82–83, 177–78n4; of Cansler (*see* Cansler, Loman); of Child (*see* Child ballads); collecting methods in, 1–3, 6–7 (*see also names of specific ballad collectors*); at Harvard University, 1–4; of Hunter (*see* Hunter, Max: ballad collecting); of George Lyman Kittredge, 2, 4; of Alan Lomax (*see* Lomax, Alan); of John Lomax, xii, 6, 7,

163, 181n54; of McCann (*see* McCann, Gordon); next generation of collectors and performers, 164–72; of O'Bryant (*see* O'Bryant, Joan); origins in Missouri, 3–7; of Parler (*see* Parler, Mary Celestia); of Randolph (*see* Randolph, Vance); of Cecil Sharp, 2–3; suppression of women and, 62–63, 92–93, 176n3
"ballet books/song ballets," 4–5, 15, 39, 57, 179n27
Bangs, Linda Hunter (MH daughter), 32, 43–44, 53, 67, 68, 116, 129, 142, 166, 172, 174
Barclay, Audrey, 132
Barnes, Willadean, 92, 93
Barton, Cathy, xii, 50–51, 57, 98, 100, 122, 135, 152, 162, 168, 170
Beaudry, Nicole, 46
Becker, Kim and Greg, 147
Belden, Henry Marvin, 61, 83; ballad collecting and, 3–7, 15, 38, 50; *Ballads and Songs Collected by the Missouri Folk-Lore Society* (1940), 4–6, 11, 14–15, 187n35, 194–95n25
Bennett, Sara J., 166
Big Muddy Folk Festival (Boonville, MO), 152
Bilyeu, Mark, 167, 170
Bird, Odis, xi, xxv, 43–44, 80–81
Black/African American folk music, 4, 6, 14–15, 17

Blevins, Brooks, 7–8, 34–35, 89, 139
Blunt, Roy, 122, 172
Bowen, Judy Domeny, 52, 168–69, 170
Bradley, Dortha, 85, 86
Breazeal, J. W., 59–60
Brewer, Pearl, xii, xxv, 60–62
Brewer, Vaughn, 83, 99
Briscoe, Mary, 149–50
broadside ballads/"stall ballads," 2, 11, 56, 58–59, 62–63, 82–83, 177–78n4
Bronson, Bertrand Harris, 126, 155, 165, 170
Bullock, Phil, 148–49
Burnett, William "Harrison," xxiv, 42, 84–86
Byrd, David, 86, 87

Campbell, Booth, xv
Cansler, Loman, xii, xvi, 123–25; awards/ honors, 163; ballad collecting and, 37–39, 123–24, 166; death (1992), 163, 213n13; Loman D. and Laura M. Cansler Collection, 124, 166; meets MH, 37–38, 123–25; Missouri Origins Project and, 162–63, 213n7; Smithsonian Folkways Recordings, 124; at the University of Missouri, 38, 123
Cantwell, Robert, 10
Carlisle, Irene Jones, 106
Carnahan, Mel, 166, 174
Carter Family repertoire, 99, 133, 152
Cawood, Georgina, 78
Cherkasky, Shirley, 153–54
Child, Francis James, 1–2, 15, 18. See also Child ballads
Child ballads (The English and Scottish Popular Ballads 1882–1898, 5 vols.), xix, 57–62; ballad collecting and, 1–2, 4–5, 15, 18, 40, 122, 165–67; in the Max Hunter Folk Song Collection, 40, 165–66, 167; MH acquires Child ballad books, 106; No. 2, 57–58; No. 3, 57, 193n8; No. 10, 61–62; No. 18, 62; No. 20, 61; No. 73, 52, 62; No. 95, 60; No. 155, 51–52, 57; No. 214, 63–67; No. 215, 102; No. 250, 6; No. 274, 34, 88; No. 289, 57; variants on, 2, 11, 51–53, 58, 61–62, 81, 88, 102
church/hymnal songs, 13, 23–24, 28, 59–60
Clayton, Otto, 143–44
Coberley, Olive, xxiv, 10, 42, 82–83, 124–25, 166
Cochran, Robert B., ix–xvi, 99, 108, 169
Coggburn, Andrew, 63

Cohen, Norm, 7, 13, 19, 73, 157
Cohen, Ronald D., xii, 11
Collins, Shirley, 92–93
Columbia, MO: Festival of Missouri Folk Music and Dance, 51–52, 122, 141; State Historical Society of Missouri–Columbia, xvii–xviii, 6, 122, 124, 135, 166. See also University of Missouri–Columbia
Copeland, Betty Lou, 12
Country Dance and Song Society, 153
Cowell, Sidney Robertson, 7
Crafton, John, 59
Crankie story scrolls, xix, 177n3

Danker, Frederick "Fred," 98, 162
Davis, Boyce, 15
Davis, Gussie L., 227
Davis, Lula and Mary Jo, xii, 62
Davis, T. M., 15
Deane, Ernie, 115, 162, 171
Dearmore, Reba, xii, 50, 58, 86–88
Driftwood, Jimmy (James Morris), xii, xiv, xv, 12, 86, 146, 150; father, Neal Morris, 92, 93, 97–98, 133; and "folk music" as term, 17; Ollie Gilbert and, 90, 96, 101; guitar playing and, 17; as Ozark Folk Center program director, xiii, xvi, 95, 100, 101, 157
Duncan, Bob, 36, 123
Dusenbury, Emma, 7, 169
Dylan, Ruby, 103–4

Eden, William, 16, 44–45, 63
Engel, Carl, 7
The English and Scottish Popular Ballads 1882–1898. See Child ballads
English folk songs. See Child ballads
Eureka Springs, AR. See Ozark Folk Festival
Everly, Elmer ("Uncle Elmer"), 26–28
Everly, Gladys ("Aunt Gladys"), 26–28, 137

Festival of American Folklife (later Smithsonian Folklife Festival), 89–90, 95, 152–54
Festival of Missouri Folk Music and Dance (Columbia, MO), 51–52, 122, 141
"folk," as term, 10–11, 17
Folk-Legacy Records, xix, 36, 122, 177n2
"folk music," as term, 17, 124, 206n23
folk revival, xiv, 10–11, 39, 85–86, 99, 133, 146–47, 152, 154, 156, 157, 163, 168

Forrest, Ashley Hull, 170
Fox, Benson and Fleecy, ix, xviii, xxv, 137
Fraser, Michael, 170

Galbraith, Art, 137–38, 158, 159
Galbraith, Emma, 5
Garcia, Flora Maria, 166
Georges, Robert A., 73
Gerould, Gordon H., 2
Gilbert, "Aunt" Ollie, x, xii, xviii, xxv, 51, 89–
    100, 101, 133, 162; banjo playing, 12, 90, 95,
    97–98; Child ballads and, 90, 94; family
    background and domestic life, 90, 92–94,
    96; festival appearances, 95–96, 154; jokes
    and stories of, 16, 98; MH and, 12, 15, 42,
    89–100, 157; visual impairment and audi-
    tory memory, 91, 95–99
Gilbert, Ewell "Oscar," 92–94
Glassie, Henry, x
Gordon, Robert Winslow, 7, 17
Gorman, Larry, x
Graves, Robert, 53
Gregory, Fern Denise, 165–66
Gummere, Francis B., 15
Guthrie, Woody, 14

Haggard, Merle, xiv
Halpert, Herbert, 17–18
Hamilton, Goldy, 5
Hammond, T. R., 58–59
Harmon, George, 102
Harvard University, 1–4; Child ballad stud-
    ies (see Child, Francis James; Child bal-
    lads); Kittredge ballad studies, 2, 4
Haslett, Iva, xxv, 78–80
Henigan, Julie, 16, 168
Heston, Joshua, xviii, xix
Hickerson Joe, xii, 88, 134
High, Fred, x–xii, xxiv, 42, 58, 70–74, 81, 113,
    149–50, 169
"hillbilly," as term, 142–43, 189n24, 206n23
Holland, Floyd, 133–34
Holland, Paul, 6
Holt, Bob, 170
Horton, Barry, 164
Horton, Charlie, 136, 164
Howell, Mike, 147
Hughes, Marion, 91
Humpy Holler Folk, 151–52
Hunter, David (MH son), 68, 129

Hunter, Ethyl Rose (MH mother), 19–28
Hunter, Harold (MH brother), ix, 24, 28
Hunter, Max (MH): birth, 19, 21; chil-
    dren, 129 (see also Bangs, Linda Hunter;
    Hunter, David; Sweet, Jenny Hunter); de-
    scribed, xiii, 24, 173; early musical inter-
    ests, 22–23, 24, 27–28; early years, 19–28,
    144; education, 29, 112, 123, 165; and fes-
    tival circuit, 145–60 (see also Mountain
    Folks Music Festival; Ozark Folk Festi-
    val); final illness and death (1999), 166,
    172–74; on "folk" as term, 10–11, 17; on
    "folk song" as term, 124, 206n23; guitar
    playing and, 24, 31–32, 40, 44, 97, 110–11,
    112; on "hillbillies" vs. "Hill People,"
    142–43, 206n23; marries Virginia Mercer
    (1939), 29, 30 (see also Hunter, Virginia
    Mercer); on "Ozarker" vs. "Ozarkian,"
    xiv–xv, 8–9, 141–42; on societal and tech-
    nological change, 163–66; Springfield as
    hometown of (see Springfield, MO); as
    traveling salesman, xxiv–xxv, 1, 10, 12,
    20–21, 29–33, 34, 37, 40–41, 116, 154; in the
    U.S. Navy, 172
—ballad collecting, 11–18, 30; academic
    world and, 1, 13, 17–18, 111, 120–23, 140–
    43, 158, 164–66; Arrow Rock interview
    (1982), 172, 173–74; authenticity require-
    ment and, xiv, 10–11, 35–37, 39–41, 48–
    53, 126–27, 135–36, 145, 146–47, 155–58,
    159–60; as avocation vs. vocation, 14–
    18, 31–33, 39–41, 45–46, 126–27, 154, 155;
    awards/honors, 163, 166, 172, 174; Child
    ballad books, 106; community songsters
    and, 83–88; documentation/transcription
    methods, 13, 16, 41, 49–53, 67, 128, 165–67;
    early contributors, 54–57; early encoun-
    ters with other collectors, 37–41; Library
    of Congress and, 30, 87–88, 126–27, 134,
    162, 172, 173–74; MH and festival circuit,
    145–60 (see also Mountain Folks Music
    Festival; Ozark Folk Festival); MH ceases
    ballad-collecting activities, 162; MH col-
    lections (see Max Hunter Folk Song Col-
    lection; Springfield–Greene County
    Library; State Historical Society of Mis-
    souri–Columbia); MH as local business-
    man and, 10, 29–33, 37, 40–41; MH "rules
    of collecting," 43, 126–27; Missouri Origins
    Project and, 162–63, 172, 173–74, 213n7;

Hunter, Max (MH) (*continued*)
—ballad collecting (*continued*): oral tradition and, 17, 137–38, 163–64, 171–72; origins of, 11–12, 29–30, 36–37; Ozarks folk culture and, 25–28, 171; "Ozarks"-only focus, 48–49, 139–44; recording equipment and methods, xiii–xiv, 30–32, 36, 39, 48–49, 63–64, 67–68, 83, 102–3; relationships with singers, 42–48, 67–74, 80–81, 171–72; religion and folklore in, 143–44; reluctant sources and, 62–63, 71; rule of not rushing, 42–48, 139; Schroeders and, 48, 62, 120–23, 159, 162; social values in, 14–18, 51–53, 74–83; songs and stories in, 12–14, 15–16, 42–48, 58–60, 81 (see also *Visits from the Ozarks/Visits With* audio recordings); years collecting (1956–1976), xxiv–xxv, 1
—musical performances: "Down in the Valley" (with Harold Hunter), ix, 28; at the Festival of Missouri Folk Music and Dance, 51–52; Folk-Legacy Records albums, 36, 122; for high school students, 161–62; at Missouri State University-Springfield, 158; Joan O'Bryant as singing partner, xii, xviii, 39, 73, 111–16; at the Ozark Folk Festival (Eureka Springs, AR), 34, 35–37, 39; at Southwest Missouri State University festival, 136, 172; at the University of Missouri–Columbia, 120–22, 158
Hunter, Roy (MH father), 19–28
Hunter, Virginia Mercer (MH wife): children, 129 (*see also* Bangs, Linda Hunter; Hunter, David; Sweet, Jenny Hunter); marries MH, 29, 30; MH ballad collecting and, 43–44, 53, 68–69, 87, 96, 104, 106, 115, 116, 118, 119, 128
Huskey, Floy, 14, 132
hymnal/church songs, 13, 23–24, 28, 59–60

indigenous/native folk music, 4, 11, 46, 58–59, 62
Ingenthron, C. W., 75–76
Irish folk songs, 75–77, 170
Ives, Edward, x

Jabbour, Alan, xii, 88, 127, 162–63
Jackson, Sue, 60–61
James, J. L., 103–4
John Quincy Wolf Jr. Collection, 92, 137

Jones, Michael A., 73
Jones, Wise, 14

Karpeles, Maud, 2–3
Kemp, Susan, 92, 96
Kinney, Nathaniel, 63
Kittredge, George Lyman, 2, 4
Knott, Sarah Gertrude, 33–34, 150, 157
Koontz, Donnie, 147

Lair, John, 157
Lamar, Bertha Everly, 26–27, 137
Lance, Carla, 55
Lance, Donald, 41, 119
Lance, Virgil, 54–56
Lansford, Kim, 170
Leadbelly (Huddie Ledbetter), x
Leary, James P., xii–xiii
Lee, Johnny, 59
Library of Congress: American Folklife Center (formerly Archive of American Folk Song), 7, 87–88, 126–27, 134, 162–63; festival song list, 158; Alan Lomax and, 6, 7, 12, 89, 92–93, 96, 100, 183n80; John Lomax and, 6, 7, 163; MH and, 30, 87–88, 126–27, 134, 162, 172, 173–74; Vance Randolph and, xv, 41; Ben and David Rice and, 6
Lomax, Alan: *The Gospel Ship* collection (1977), 89; Library of Congress recordings and, 6, 7, 12, 89, 92–93, 96, 100, 183n80; MH and, 11; Southern Folk Heritage Series, 12, 183n80; *Southern Journey* collection (1959), 89
Lomax, John, xii, 6, 7, 163, 181n54
Long, James, 56–57
Louvin, Ira, xiv
Lunsford, Bascom Lamar, 12
Lynn, Loretta, 12

Machado, Adam, xii
Majors, Frances, 12, 52, 110–11
Max Hunter Collection. *See* Springfield-Greene County Library; State Historical Society of Missouri–Columbia
Max Hunter Folk Song Collection: ballad collecting for (*see* Hunter, Max: ballad collecting); a capella singing in, 12–13; Child ballads in, 40, 165–66, 167; digitization, 135, 159, 166–68; Hunter Map of

Contributors, xxiv–xxv; as resource for performers, 170–71; transcription and notation issues, 165–67
McCann, Gordon, 170, 172; Art's Country Pickers and, 158; fiddle contests, xii, 159; McCann Collection, Missouri State University, 9–10; MH and, 159–60; Ozark Heritage Series concerts and, 137–38; Springfield as hometown of, 9–10, 23
McCord, May Kennedy, xii, xvi, xxiv, 115, 122, 136, 171; *Hillbilly Heartbeats* column and radio show, 5, 23, 77–78; Ozark Folk Festival and, 33–34, 35, 148–49, 151; as "Queen of the Hillbillies," xvi, 148–49, 180n39
McDaniels, Harry, 118
McDonald, Laura, 122
McGuire, Lizzie, 81–82
McNeil, W. K., x–xi, xv, 10, 63, 139
Mercer, Myrl (MH father-in-law), 29–31, 132–33, 137
Missouri Arts Council, 170; Missouri Arts Council Award (1998), 166, 172, 174; Springfield Art Museum concerts and, 121–22, 157–58, 168–69
Missouri Folklore Society, 3–5, 119; Award for Distinguished Achievement, 163; *Ballads and Songs Collected by the Missouri Folk-Lore Society* (Belden, 1940), 4–6, 11, 14–15, 187n35, 194–95n25; *Missouri Folklore Society Journal*, 170; Schroeders and, 120
Missouri Origins Project, 162–63, 172, 173–74, 213n7
Missouri State University–Springfield, 146–47; digitization of the Max Hunter Folk Song Collection and, 135, 159, 166–68; Gordon McCann Collection (fiddle tunes), 9–10; MH performances and lectures, 158; song swaps, 146
Moody, Kermit, 133–34
Morris, Jimmy. *See* Driftwood, Jimmy (James Morris)
Morris, Neal, 92, 93, 97–98, 133
Morrow, Lynn, 8
Mountain Folks Music Festival (Silver Dollar City, MO), xiii, xviii, 117, 145–48, 153–58
Mountain Home Folk Festival, 86
Mullins, Johnny, 12

Murray, Kathleen and Michael, 166–67
Musick, Ruth Ann, 5–6
*Music of the Mountains* (video), 145, 147
Myers-Phinney, Linda, 8

National Folk Festival, 33, 150
National Folk Festival Association, 158
native/indigenous folk music, 4, 11, 46, 58–59, 62
Nichols, Dwight "Nick," 115
Nichols, Jean, 155–56
Nix, Toby, 147–48, 149

O'Bryant, Joan, xxiv, 111–16; ballad collecting and, 39, 55, 112–14, 122, 124, 163; death, xii, 112, 117, 122; Joan O'Bryant Kansas Folklore Collection, 112, 122–23, 124; meets MH, 39, 40; as MH singing partner, xii, xviii, 39, 73, 107, 111–16; RCA recording, 122; Smithsonian Folkways Recordings, 114–15; at Wichita State University, xviii, 39, 163
Ohrlin, Glenn, 48, 71, 96
Old Time Music Heritage Festival, 170–71
Olson, Betsy, 140
Opportune Records, 114
O'Reilly, Julia, 146–47
Orr, Doug, 13
Osterloh, Samuel, 147–48, 149
Owen, Mary Alicia, 4
Owens, Bessie, 59
"Ozarker/Ozarkian," as terms, xiv–xv, 8–9, 141–42
Ozark Folk Center (Mountain View, AR), xiii, xvi, 95, 100, 101, 157
Ozark Folk Festival (Eureka Springs, AR), 95, 105, 109, 114–17; of 1934, 33–34; of 1948 ("Original" or "Annual"), 34–35; of 1957, 34–41; of 1958, 123; of 1959, 34; of 1975 (MH boycotts), 145, 148; of 1976 (MH as "master of ceremonies"), xiii, 148–54; of 1977, 158; Crescent Hotel gatherings, 114–15; MH as producer and director (1976–1988), xiii, 146–47, 148–54, 157–60, 172–73; MH performs at, 34, 35–37, 39
Ozark Folklore Society, 127, 140
Ozark Folksong Collection (University of Arkansas), xix, 8, 37, 75–76, 89, 176n3
Ozark Heritage Series concerts (Springfield–Greene County Library), 137–38

Ozark Highballers, 171
Ozark Opry, 10

Para, Dave, 100, 152, 170
Parker, Allie Long, xii, xxiv, 42, 43, 45, 52, 56–57, 67–68, 164
Parker, Geraldine, 5
Parker, Krisanne, xvii, xviii, 14, 146–49
Parler, Mary Celestia, xii, xxiv; ballad collecting and, 16, 40, 55–56, 60, 77, 109–10, 113–14, 126, 134, 166, 176n3; dubbed MH tapes, 40, 109, 126, 166, 176n3; guitar playing and, 110–11; marries Vance Randolph, 107; meets MH, 35–37, 39–41; as MH mentor and collecting partner, xii, xiii, 39–41, 44–45, 47, 54–57, 105–11, 113–16, 117; record liner notes for friends, xv, 36, 73; University of Arkansas, Fayetteville classes, 36, 37, 40, 54, 60, 77–78, 85–86, 105–6, 108, 109–11, 163
Paton, Caroline, xix
Pentlin, Susan, 4
Petrus, Stephen, xii
Philbrick, Herbert Charles, 10, 48, 63–67, 102, 109
Phillips, Bob, 145, 147
Pickering, M. J., 150
Poole, George, 102
Pound, Louise, 4, 5, 7
Prickett, David, xviii, 58
Prickett, Fannie, 45

Quigley, Lucy, 13

Rackensack Folklore Collection, xv, 83
Rafferty, Milton, 139
Randolph, Vance, x–xiii, xxiv, 171; ballad collecting and, 5–7, 8, 39, 63, 105–9, 139, 169; biography, xiv, xv–xvi; death, 162; economic challenges of, 108–9, 117–18; health issues, 106–7, 117–19; library archives and, 134–35; Library of Congress recordings, xv, 41; marries Mary Parler, 107; meets MH, 35–37, 39–41; as MH mentor, xii, xiii, 39–41, 47–48, 49, 105–11, 117–19, 139, 140, 154, 164; Ozark Folk Festival (1934) and, 33–34; *Ozark Folksongs* (1946–1950, 4 vols.), x–xi, xv, 5, 6, 17, 41; Ozarks folk culture and, 8, 9, 25–27, 36, 108–9, 182n62; privacy needs

of, 117, 134–35; recording equipment, 108, 203nn20–21; record liner notes for friends, xv, 36, 73
Rayburn, Otto Ernest, xv, 140, 142, 171; as Ozark Folk Festival producer and director, 34–35; publications, 5, 35, 188n23
RCA, 114, 122
Reed, Ola Belle, x
Rice, Ben and David, 6
Riddle, Almeda, x, xii, xxv, 147; Child ballads and, 102–3; festival appearances, 104, 136; "Heber Springs Tornado," 103–4; "Lady Margaret," 67, 102; "The Maid of Dundee," xiii–xiv, 48–49, 102–3; MH and, 12, 14, 100–104, 136
Rinzler, Ralph, 96
Ritchie, Fiona, 13
Ritchie, Jean, 146
Robertson, Lonnie, 10
Rost, Mary, 87

Sandburg, Carl, 7, 14, 38
Sanders, Raymond, xxv, 48, 83–84, 90
Scarborough, Dorothy, 17
Schott, Goldie, 75–76, 164
Schroeder, Adolf "Dolf," xii; Festival of Missouri Folk Music and Dance, 51–52, 122, 141; Missouri Origins Project and, 162–63, 172, 173–74, 213n7; relationship with MH, 48, 62, 120–23, 159, 162; and the State Historical Society of Missouri–Columbia, xvii–xviii, 122, 124, 135, 166; at the University of Missouri–Columbia, 3, 48, 120–23
Schroeder, Rebecca "Becky," xii, 4; as editor for the University of Missouri Press Heritage Series, 120; fundraising by, 158; relationship with MH, 62, 120–23, 159, 162; and the State Historical Society of Missouri–Columbia, xvii–xvii, 122, 124, 135, 166
Scott, Joe, x
Scottish folk songs, 2, 170. *See also* Child ballads
Seeger, Charles, 7
shape-note hymnals, 60
Sharp, Cecil, 2–3
Shelly, W. H., 16
*Shepherd of the Hills* (Wright), 8
Silver Dollar City, Mountain Folks Music Festival, xiii, xviii, 117, 145–48, 153–58

Smith, Fred, xxiv, 77–78, 114
Smithsonian Institution: Festival of American Folklife (later Smithsonian Folklife Festival), 89–90, 95, 152–54; Smithsonian Folkways Recordings, 114–15, 124
Southern Folk Heritage Series, 12, 183n80
Southwest Missouri State University (Springfield), 136, 153, 172
Spencer, Ralph and Minnie, 151–52
Springfield, MO: All-Ozarks Festival (1934), 23; Campbell Street Methodist Church, 29, 30, 143–44; fiddle contests, 151, 159–60; local song collections, 5–6, 59–60 (*see also* Springfield–Greene County Library); as MH hometown, ix, xvii, 5, 8–9, 14–15, 19, 21, 22–24, 143, 151; MH local recognition as ballad expert, 161–63; Ozark Opry, 10; Southwest Missouri State University, 136, 153, 172; Springfield Art Museum folk music series, 121–22, 157–58, 168–69
Springfield–Greene County Library, 128–29, 162; Library of Congress celebration of MH, 172, 173–74; Ozark Heritage Series concerts and, 137–38; as permanent home for Max Hunter Collection, xvii, 134–38, 165, 166, 168–69. See also *Visits from the Ozarks/Visits With* audio recordings
Stanley, Lola, 102
State Historical Society of Missouri–Columbia, xvii–xviii, 6, 122, 124, 135, 166
*State of the Ozarks* online newsletter, xviii
Stilley, Ed, 45–46
Stone County, AR: Ozark Folk Center (Mountain View), xiii, xvi, 95, 100, 101, 157. *See also* Gilbert, "Aunt" Ollie; Riddle, Almeda
Sweet, Jenny Hunter (MH daughter), 46–47, 129, 135–36, 166, 172

Thompson, Carol, 150, 156–57
TradMad, 169–70

University of Arkansas, 17–18; MH contribution to Folklore Research Project, 40, 109, 126, 134, 166, 176n3; Ozark Folksong

Collection, xix, 8, 37, 75–76, 89, 176n3; Mary Parler ballad-collecting class, 36, 37, 40, 54, 60, 77–78, 85–86, 105–6, 108, 109–11, 163
University of Missouri–Columbia, 152; Belden folklore studies and collection, 3–7, 11, 14–15; Loman Cansler and, 38, 123; MH performances and lectures, 120–22, 158; Dolf Schroeder and, 3, 48, 120–23
Upton, Lucile Morris, 5

Van Ravenswaay, Charles, 6
*Visits from the Ozarks/Visits With* audio recordings, 127–34; Audrey Barclay, 132; Otto Clayton, 143–44; Benson and Fleecy Fox, 137; Ollie Gilbert, x, 90, 92, 93, 133; Floyd Holland, 133–34; Charlie and Barry Horton, 136, 164; Floy Huskey, 14, 132; Bertha Lamar, 26–27, 137; Myrl Mercer, 132–33, 137; MH introduction to, 129–32, 154–55; Kermit Moody, 133–34; nature of, x, xviii; Herbert Charles Philbrick, 63–67; Joe Walker, 15

Walker, Joe, 15
Weddington, Paralee, 58, 149, 151, 153
Western Historical Manuscript Collection. *See* State Historical Society of Missouri–Columbia
Wheat, C. V., 6
White Top Festival, 34
Wichita State University, xviii; Joan O'Bryant Kansas Folklore Collection, 112, 122–23, 124; Joan O'Bryant classes, 39, 163
Wilgus, D. K., 99, 118
Williams, Maude, 3
Williams, Michael Ann, 157
Witt, Leander, 67, 75
Wolf, John Quincy, Jr., xii, 11–12, 71–72, 86, 89, 96
Wolz, Lyn, 5, 170
Wood, Emmanuel, 10
Woolf, Cindy, 167, 170
Wright, Harold Bell, 8

# SONG INDEX

"After the Ball," 27
"Angel Band," 94–95

"The Baggage Coach Ahead," 58–59
"Bailiff's Daughter," 82–83
"Barbara Allen," 17, 24, 90, 102, 106
"Battle of New Orleans," 97
"Battle of Pea Ridge," 43
"Battle of Prairie Grove," 71
"Bawdy Strawberry Roan," 71
"Bill Stafford," 55–56
"Blackest Crow," xviii
"The Blind Child," 24, 168
"Branigan's Pup," 75–76
"The Brown Girl," 52, 62
"Buffalo Girls," 97

"California Joe," 16
"Charley Brooks," 83
"Charming Beauty Bright," 122
"The Cruel Mother," 61

"Darling Little Joe," 28
"The Dewey Dens of Yarrow," 63–67, 102,
   109
"Down by the Greenwood Side," 61
"Down in the Valley," 28, ix
"The Drown'd Boy," 102
"The Drunken Fool," 24
"Dying Soldier Boy-Mill Spring," 84

"Erin's Green Shores"/"Rose of Erin," 56

"Fair Willie Drowned in Yarrow," 102
"Four Marys," 102
"Fy Foley," 86

"Go Tell Aunt Rhody," 133
"Green Corn," 90, 97

"Hangman, Hangman, Hold Your Hand," 60
"Heber Springs Tornado," 103–4

"I'm a Good Old Rebel," xv
"In a Hog Pen," 71
"In the Garden," 98
"The Irish Wake," 75–76
"It Rained a Mist"/"The Jew's Garden,"
   51–52, 57, 90
"I Wish I Was a Little Bird," 75

"Jesse James," 104
"The Jew's Garden," 51–52, 57, 90
"Johnny German," 67–68
"Johnny Lee Ballad," 59

"Kitty Wells," 161
"The Knoxville Girl," 17, 58

"The Lady from the West Countree," 110–11
"Lady Margaret," 27, 67, 102
"The Lightning Express," 168
"Little Billy," 81
"Little Colleen," 16
"Little Darling," 16

"Little Omie," 85
"The Little Rosewood Casket," 24
"Lonesome Scenes of Winter," 83
"Lord Randall," 90, 132
"Lord Thomas," 62
"Lovely Jane"/"Sweet Lovely Jane," 56

"The Maid of Dundee," 48–49, 102–3, xiii–xiv
"The Mermaid," 57
"My Home in the White River Hills," 55
"My Kind Ole Husband," 75–76

"The Nightingale," 27, 137
"Nightman," 57
"Notchville Girl," 12

"The Office Boy," 227
"Oh Miss, I Have a Very Fine Farm," 81–82
"The Old Armchair," 168
"Old Bangum," 62
"The Old Hickory Cane," 27
"Old Joe Clark," 17
"The Old Woman Lived on a Sea Shore," 61–62
"O Miss, You Have a Very Fine Farm," 114
"One Morning in May," 133
"Orphan Child," 102
"Orphan Girl," 28
"Our Goodman," 34, 88

"The Peaceful Farm"/"The Peaceful Old Farm," 50
"Poor Boy," 37–38

"A Pretty Fair Maid in Yonders Garden," 45
"Pretty Polly," 81
"Prisoner for Life," 85

"The Rising Sun," 33
"Roll the Tater," 137
"Rosemary and Thyme," 57–58, xviii–xix

"A Sailor Cut Down His Prime," 51
"Sally Goodin," 90
"Shoot the Cat," 71
"Sing Low, Laurie O," 57
"Sir Lionel," 62
"The State of Arkansas," 55–56
"The Streets of Laredo," 51
"Sugar Hill," 97

"The Taylor Boys," 62
"Tell Ye the Story," 83
"Three Little Babes," 94
"Three Nights Drunk," 34
"The Tiehackers Song," 15
"Time Enough Yet," 83
"Twenty One Years," 49
"Two Sisters," 61–62, 90

"Where the Ole White River Flows," 55
"The Wild Hog," 62
"Will the Weaver," 71
"A Wounded Soldier"/"Dying Soldier Boy-Mill Spring," 84

The Office Boy.

The office had just opened
An old worn in years
Just listed on his care-worn face
Shown signs of grief and tears
Not as the clerk approached him
With a trembling voice he said
"I'm looking for my boy sir
He's coming home today."

II

"You've made a slight mistake sir
For surely you may know
This is an express office sir
and not a town depot
and if your boy is coming home"
The clerk with a smile did say
"You'll find him with the passengers
at the depot o'er the way."

III

"You do not understand me"
The old man shook his head

Lyrics to "The Office Boy" written in the hand of a Hunter contributor (undated), author Gussie L. Davis (1899). (Courtesy of the Springfield–Greene County Library)

SARAH JANE NELSON is a writer and musical performer. She has written on music for *Old-Time Herald, Ozarks Watch, Fiddler Magazine,* and other publications.

# MUSIC IN AMERICAN LIFE

Only a Miner: Studies in Recorded Coal-Mining Songs   *Archie Green*
Great Day Coming: Folk Music and the American Left   *R. Serge Denisoff*
John Philip Sousa: A Descriptive Catalog of His Works   *Paul E. Bierley*
The Hell-Bound Train: A Cowboy Songbook   *Glenn Ohrlin*
Oh, Didn't He Ramble: The Life Story of Lee Collins, as Told to Mary Collins
    *Edited by Frank J. Gillis and John W. Miner*
American Labor Songs of the Nineteenth Century   *Philip S. Foner*
Stars of Country Music: Uncle Dave Macon to Johnny Rodriguez
    *Edited by Bill C. Malone and Judith McCulloh*
Git Along, Little Dogies: Songs and Songmakers of the American West   *John I. White*
A Texas-Mexican *Cancionero*: Folksongs of the Lower Border   *Américo Paredes*
San Antonio Rose: The Life and Music of Bob Wills   *Charles R. Townsend*
Early Downhome Blues: A Musical and Cultural Analysis   *Jeff Todd Titon*
An Ives Celebration: Papers and Panels of the Charles Ives Centennial
    Festival-Conference   *Edited by H. Wiley Hitchcock and Vivian Perlis*
Sinful Tunes and Spirituals: Black Folk Music to the Civil War   *Dena J. Epstein*
Joe Scott, the Woodsman-Songmaker   *Edward D. Ives*
Jimmie Rodgers: The Life and Times of America's Blue Yodeler   *Nolan Porterfield*
Early American Music Engraving and Printing: A History of Music Publishing in
    America from 1787 to 1825, with Commentary on Earlier and Later Practices
    *Richard J. Wolfe*
Sing a Sad Song: The Life of Hank Williams   *Roger M. Williams*
Long Steel Rail: The Railroad in American Folksong   *Norm Cohen*
Resources of American Music History: A Directory of Source Materials from Colonial
    Times to World War II   *D. W. Krummel, Jean Geil, Doris J. Dyen, and Deane L. Root*
Tenement Songs: The Popular Music of the Jewish Immigrants   *Mark Slobin*
Ozark Folksongs   *Vance Randolph; edited and abridged by Norm Cohen*
Oscar Sonneck and American Music   *Edited by William Lichtenwanger*
Bluegrass Breakdown: The Making of the Old Southern Sound   *Robert Cantwell*
Bluegrass: A History   *Neil V. Rosenberg*
Music at the White House: A History of the American Spirit   *Elise K. Kirk*
Red River Blues: The Blues Tradition in the Southeast   *Bruce Bastin*
Good Friends and Bad Enemies: Robert Winslow Gordon and the Study of American
    Folksong   *Debora Kodish*
Fiddlin' Georgia Crazy: Fiddlin' John Carson, His Real World, and the World of His
    Songs   *Gene Wiggins*
America's Music: From the Pilgrims to the Present (rev. 3d ed.)   *Gilbert Chase*
Secular Music in Colonial Annapolis: The Tuesday Club, 1745–56   *John Barry Talley*
Bibliographical Handbook of American Music   *D. W. Krummel*
Goin' to Kansas City   *Nathan W. Pearson Jr.*
"Susanna," "Jeanie," and "The Old Folks at Home": The Songs of Stephen C. Foster from
    His Time to Ours (2d ed.)   *William W. Austin*

Songprints: The Musical Experience of Five Shoshone Women   *Judith Vander*
"Happy in the Service of the Lord": Afro-American Gospel Quartets in Memphis
   *Kip Lornell*
Paul Hindemith in the United States   *Luther Noss*
"My Song Is My Weapon": People's Songs, American Communism, and the Politics of
   Culture, 1930–50   *Robbie Lieberman*
Chosen Voices: The Story of the American Cantorate   *Mark Slobin*
Theodore Thomas: America's Conductor and Builder of Orchestras, 1835–1905
   *Ezra Schabas*
"The Whorehouse Bells Were Ringing" and Other Songs Cowboys Sing
   *Collected and Edited by Guy Logsdon*
Crazeology: The Autobiography of a Chicago Jazzman   *Bud Freeman,*
   *as Told to Robert Wolf*
Discoursing Sweet Music: Brass Bands and Community Life in Turn-of-the-Century
   Pennsylvania   *Kenneth Kreitner*
Mormonism and Music: A History   *Michael Hicks*
Voices of the Jazz Age: Profiles of Eight Vintage Jazzmen   *Chip Deffaa*
Pickin' on Peachtree: A History of Country Music in Atlanta, Georgia
   *Wayne W. Daniel*
Bitter Music: Collected Journals, Essays, Introductions, and Librettos   *Harry Partch;*
   *edited by Thomas McGeary*
Ethnic Music on Records: A Discography of Ethnic Recordings Produced in the
   United States, 1893 to 1942   *Richard K. Spottswood*
Downhome Blues Lyrics: An Anthology from the Post–World War II Era
   *Jeff Todd Titon*
Ellington: The Early Years   *Mark Tucker*
Chicago Soul   *Robert Pruter*
That Half-Barbaric Twang: The Banjo in American Popular Culture   *Karen Linn*
Hot Man: The Life of Art Hodes   *Art Hodes and Chadwick Hansen*
The Erotic Muse: American Bawdy Songs (2d ed.)   *Ed Cray*
Barrio Rhythm: Mexican American Music in Los Angeles   *Steven Loza*
The Creation of Jazz: Music, Race, and Culture in Urban America   *Burton W. Peretti*
Charles Martin Loeffler: A Life Apart in Music   *Ellen Knight*
Club Date Musicians: Playing the New York Party Circuit   *Bruce A. MacLeod*
Opera on the Road: Traveling Opera Troupes in the United States, 1825–60
   *Katherine K. Preston*
The Stonemans: An Appalachian Family and the Music That Shaped Their Lives
   *Ivan M. Tribe*
Transforming Tradition: Folk Music Revivals Examined   *Edited by Neil V. Rosenberg*
The Crooked Stovepipe: Athapaskan Fiddle Music and Square Dancing in Northeast
   Alaska and Northwest Canada   *Craig Mishler*
Traveling the High Way Home: Ralph Stanley and the World of Traditional Bluegrass
   Music   *John Wright*
Carl Ruggles: Composer, Painter, and Storyteller   *Marilyn Ziffrin*

Never without a Song: The Years and Songs of Jennie Devlin, 1865–1952
  *Katharine D. Newman*
The Hank Snow Story  *Hank Snow, with Jack Ownbey and Bob Burris*
Milton Brown and the Founding of Western Swing  *Cary Ginell,*
  *with special assistance from Roy Lee Brown*
Santiago de Murcia's "Códice Saldívar No. 4": A Treasury of Secular Guitar Music from
  Baroque Mexico  *Craig H. Russell*
The Sound of the Dove: Singing in Appalachian Primitive Baptist Churches
  *Beverly Bush Patterson*
Heartland Excursions: Ethnomusicological Reflections on Schools of Music
  *Bruno Nettl*
Doowop: The Chicago Scene  *Robert Pruter*
Blue Rhythms: Six Lives in Rhythm and Blues  *Chip Deffaa*
Shoshone Ghost Dance Religion: Poetry Songs and Great Basin Context
  *Judith Vander*
Go Cat Go! Rockabilly Music and Its Makers  *Craig Morrison*
'Twas Only an Irishman's Dream: The Image of Ireland and the Irish in American
  Popular Song Lyrics, 1800–1920  *William H. A. Williams*
Democracy at the Opera: Music, Theater, and Culture in New York City, 1815–60
  *Karen Ahlquist*
Fred Waring and the Pennsylvanians  *Virginia Waring*
Woody, Cisco, and Me: Seamen Three in the Merchant Marine  *Jim Longhi*
Behind the Burnt Cork Mask: Early Blackface Minstrelsy and Antebellum American
  Popular Culture  *William J. Mahar*
Going to Cincinnati: A History of the Blues in the Queen City  *Steven C. Tracy*
Pistol Packin' Mama: Aunt Molly Jackson and the Politics of Folksong  *Shelly Romalis*
Sixties Rock: Garage, Psychedelic, and Other Satisfactions  *Michael Hicks*
The Late Great Johnny Ace and the Transition from R&B to Rock 'n' Roll
  *James M. Salem*
Tito Puente and the Making of Latin Music  *Steven Loza*
Juilliard: A History  *Andrea Olmstead*
Understanding Charles Seeger, Pioneer in American Musicology
  *Edited by Bell Yung and Helen Rees*
Mountains of Music: West Virginia Traditional Music from *Goldenseal*
  *Edited by John Lilly*
Alice Tully: An Intimate Portrait  *Albert Fuller*
A Blues Life  *Henry Townsend, as told to Bill Greensmith*
Long Steel Rail: The Railroad in American Folksong (2d ed.)  *Norm Cohen*
The Golden Age of Gospel  *Text by Horace Clarence Boyer;*
  *photography by Lloyd Yearwood*
Aaron Copland: The Life and Work of an Uncommon Man  *Howard Pollack*
Louis Moreau Gottschalk  *S. Frederick Starr*
Race, Rock, and Elvis  *Michael T. Bertrand*
Theremin: Ether Music and Espionage  *Albert Glinsky*
Poetry and Violence: The Ballad Tradition of Mexico's Costa Chica  *John H. McDowell*

The Bill Monroe Reader   *Edited by Tom Ewing*
Music in Lubavitcher Life   *Ellen Koskoff*
Zarzuela: Spanish Operetta, American Stage   *Janet L. Sturman*
Bluegrass Odyssey: A Documentary in Pictures and Words, 1966–86
     *Carl Fleischhauer and Neil V. Rosenberg*
That Old-Time Rock & Roll: A Chronicle of an Era, 1954–63   *Richard Aquila*
Labor's Troubadour   *Joe Glazer*
American Opera   *Elise K. Kirk*
Don't Get above Your Raisin': Country Music and the Southern Working Class
     *Bill C. Malone*
John Alden Carpenter: A Chicago Composer   *Howard Pollack*
Heartbeat of the People: Music and Dance of the Northern Pow-wow   *Tara Browner*
My Lord, What a Morning: An Autobiography   *Marian Anderson*
Marian Anderson: A Singer's Journey   *Allan Keiler*
Charles Ives Remembered: An Oral History   *Vivian Perlis*
Henry Cowell, Bohemian   *Michael Hicks*
Rap Music and Street Consciousness   *Cheryl L. Keyes*
Louis Prima   *Garry Boulard*
Marian McPartland's Jazz World: All in Good Time   *Marian McPartland*
Robert Johnson: Lost and Found   *Barry Lee Pearson and Bill McCulloch*
Bound for America: Three British Composers   *Nicholas Temperley*
Lost Sounds: Blacks and the Birth of the Recording Industry, 1890–1919   *Tim Brooks*
Burn, Baby! BURN! The Autobiography of Magnificent Montague   *Magnificent
     Montague with Bob Baker*
Way Up North in Dixie: A Black Family's Claim to the Confederate Anthem
     *Howard L. Sacks and Judith Rose Sacks*
The Bluegrass Reader   *Edited by Thomas Goldsmith*
Colin McPhee: Composer in Two Worlds   *Carol J. Oja*
Robert Johnson, Mythmaking, and Contemporary American Culture
     *Patricia R. Schroeder*
Composing a World: Lou Harrison, Musical Wayfarer   *Leta E. Miller
     and Fredric Lieberman*
Fritz Reiner, Maestro and Martinet   *Kenneth Morgan*
That Toddlin' Town: Chicago's White Dance Bands and Orchestras, 1900–1950
     *Charles A. Sengstock Jr.*
Dewey and Elvis: The Life and Times of a Rock 'n' Roll Deejay   *Louis Cantor*
Come Hither to Go Yonder: Playing Bluegrass with Bill Monroe   *Bob Black*
Chicago Blues: Portraits and Stories   *David Whiteis*
The Incredible Band of John Philip Sousa   *Paul E. Bierley*
"Maximum Clarity" and Other Writings on Music   *Ben Johnston,
     edited by Bob Gilmore*
Staging Tradition: John Lair and Sarah Gertrude Knott   *Michael Ann Williams*
Homegrown Music: Discovering Bluegrass   *Stephanie P. Ledgin*
Tales of a Theatrical Guru   *Danny Newman*
The Music of Bill Monroe   *Neil V. Rosenberg and Charles K. Wolfe*

Pressing On: The Roni Stoneman Story  *Roni Stoneman, as told to Ellen Wright*
Together Let Us Sweetly Live  *Jonathan C. David,*
    *with photographs by Richard Holloway*
Live Fast, Love Hard: The Faron Young Story  *Diane Diekman*
Air Castle of the South: WSM Radio and the Making of Music City
    *Craig P. Havighurst*
Traveling Home: Sacred Harp Singing and American Pluralism  *Kiri Miller*
Where Did Our Love Go? The Rise and Fall of the Motown Sound  *Nelson George*
Lonesome Cowgirls and Honky-Tonk Angels: The Women of Barn Dance
    Radio  *Kristine M. McCusker*
California Polyphony: Ethnic Voices, Musical Crossroads  *Mina Yang*
The Never-Ending Revival: Rounder Records and the Folk Alliance  *Michael F. Scully*
Sing It Pretty: A Memoir  *Bess Lomax Hawes*
Working Girl Blues: The Life and Music of Hazel Dickens  *Hazel Dickens*
    *and Bill C. Malone*
Charles Ives Reconsidered  *Gayle Sherwood Magee*
The Hayloft Gang: The Story of the National Barn Dance  *Edited by Chad Berry*
Country Music Humorists and Comedians  *Loyal Jones*
Record Makers and Breakers: Voices of the Independent Rock 'n' Roll Pioneers
    *John Broven*
Music of the First Nations: Tradition and Innovation in Native North America
    *Edited by Tara Browner*
Cafe Society: The Wrong Place for the Right People  *Barney Josephson,*
    *with Terry Trilling-Josephson*
George Gershwin: An Intimate Portrait  *Walter Rimler*
Life Flows On in Endless Song: Folk Songs and American History  *Robert V. Wells*
I Feel a Song Coming On: The Life of Jimmy McHugh  *Alyn Shipton*
King of the Queen City: The Story of King Records  *Jon Hartley Fox*
Long Lost Blues: Popular Blues in America, 1850–1920  *Peter C. Muir*
Hard Luck Blues: Roots Music Photographs from the Great Depression
    *Rich Remsberg*
Restless Giant: The Life and Times of Jean Aberbach and Hill and Range Songs
    *Bar Biszick-Lockwood*
Champagne Charlie and Pretty Jemima: Variety Theater in the Nineteenth Century
    *Gillian M. Rodger*
Sacred Steel: Inside an African American Steel Guitar Tradition  *Robert L. Stone*
Gone to the Country: The New Lost City Ramblers and the Folk Music Revival
    *Ray Allen*
The Makers of the Sacred Harp  *David Warren Steel with Richard H. Hulan*
Woody Guthrie, American Radical  *Will Kaufman*
George Szell: A Life of Music  *Michael Charry*
Bean Blossom: The Brown County Jamboree and Bill Monroe's Bluegrass Festivals
    *Thomas A. Adler*
Crowe on the Banjo: The Music Life of J. D. Crowe  *Marty Godbey*
Twentieth Century Drifter: The Life of Marty Robbins  *Diane Diekman*

Henry Mancini: Reinventing Film Music   *John Caps*
The Beautiful Music All Around Us: Field Recordings and the American Experience
   *Stephen Wade*
Then Sings My Soul: The Culture of Southern Gospel Music   *Douglas Harrison*
The Accordion in the Americas: Klezmer, Polka, Tango, Zydeco, and More!
   *Edited by Helena Simonett*
Bluegrass Bluesman: A Memoir   *Josh Graves, edited by Fred Bartenstein*
One Woman in a Hundred: Edna Phillips and the Philadelphia Orchestra
   *Mary Sue Welsh*
The Great Orchestrator: Arthur Judson and American Arts Management
   *James M. Doering*
Charles Ives in the Mirror: American Histories of an Iconic Composer   *David C. Paul*
Southern Soul-Blues   *David Whiteis*
Sweet Air: Modernism, Regionalism, and American Popular Song
   *Edward P. Comentale*
Pretty Good for a Girl: Women in Bluegrass   *Murphy Hicks Henry*
Sweet Dreams: The World of Patsy Cline   *Warren R. Hofstra*
William Sidney Mount and the Creolization of American Culture   *Christopher J.
   Smith*
Bird: The Life and Music of Charlie Parker   *Chuck Haddix*
Making the March King: John Philip Sousa's Washington Years, 1854–1893
   *Patrick Warfield*
In It for the Long Run   *Jim Rooney*
Pioneers of the Blues Revival   *Steve Cushing*
Roots of the Revival: American and British Folk Music in the 1950s   *Ronald D. Cohen
   and Rachel Clare Donaldson*
Blues All Day Long: The Jimmy Rogers Story   *Wayne Everett Goins*
Yankee Twang: Country and Western Music in New England   *Clifford R. Murphy*
The Music of the Stanley Brothers   *Gary B. Reid*
Hawaiian Music in Motion: Mariners, Missionaries, and Minstrels   *James Revell Carr*
Sounds of the New Deal: The Federal Music Project in the West   *Peter Gough*
The Mormon Tabernacle Choir: A Biography   *Michael Hicks*
The Man That Got Away: The Life and Songs of Harold Arlen   *Walter Rimler*
A City Called Heaven: Chicago and the Birth of Gospel Music   *Robert M. Marovich*
Blues Unlimited: Essential Interviews from the Original Blues Magazine
   *Edited by Bill Greensmith, Mike Rowe, and Mark Camarigg*
Hoedowns, Reels, and Frolics: Roots and Branches of Southern Appalachian Dance
   *Phil Jamison*
Fannie Bloomfield-Zeisler: The Life and Times of a Piano Virtuoso
   *Beth Abelson Macleod*
Cybersonic Arts: Adventures in American New Music   *Gordon Mumma,
   edited with commentary by Michelle Fillion*
The Magic of Beverly Sills   *Nancy Guy*
Waiting for Buddy Guy   *Alan Harper*
Harry T. Burleigh: From the Spiritual to the Harlem Renaissance   *Jean E. Snyder*

Music in the Age of Anxiety: American Music in the Fifties  *James Wierzbicki*
Jazzing: New York City's Unseen Scene  *Thomas H. Greenland*
A Cole Porter Companion  *Edited by Don M. Randel, Matthew Shaftel,*
  *and Susan Forscher Weiss*
Foggy Mountain Troubadour: The Life and Music of Curly Seckler  *Penny Parsons*
Blue Rhythm Fantasy: Big Band Jazz Arranging in the Swing Era  *John Wriggle*
Bill Clifton: America's Bluegrass Ambassador to the World  *Bill C. Malone*
Chinatown Opera Theater in North America  *Nancy Yunhwa Rao*
The Elocutionists: Women, Music, and the Spoken Word  *Marian Wilson Kimber*
May Irwin: Singing, Shouting, and the Shadow of Minstrelsy  *Sharon Ammen*
Peggy Seeger: A Life of Music, Love, and Politics  *Jean R. Freedman*
Charles Ives's *Concord*: Essays after a Sonata  *Kyle Gann*
Don't Give Your Heart to a Rambler: My Life with Jimmy Martin, the King of Bluegrass
  *Barbara Martin Stephens*
Libby Larsen: Composing an American Life  *Denise Von Glahn*
George Szell's Reign: Behind the Scenes with the Cleveland Orchestra
  *Marcia Hansen Kraus*
Just One of the Boys: Female-to-Male Cross-Dressing on the American Variety Stage
  *Gillian M. Rodger*
Spirituals and the Birth of a Black Entertainment Industry  *Sandra Jean Graham*
Right to the Juke Joint: A Personal History of American Music  *Patrick B. Mullen*
Bluegrass Generation: A Memoir  *Neil V. Rosenberg*
Pioneers of the Blues Revival, Expanded Second Edition  *Steve Cushing*
Banjo Roots and Branches  *Edited by Robert Winans*
Bill Monroe: The Life and Music of the Blue Grass Man  *Tom Ewing*
Dixie Dewdrop: The Uncle Dave Macon Story  *Michael D. Doubler*
Los Romeros: Royal Family of the Spanish Guitar  *Walter Aaron Clark*
Transforming Women's Education: Liberal Arts and Music in Female Seminaries
  *Jewel A. Smith*
Rethinking American Music  *Edited by Tara Browner and Thomas L. Riis*
Leonard Bernstein and the Language of Jazz  *Katherine Baber*
Dancing Revolution: Bodies, Space, and Sound in American Cultural History
  *Christopher J. Smith*
Peggy Glanville-Hicks: Composer and Critic  *Suzanne Robinson*
Mormons, Musical Theater, and Belonging in America  *Jake Johnson*
Blues Legacy: Tradition and Innovation in Chicago  *David Whiteis*
Blues Before Sunrise 2: Interviews from the Chicago Scene  *Steve Cushing*
The Cashaway Psalmody: Transatlantic Religion and Music in Colonial Carolina
  *Stephen A. Marini*
Earl Scruggs and Foggy Mountain Breakdown: The Making of an American Classic
  *Thomas Goldsmith*
A Guru's Journey: Pandit Chitresh Das and Indian Classical Dance in Diaspora
  *Sarah Morelli*
Unsettled Scores: Politics, Hollywood, and the Film Music of Aaron Copland and
  Hanns Eisler  *Sally Bick*

Hillbilly Maidens, Okies, and Cowgirls: Women's Country Music, 1930–1960
    *Stephanie Vander Wel*
Always the Queen: The Denise LaSalle Story    *Denise LaSalle with David Whiteis*
Artful Noise: Percussion Literature in the Twentieth Century    *Thomas Siwe*
The Heart of a Woman: The Life and Music of Florence B. Price    *Rae Linda Brown,*
    *edited by Guthrie P. Ramsey Jr.*
When Sunday Comes: Gospel Music in the Soul and Hip-Hop Eras
    *Claudrena N. Harold*
The Lady Swings: Memoirs of a Jazz Drummer    *Dottie Dodgion and Wayne Enstice*
Industrial Strength Bluegrass: Southwestern Ohio's Musical Legacy
    *Edited by Fred Bartenstein and Curtis W. Ellison*
Soul on Soul: The Life and Music of Mary Lou Williams    *Tammy L. Kernodle*
Unbinding Gentility: Women Making Music in the Nineteenth-Century South
    *Candace Bailey*
Punks in Peoria: Making a Scene in the American Heartland    *Jonathan Wright*
    *and Dawson Barrett*
Homer Rodeheaver and the Rise of the Gospel Music Industry    *Kevin Mungons*
    *and Douglas Yeo*
Americanaland: Where Country & Western Met Rock 'n' Roll    *John Milward,*
    *with Portraits by Margie Greve*
Listening to Bob Dylan    *Larry Starr*
Lying in the Middle: Musical Theater and Belief at the Heart of America
    *Jake Johnson*
The Sounds of Place: Music and the American Cultural Landscape    *Denise Von Glahn*
Peace Be Still: How James Cleveland and the Angelic Choir Created a Gospel Classic
    *Robert M. Marovich*
Politics as Sound: The Washington, DC, Hardcore Scene, 1978–1983
    *Shayna L. Maskell*
Tania León's Stride: A Polyrhythmic Life    *Alejandro L. Madrid*
Elliott Carter Speaks: Unpublished Lectures    *Edited by Laura Emmery*
Interviews with American Composers: Barney Childs in Conversation
    *Edited by Virginia Anderson*
Queer Country    *Shana Goldin-Perschbacher*
On the Bus with Bill Monroe: My Five-Year Ride with the Father of Blue Grass
    *Mark Hembree*
Mandolin Man: The Bluegrass Life of Roland White    *Bob Black*
Music and Mystique in Muscle Shoals    *Christopher M. Reali*
Buddy Emmons: Steel Guitar Icon    *Steve Fishell*
Music in Black American Life, 1600–1945: A University of Illinois Press Anthology
    *Compiled by Laurie Matheson*
Music in Black American Life, 1945–2020: A University of Illinois Press Anthology
    *Compiled by Laurie Matheson*
Ballad Hunting with Max Hunter: Stories of an Ozark Folksong Collector
    *Sarah Jane Nelson*

The University of Illinois Press
is a founding member of the
Association of University Presses.

---

University of Illinois Press
1325 South Oak Street
Champaign, IL 61820-6903
www.press.uillinois.edu